HUMAN RIGHTS

N. Jayapalan

ATLANTIC
PUBLISHERS & DISTRIBUTORS (P) LTD

Published by

ATLANTIC

PUBLISHERS & DISTRIBUTORS (P) LTD

7/22, Ansari Road, Darya Ganj, New Delhi-110002
Phones : +91-11-40775252, 23273880, 23275880, 23280451
Fax : +91-11-23285873
Web : www.atlanticbooks.com
E-mail : orders@atlanticbooks.com

Branch Office
5, Nallathambi Street, Wallajah Road, Chennai-600002
Phones : +91-44-64611085
E-mail : chennai@atlanticbooks.com

Printed in India at Nice Printing Press, A-33/3A, Site-IV,
Industrial Area, Sahibabad, Ghaziabad, U.P.

Preface

It gives me great pleasure to place this book in the hands of the readers. It is quite comprehensive and covers all aspects. It covers the entire syllabus prescribed by several universities. I have narrated all the events chronologically from the beginning to the end. I have also made a serious attempt to present the matter in a simple and lucid manner.

There is a plethora of books on 'Human Rights'. Most of them are bulky. Hence, I have written this book in a sizable Volume *i.e.,* neither too small nor too big. In addition to this I have given importance to the United Nations Charter and Indian Constitution so as to give a clear picture about the Human Rights and the role of Dissents for the welfare of the people.

My experience of teaching the subject at the college level for several years has prompted me to write this book for the students of our universities mainly to fulfil their requirements. In addition to this it has been designed to meet the requirements of the examinees of Civil Services Examination in History and Political Science. I hope that the present book will prove more useful to the students than any other book on the subject.

I am thankful to the M/s Atlantic Publishers and Distributors, New Delhi for readily agreeing to publish this book and bringing it out expeditiously and efficiently.

Suggestions, if any, for the improvement of the book in the subsequent editions will be highly appreciated.

N. JAYAPALAN

Contents

1

Introduction

The study of Human Rights occupies a very important place in the world. In other words Human Rights are of Universal importance. They are no doubt the inherent rights of a man. They are common to all regardless of caste, colour, religion, race etc.

All world countries strive hard to safe guard human rights through their well established constitutions as per the provisions of the Universal Declaration of Human Rights, International Convenants on Civil and Political Rights, Economic, Social and Cultural Rights and Optional Protocols. Indian Constitution guarantees these rights in its Parts III and IV. Yet, violations of Human Rights, occur in the name of religion, race, creed, caste, colour, sex, region etc.

Human Rights belong to a person and affirm his human dignity. The concept of human rights was unknown during ancient and medieval period. In these days the ruler of a country was considered to be the fountain of all sources. He possessed vast powers in his hands. The autocratic rulers just safeguarded the country from foreign invasions and the subjects in turn obeyed the dictation of the ruler.

It goes without saying that rights do not exist in a state of anarchy. It is essential to enquire into the relation between the conceptions of the law of nature and the natural rights of man. The concept of human rights has been evolved from the concept of natural rights. These natural rights are derived from Natural Law, which helped the development of human rights. This idea is beautifully given by F. Castleberg in his 'Natural Law and Human Rights'.

Meaning of Rights

Rights are those conditions of social life without which man cannot be as his best or give of his best, or what is needful to the adequate development and expression of his personality.

Various definitions of human rights have been given by different scholars. Prof. Laski has aptly said that every "State is known by the rights that it maintains". According to Bosanquet, "A right is a claim recognised by society and enforced by the state". E. Barker opines, "Rights are the external conditions necessary for the greatest possible development of the capacities of the personality".

Right exist within society. If there is no society, there cannot be any rights either.

Rights imply duties. Rights are related to certain ends. They are essential to the development of individual personality.

Further rights have a tendency to grow. As the older social and political orders give way to new ones, the new rights also frequently came into existence.

The above definitions clearly vindicate and indicate that there are certain inherent characteristics of rights.

Characteristics of Rights

All we have said about rights above, may be summed up as follows :

1. Rights arise only in society because they are the result of the society and nature of man. Without society, there can be no rights.
2. A claim of an individual is not a right. To become a right, the claim should have the recognition and acceptance of the society as a whole. A claim, by its very nature, implies selfishness and it may harm the interests of a person or persons in society. A right, on the other hand, aims at the good of all and it has a moral end to serve.
3. Rights are compatible with the common good. The society gives recognition to only those rights which are for the welfare of the society as a whole and which promote some common end or moral good.
4. The state does not create rights though they exist within the state. It simply maintains, protects and co-ordinates them. By giving them a legal sanction, the state ensures to every one the enjoyment of his rights.

5. Rights must be definite and universally applicable. They are given equally to all individuals in the society. There can be no discrimination on the basis of religion, race, caste, sex, class or creed. If rights are given to one section of society as against the other, they become privileges.
6. Rights and duties are correlated. They are the two sides of a coin and can never be separated. Every side has a corresponding obligation. The rights of an individual become the duties of all the other individuals of society. An eminent writer expresses the relationship of rights and duties in the following words : "Rights without duties are like men without shadows : They only exist in fairy tales."
7. Rights have a tendency to grow. With change in the social, political and economic environment and the needs of man, the rights also grow, develop and expand. During the middle ages, the rights to life and property were considered important. After the French Revolution, the right to liberty, equality and fraternity became indispensable. In modern times the granting of social and economic rights along with other rights have become the order of the day.

Thus, while the older social and political orders recognised rights to a very small extent, in course of time new rights have frequently come into existence.

Classification of Rights

Broadly speaking, rights are divided into two categories — 'Civil Rights' and 'Political Rights'. But in modern times this classification is not strictly adhered to. It has been seen that in the "Bill of Rights" or lists of 'Fundamental Rights' in the constitutions of many states there are certain rights which fall under both the categories. However, the two-fold division of rights — 'Civil and 'Political' — has an important historical significance. Civil rights were achieved by the people earlier and they have existed and can exist even in those countries where political rights are denied to the people. It is, therefore, necessary to understand the distinction between them and to enumerate civil and political rights separately.

However, it may be mentioned that a distinction is also generally made between two other kinds of rights, *i.e.,* 'moral' and 'legal' rights. First, we may consider these rights briefly before we explain in detail the 'civil' and 'political' rights.

Moral Rights

A moral right is one which merely rests on social recognition only but has not yet been recognised by the state and cannot be enforced by any legal process or through the courts. Moral rights are based upon the moral conscience of the community. They are those claims which the ethical conscience of the society recognises. For instance, a child has a moral claim to be properly fed, brought up and educated by the parents; a wife has a moral claim to be affectionately treated by the husband; a teacher has a moral claim to be respected by his pupils. The society realises that these claims are essential for harmony and human progress. But they are not supported by the laws of the state. There is no legal force behind these claims. If the husband or the parents neglect their duty it cannot be legally enforced. These claims are based on the moral notions of the people and sanctioned by the prevalent ethical conceptions of the society. Moral claims, on the other hand, when recognised by the state or guaranteed by it and can be legally enforced, turn into legal rights. Moral rights lack the force of law. Their violation is not accompanied by the physical force of punishment though they may invite public approbation or condemnation.

Legal Rights

Legal rights are those privileges of man which are recognised, sanctioned and enforced by the state. Leacock says : "A legal right is a privilege enjoyed by a citizen as against his fellow-citizens granted and upheld by the sovereign power of the state." The test of a legal right is that it can be enforced in a court of law. The Indian Constitution includes for this reason, the Right to Constitutional Remedies among the Fundamental Rights guaranteed to Indian citizens.

Legal rights may be further classified into civil rights and political rights.

Civil Rights

Those rights which relate to the protection and enjoyment of life and property by the individual and are regarded as essential to civilised existence are known as 'Civil Rights'. They are called 'Civil' because they are essential conditions of a civilised society. Without them, civilised life is not possible. They are given to all. Every man living in a state enjoys these rights because he is a social being. It is only through the enjoyment of these rights that all-sided development of a man is possible. Civil rights vary from state to state and from time to time. But all the democratic states value them greatly and provide safeguards against their encroachment either by the government or by the individuals. The following are generally included in the category of civil rights :

The Right to Life: Obviously, this is a basic right for without life and security of a person, other rights are of no avail. T.H. Green regarded it as the most fundamental of all rights. Even Hobbes regarded the security of life as important. It means that the state must provide protection to the individual against all foes, internal and external, even against himself, because he must be prevented from committing suicide. Thus, the right to life implies the duty to live. As Gilchrist says : "From the point of view of the general welfare, every life is valuable, and to murder another or murder oneself means the elimination of an individuality which has duties as well as rights." Suicide, says Aquinas, "is an offence to oneself, an offence to community, as well as offence to God Himself."

The right to life also includes the right to use force in selfdefence. But the force used must be both necessary and reasonable and it is for the courts to decide whether in the particular circumstances of a case the force used was justified.

At the same time, the right to life is not absolute. During the times of war or any other national emergency, the citizen owes a duty to the state. The state may even order compulsory conscription. It may also be noted that, since the laws exist to maintain a system of rights, action has to be taken to preserve the system if the laws are violated. The right to life may be suspended if laws are violated. If the violation of laws is not punished, it may lead to anarchy and disorder in the state.

Right to Personal Liberty

The right to life also involves the right to personal liberty or freedom. A number of liberties or freedoms are generally grouped together under this head. They enable a citizen to exercise his inner faculties without restraint or hindrance. As Gettell points out, "Mere life without the right to exercise one's faculties and to determine the general conditions of life would be valueless." This right also guarantees to all the citizens the freedom of movement throughout the country. A citizen may travel or reside in any part of his country, though restrictions may be put on foreigners and aliens. In this regard Gilchrist remarks : "Mere life without movement would be meaningless and without the exercise of the human faculties it would not rise above the level of that of animals."

Slavery, which is the antithesis of liberty, is severely condemned because it deprives a man of his right to personal liberty. This right also involves freedom from arbitrary arrest. In case a man is wrongfully arrested or detained, he may move a court of law for necessary remedy. In India, the right of personal liberty is safeguarded by the Constitution.

The right to personal liberty arises from the fact that every man has to contribute something to the good of the society. However, this right too is not absolute. During an emergency the government has the right to limit our freedom, although this should not be resorted to in times of peace.

Right to Freedom of Thought and Expression

The right to freedom of thought and expression along with the freedom of speech and press has been highly valued by all the democratic states. It is considered as fundamental for the development of human personality. Therefore, poets, philosophers and political scientists have passionately pleaded for freedom of thought and expression. Milton said : "Give me the liberty to know, to utter and to argue freely, according to conscience, above all liberties." J.S. Mill strongly advocated for the liberty of thought and speech and wrote : "If all mankind minus one were of one opinion, mankind would be no more justified in silencing mankind." Renan described liberty of thought as the great solvent of all fanaticisms. Laski calls freedom of speech the catharsis of discontent and the condition of necessary reform. Hocking, Bury, and Laski also consider that liberty of thought is essential for the development of the individual. According to Bury, it is "one supreme condition of mental and moral progress." And, Laski opines : "To allow a man to say what he thinks is to give his personality the only ultimate channel of free expression, and his citizenship the only means of moral adequacy."

The right to speech "means freedom to express one's view of general subjects." It means that every individual is free to think and express his opinion in public without any interference by government. It implies that every individual should be free to criticise the policy pursued by the government. The freedom to think as you will, and to speak as you think are the only indispensable means to the discovery and spread of political truth. Prof. C.E.M. Joad has put it thus : "There is, then, a case for the free exercise of reason and its free expression in speech, writing and discussion, simply because to reason, to speak, to write and to discuss are natural human propensities in the exercise of which men express their natures. To forbid men to express their natures is to forbid them to realise all that they have it in them to be; it is, in a word, to forbid them to be themselves." Pointing out the evil of suppressing the right to freedom of speech and expression, Mill says : "The peculiar evil of silencing the expression of an opinion is that it is robbing the human race, posterity as well as the existing generation, those who dissent from the opinion, still more than those who hold it."

The freedom of speech and expression is also the cornerstone of democracy. A government can always learn more from the criticism of its opponents than from the eulogy of its supporters. Democracy is a government by talk, discussion, clash of ideas and conflict of opinion. Out of this clash and conflict emerges the truth. Criticism of government policy creates enlightened public opinion. It is, thus, a potent factor for the redress of public grievances. When freedom of speech is allowed, government too, possesses the means to benefit from the expression of views of the public. It is a barometer of public opinion and government which stifles public opinion prepares for its own destruction. Prof. Laski has beautifully summed up this point. He says : "To allow a man to say what he thinks is to give his personality the only ultimate channel of full expression and his citizenship the only means of moral adequacy. To act otherwise is to favour those who support the *status quo*, and thus either drive the activities of men underground and, therefore, into dangerous channel, or to suppress experience not less entitled than any other to interpret publicly its meaning."

But Laski also urges that the citizen has the right "to preach the complete inadequacy of the social order. He may demand its overthrow by armed revolution." He does not accept the argument of "reasons of state" and that the preaching of overthrow of government by armed revolution would mean anarchy in the state. He says : "It is no answer to this view to urge that it is the coronation of disorder. If views which imply violence have a sufficient hold upon the state to disturb its foundations, there is something radically wrong with the habits of state." It might be anarchy and, in fact, it is. But, he argues, it does not matter, for the peace in which injustice and tyranny go unquestioned is unworthy of human existence. This is an extreme view which no state can permit, not even an advanced democracy, and every where restrictions — 'reasonable restrictions' are laid down on the exercise of this important right in the interest of clean public life and non-violence. Restrictions are apt to be tightened and increased during war time and in periods of natural emergencies.

Thus, the right to freedom of speech and expression is not absolute. Its exercise is permitted only within certain limits. In all free countries this right is made subject to the law of defamation, libel, obscenity, blasphemy and sedition and, it is well understood, that it does not mean that a person has the right to abuse others or to spread communal or class hatred or to preach the overthrow of government of social order by use of violence. Therefore, the right to freedom of speech does not mean the right to say anything at any time; it simply means the right to speak or to unite in so far as it is consistent with the public well-being, international peace and democratic process.

The Right to Property

The right to property is also one of the important civil rights of man. Less than a century ago this right was considered as important as the right to security of person and the two rights were generally lumped together. This right is based on the assumption that owning property is a natural instinct in man and it provides incentive to hard work. Thus, since the early days of human society, the idea of property has been a supreme right in the evolution of civilisation. And, it would not be an exaggeration to say that the foundations of modern civilisation are deeply rooted in the institution of property which has always existed in some form or the other.

The right to property means the freedom to the individual to enjoy his property. It implies that the individual has the right to 'acquire, hold and dispose of property' without any restriction or hindrance. It also means that he is free to alienate property by way of gift, exchange or will.

Most of the democratic states recognise, in one form or the other, the right to private property and give protection to it. Even the U.S.S.R. recognises the right to private property to a limited extent. In spite of that a fierce controversy has been perpetually, raging regarding the uses and abuses of private property and the desirability of its retention or abolition. We shall now discuss the details of this controversy here because they have been exhaustively dealt with in a separate section in this book. Suffice is to say that the right to property is not considered sacrosanct today.

As a matter of fact the whole concept of property has undergone radical changes in recent times and the process is continuing at present. While it is true that the institution of property continues to be of great importance in modern times, it is also a fact that it has been subjected to serious attacks in recent years and varied restrictions have been imposed by governments on the control and use of property and the rights that go with it. As Professor Laski puts it, "The history of the Right of Property is largely the record of its circumspection." This is particularly the case in all democratic countries, where the state has the right to acquire compulsorily private property in public interest; frame the tax policy and structure in such a manner as to reduce economic inequalities, mitigate the hardships which such inequalities entail; to tax inheritance, levy death duties and a super-tax on higher incomes and to tax unearned incomes at a higher rate than the earned incomes.

However, the crux of the problem is not the 'restriction' or 'regulation' of private property. First, can the state permit private persons to own the means and implements of production and exploit the individual without safeguarding the interest of society and the individual? Secondly, to what extent can disparity in wealth be permitted and when does it become a danger to the democratic foundations of the state? Laski's answer to these questions is that a state which holds the lives of its citizens at its disposal is entitled in a far higher degree to hold their property at its disposal also. In other words, if conscription of men for war is justified, why not conscription of property for the sake of social good?

The Right to Freedom of Religion and Conscience

The right to freedom of religion and conscience guarantees to every citizen the right to liberty, belief and worship. It means that everyone is free to profess and follow any religion and perform the necessary rites connected with his religious practices. While at one time the state permitted only a particular religious faith and worship, the modern secular states remain neutral between different religious faiths and permit the citizens to enjoy the right to profess, to propagate and practise any religion. The Constitution of India also guarantees this right to all the Indian citizens. It says : "Subject to public order, morality and health.... all persons are equally entitled to freedom of conscience and the right freely to profess, practise and propagate religion."

However, the right to religion and conscience does not preclude the state from making any law regulating or restricting any economic, financial, political or other secular activity which may be associated with religious practice. In fact it has to regulate religious activities of the people in the interest of public order or public morality.

Also, under the pretext of freedom of conscience, the individual cannot disobey the laws of the state on the ground that they come into conflict with the religious ideas. Long ago, Rousseau said : "Tolerance should be given to all religions that tolerate others, so long as their dogmas contain nothing contrary to the duties of citizenship." The modern democratic states follow this sound dictum and accept the principle of religious tolerance.

The Right to Equality

The right to equality is also given importance in the modern democratic states. This right means the absence of legal discrimination against any one individual, group, class or race. In earlier times certain classes possessed special privileges or were judged by special law. In modern times the tendency is to enforce the same law over all persons in the state and to give to all persons equal rights and privileges in the protection of their civil liberty.

Democracy can only exist and flourish in a society of equals. The Constitution of India makes social and civil equality the bedrock of Indian polity. It guarantees equality of all persons before law, prohibits discrimination on grounds of religion, race, caste, sex or place of birth or between citizens, and abolishes untouchability, on the one hand, and titles on the other.

The Right to Association and Assembly

All democratic countries recognise the right of the people to form associations. They consider it as important as freedom of opinion. Associations, according to Gierke and Maitland, are instinctive to man. The pluralists even regard the state as an association and plead for the autonomy of groups and associations. Though the contention of the pluralists is not fully accepted, yet there is no denying the fact that the individual can forcefully put forward his views only in concert with his fellows. And, there are many objectives which he cannot achieve alone, but only in association with others. Therefore, it is necessary that the citizens should be free to form associations and assemble very often to propagate their views. In all matters of public interest and policy they should be free to publicly discuss and express honest opinion. It also includes the right of petition and protest.

But the right to association is limited by the necessities of the state. So long as states preserve their sovereign national character, the proposition that the state is an association cannot be accepted. The state is sovereign and it must ensure its continued existence. The associations must function under the legal control of the state. The state may declare an association or a public meeting unlawful, if a breach of peace or the security of the government established by law is apprehended. It may also forbid some activities which endanger the security of the state or are against social welfare.

The Right to Family

Previously, we have discussed the importance of Rights in the State. In the continuance of the state the family is its hope and the cradle of civilisation.

The right to family is, therefore, one of the most fundamental rights. Thus, it is natural that the state should recognise the right to family.

This right implies the right to marriage, the right against others in maintaining the purity to marriage relations, the right to the custody and control of children and the right of inheritance. Article 16 of the Universal Declaration of Human Rights declares : "(1) Men and Women of full age, without any limitation due to race, nationality or religion, have the right to marry and to found a family. They are entitled to equal rights as to marriage, during marriage and its dissolution. (2) Marriage shall be entered into only with the free consent of the intending spouses. (3) The family is the natural and fundamental group unit of society and is entitled to protection by society and the state."

However, all the family rights are to be exercised with due regard to the good of the community. And, the state may restrict the right to family if it is being used in a manner which is opposed to the general good of the society.

There are two other Civil Rights — *(a)* the Right to Work and *(b)* the Right to Education — which have acquired great prominence and importance in modern times. In India, these rights are not included in the list of Fundamental Rights. But they find a prominent place in the Directive Principles of State Policy and the government is to endeavour to implement them as far as possible and permitted by our limited resources.

In conclusion, it may be emphasised that none of the civil rights discussed above, is absolute. These rights exist within the state and are conferred by the state on its individual members. The state may regulate and control their enjoyment in a manner it thinks desirable for the protection of its own interests as well as for furthering general welfare.

Political Rights

Political rights are the foundation of a democratic polity. In fact, it is only through the exercise of these rights that democracy actually comes into existence, and it is only a democratic constitution which provides political rights to the people.

Political rights are exercised by those persons whom the state permits to share in the legal expression and administration of its sovereign power. They give the right, an equal opportunity, to the individual, if he is worthy of it, to take part in the political affairs of his community and influence the policy of his government. They provide the people with "channels of direct access to the sources of authority".

Before we discuss the important political rights, it may be useful to point out that the classification of rights between 'Civil' and 'Political' is neither scientific, nor very useful today because some important rights fall under both the categories. For intance, Freedom of Speech and Expression, including Freedom of the Press, Freedom of Association, Freedom of Assembly, including that of holding Public Meetings, the Right to Equality of Opportunity in matters of Public Employment, are both Civil and Political Rights. However, there are certain rights which are *par-excellence* "Political", such as : The Right to Vote; The Right to be Elected; The Right to Public Office; The Right to Petition; The Right of Criticising the Government; and the Right to Resistance.

The Right to Vote

The right to vote, also called the 'franchise', is both a condition and product of democracy. Modern democracies, because of their large areas and populations, are not direct but indirect or representative democracies. And, effective participation in the government is possible for the people only through their representations. Consequently, the right to choose the representative or the right to vote at elections is of fundamental importance.

By the right to vote we mean that every adult citizen has the right to express his opinion by casting a vote at the time of election what persons he desires should undertake the task of government. It is contended that the right to vote should be as wide as possible and neither sex nor property, neither race nor creed, neither religion nor education should be the criterion for the grant of the right to vote. One man one vote ought to be the maxim of a democratic government.

However, it has been seen that even democratic governments do not grant this right to every citizen. Aliens, bankrupts, paupers, certain types of criminals and minors are denied the right to vote. In fact, each state determines the qualifications for voters. Some states place limitations on the right to vote. Laski opines : "Neither sex nor property, neither race nor creed, ought to prevent the citizen from aiding in the choice of his rulers." He adds : "Whenever the body of voters is limited, the welfare realised usually excludes that of the persons excluded." Since, no test so far has been devised to limit the franchise in such a way as to equate civil virtue with its possession, the tendency in the modern world in favour of widening the franchise.

The Right to be Elected

The right to be elected or to represent the people is another important political right. In a democracy, particularly a parliamentary democracy, this right acquires an added significance. The right is a corollary to the right to vote and most of the democratic states grant to their citizens the privilege of contesting elections to different legislative bodies.

The legislature is the supreme body in a parliamentary democracy. The responsibilities of representatives are enormous and difficult, because they make laws, control and determine the national expenditure and revenues, and in a parliamentary democracy control the executive and the national policy. It is, therefore, essential that every voter should also have the 'Right to be Elected' to the legislature in case he can shoulder the onerous tasks of an elected representative.

It has been argued by some that it would be desirable from the functional standpoint to prescribe a qualification, demanding experience of work on a representative body. Laski is of the opinion that this right should be made contingent upon three years' service in a local public authority. He writes : "Absence of limitation may give us a Younger Pitt, but gives us a large number of members who go to the legislative assembly merely for the prestige which membership confers." That frustrates the ideal of democracy and representation. He, therefore, suggests a representative must possess previous experience and adequate knowledge of the working of a local body.

The Right to Public Office

This right implies equal opportunities for all citizens in the matter of holding public offices. In a democracy every citizen has the right of equal eligibility for any office, executive, administrative or judicial and to be protected against discrimination "on grounds only of religion, race, caste, sex, descent, place of birth, residence or any of them", as Art. 16(2) of the Indian Constitution puts it. Art. 16(1) ensures to all citizens in India "equality of opportunity...in matters relating to employment or appointment to any office under the state." This right, thus, is the gift of democracy which gives equal rights to all the citizens. This shows that even the will of an average citizen has channels of direct access to the sources of authority spreading over all public offices, executive, legislative and judicial. To entrust the power to the mass of people means, naturally, a more close and stringent scrutiny of public administration.

It does not, however, mean that academic, professional and other qualifications cannot be laid down for filling the various posts — all that it means is, that whatever qualifications are prescribed and whatever made is adopted for filling the posts they should not discriminate between the candidates "on grounds only of religion, race, caste, sex, dissent, place of birth, residence or any of them." Discrimination in respect of public offices, unjustified by wider canons of social justice, is the very antithesis of democracy. But in India, on account of certain historical reasons an exception has been made in the case of Scheduled Castes and Scheduled Tribes by reserving a certain percentage of seats for them. But this has been done with a view to bring about their more rapid development and to protect their interests for the time being.

The Right to Petition

The right to send petition for the redress of grievances is an old and valued right of the people. This right entitles every citizen to send petitions, either individually or collectively, to the competent authority, executive or legislative, for the redress of grievances. In a democracy, the governors cannot ignore the legitimate desires and grievances of the people, because they are the ultimate sovereigns. The government must always be alive to the grievances of the people and promptly respond to their needs. Otherwise, it hazards its own existence.

The Right of Criticising the Government

This right is available only in free and democratic states. This right is beneficial not only for the people but also for the government. It is necessary for keeping the government on the right path and to protect the interests of the people. Public criticism of governmental policies and actions helps to make the government efficient and good — alert and mindful of the interests of the people. And, it is for this reason that a responsible and constructive opposition party in the legislature is considered essential. The role and importance of healthy public criticism in a democracy cannot be overemphasised. Democracy is really a government by criticism, for truth only comes by the clash of opinion with opinion and every citizen has something of value to contribute and he must not be hindered in bringing it forward. Thus, the right of criticising the government must be adhered to both in letter and spirit.

The Right to Resist

It is sometimes claimed that a citizen has the right to resist the authority of the state if he honestly feels that a particular law or action of the government is inimical to his moral sense of justice. But the resistance of this type is only a moral right and not a legal right. Obviously, no state can permit an action which defies its authority and may jeopardise even its existence. T.H. Green has suggested that, as the consequences of disobedience are apt to be most serious and may even prove disastrous, great care should be exercised in making use of the "Right". A citizen must carefully consider whether the good which might accrue would greatly outweigh the harm which disobedience is bound to cause and, in any case, he should, in the first instance, win over the majority of the citizens to his view before attempting to upset the existing fabric of society. In the light of Green's proposition it may be conceded that if the majority of citizens really feel and believe that the laws of the state or the actions of the government are tyrannical, repugnant to the moral sense of justice, and are against the true interest of the people and their obedience may have demoralising and degenerating effects on them, they may resist such laws and authority.

To conclude our discussion on 'Civil' and 'Political' rights, it may be emphasised that these rights are not an end in themselves. They are the means for the development of human personality; and the creation of a healthy society and democratic polity. Therefore, they have to be guaranteed only to those who could use them wisely and judiciously. To give these rights to those who are ignorant and incapable of understanding the vital issues at stake is to endanger the foundations of democracy. But then what sort of democracy would it be where large sections of people do not enjoy 'civil' and 'political' rights?

2

Theories of Human Rights

It is very interesting to explore the origin and development of human rights. It could be done clearly with theories of human rights. Various theories have been propounded about human rights by different writers from time to time. We consider the following as important theories :

Various Theories of Rights

Various explanations of rights have been offered from time to time, but we consider the following important theories :

1. The Liberal-Individualist Theory of Natural Rights.
2. The Legal Theory of Rights.
3. The Historical Theory of Rights.
4. The Idealist or Personality Theory of Rights.
5. The Social Welfare Theory of Rights.

1. The Liberal-Individualist Theory of Natural Rights

The liberal theory of rights was propagated by the exponents of liberalism in the seventeenth and eighteenth centuries. The ideas which together are known by the term "liberalism", classical and modern, may often appear to be contradictory. However, certain tenets can be made out of them. Freedom of thought and political freedom are its first principles which were born with the struggle of the middle classes against feudalism. The liberal principles that have gone to influence the concept about rights included the principles of civil, fiscal, personal, social and economic liberty.

The liberal concept of rights explains that liberty issues in the form of individual rights. As Laski said, "Liberty is the atmosphere created by rights." Liberty consists in the maintenance of a system of rights. Individuals can enjoy their rights only when these are recognised and guaranteed by the law of the land. Rights are regarded as inviolate and fundamental of the state. The crown and glory of liberalism was political liberty and popular sovereignty.

The Liberal-Individualist Theory of Natural Rights is the earliest theory of rights. Though it can be traced back to the Greek times, yet it came to the fore in the seventeenth century when a persistent and powerful body of opinion in the West popularised the idea that all men possess certain rights by nature, irrespective or particular political, social or legal institutions. It meant that these rights are the gifts of nature. The individual has some natural, inalienable, fundamental, inherent, absolute and sacred rights by birth. They are as much a part of man's nature as the colour of his skin. They do not require any justification. They are self-evident truths. They are independent of society and the state. They can either be taken away by any other individual or the society. The state cannot deprive any man of rights which are born with him. They are the intrinsic properties of man 'as men'.

According to the exponents of the theory, the natural rights are pre-political and, according to some, they are pre-social also. They can be asserted any where and everywhere. In fact, these natural rights are an end in themselves. Locke says, all men are born free and rational. God has given authority to no man to compel another to carry out his wishes or orders. According to him, these natural and inalienable rights are the rights to "life, liberty and pursuit of happiness."

Although this theory is the oldest theory of rights yet it gained distinct recognition from the authors of the Social Contract Theory. John Locke, Hobbes and Thomas Paine made much use of it. In practical politics it exerted great influence on the constitutional struggle of America and France. Thus, the Virginian Constitution declares, "That all men are by nature equally free and independent, and have certain inherent rights, of which, when they enter into a state of society, they cannot be any compact deprive or divest their posterity; namely, the enjoyment of life and liberty, with the means of acquiring and possessing property, and pursuing, and obtaining happiness and safety." The American Declaration of Independence, 1776, holds these truths natural and declares that all men are created equal and are endowed by their Creator with certain inalienable rights.

Locke said that the individuals enjoyed the right to life, the right to property and liberty in the state of nature, that is, before the political state was born. These rights were called natural because they did not depend for their validity on the recognition and enforcement by the state. Hobbes adopts a totally different point of view. According to him, one's natural rights are one's natural powers. He says : "Every man has a right to everything, even to one another's body." Herbert Spencer holds that in the state of nature, one fundamental right of all men is the right to do that which he wills, provided he infringes not the equal freedom of others. Individualists also believed in the theory of natural rights. The Sociological School of Philosophers gives new meaning and significance to this theory. They opine that natural rights should be maintained even after the state came into existence because these are the essential conditions for human existence in society. Even in modern times it is far from dead. In many quarters of the world, the right to food, clothing and shelter, the right to work and political rights life the right to vote are asserted and carry with them the flavour of natural rights.

Criticism of the Liberal Individualist Theory of Natural Rights

The doctrine of natural rights has been strongly criticised. *First,* it is variously interpreted and there is no universal concept of natural rights. It is very difficult, if not impossible, to define the term "natural". D.G. Ritchie has written a whole volume on natural rights and brings out the various senses in which the term has been used. In which of the senses are we to understand the term 'nature' in speaking of natural rights? Will it mean the whole universe, or the non-human part of the universe, the ideal or the original or average? To use the paradoxical language of Prof. Hocking, it is natural for human beings to be artificial. Wearing clothes which was artificial at one time, is natural today. If "natural" means the whole process of nature, its normal meaning, the civilised condition is just as much natural as the savage condition. There is no reason why we should equate 'natural' with 'primitive.' To some, wife-beating is a matter conscience just as much as wife adoration may be to others. According to Muslims, one man can keep four wives and it appears natural to them, whereas it is illegal for others. The trouble with commonsense is that is not common and its verdict varies with individuals.

Secondly, among the supporters of this theory is no official, or complete or generally agreed list of natural rights. Some justify slavery as natural, others condemn it as being unnatural and artificial. Some assert that by nature men and women are equal; other deny it. Some hold that men are naturally good, others believe that by nature the are wicked. In the light of all this, we are inclined to agree with Ritchie's statement : "If you appeal to nature we may not be able to prove you wrong in you own court of appeal; but neither can you prove yourself right."

Thirdly, to so-called natural rights conflict with one another. The French Revolution declared liberty, equality and fraternity to be the absolute rights of man. But when we begin to apply them we are faced with endless difficulties. In no rational system can there be a place for absolute liberty and absolute equality. On the other hand, if we start with absolute equality, liberty soon vanishes. The theory of natural rights cannot give us a self-evident way of reconciling liberty and equality. Has a milk dealer, for example, the right to empty the cans of milk into the gutters in order to maintain a high price? Can a mill owner close his mill at any time that he likes without giving ample notice to his employees? These are questions which cannot be answered by the theory of natural rights. As Prof. Hocking points out, "My natural right does not tell me what my limits are. The trouble with such rights is that they present us with too many absolutes."

Fourthly, the implication of the theory of natural rights is that the state and social institutions in general are artificial and that they have robbed man of certain inherent rights which belonged to him in a state of nature. Rights represent, according to Laski, "The recovery of a lost inheritance. The state is a natural growth. Institutions are not artificial. They are embodiments of ethical ideas."

Fifthly, rights cannot exist in the state of nature. What man receives from nature is powers and not rights. For instance, nature gives man not the right but the power to defend himself from his enemies. We have rights only as members of the society. Rights antecedent to society are meaningless. They arise from the fact that man is a social animal. Membership in a common order is the foundation of rights. In the words of Bosanquet, "A right is a claim, recognised by society and enforced by the state." These two conditions exist only in a politically organised society. Rights become empty claims when not recognised and enforced by the state.

In spite of the above defects, the theory contains a large amount of truth. If by natural rights we mean rights which we had in the dim, prehistoric past and which we have since lost, it is an absurd conception. If, on the other hand, we interpret natural rights as ideal rights or moral rights which we ought to have in future, the conception is a very valuable one. Thus, the right to work is a natural right in the sense that in a well-ordered state it is desirable that every one has the opportunity to earn enough at least for his food, shelter and clothing. We may, therefore, define natural rights as those conditions which are required for the development of personality. As Laski observes : “Rights are not historic conditions possessed by man in the childhood of the race, but since lost.”

2. The Legal Theory of Rights

By the end of the eighteenth century and the beginning of the nineteenth century, the limitations and shortcomings of the Liberal-Individualist Theory of Rights were fully exposed. For instance, it was clear that the individuals could not enjoy the so-called ‘natural rights’ unless they were recognised by the state and protected by the laws of the state. Thus, the rise of the legal theory of rights was a logical corollary of the necessity of the recognition and protection of the natural rights of the individual.

The Legal Theory of Rights was also the outcome of the acceptance of the monistic view of sovereignty. According to this theory, political power is vested in the hands of a determinate authority and all the laws, policies and rights, etc., flow from this authority. Further, rights are the creation of the state. They are determined by the law of the state; granted by the laws of the state; and protected by the laws of the state.

Exponents of the Legal Theory of Rights

The Legal Theory of Rights was propounded by Hobbes; developed by Bentham and Austin; and supported by Ritchie and Solmond. While Hobbes established the relationship between rights and authority and maintained that there could be no rights without the existence of an authority, Bentham expressed the view that “Rights are the fruits of law and of the law alone. There are no rights without law — no rights contrary to law — no rights anterior to the law.” Barker also says : “Law contains rights and indeed is rights. Law and rights are simply two aspects of something which is essentially one....” Ritchie also holds the view that a “Legal right is the claim of an individual upon others recognised by the state.”

Statement of the Legal Theory of Rights

According to this theory, rights are the creation of the state. What the law gives or permits an individual are his rights, and what it does not give him are not his rights. Rights are neither absolute nor inherent as was advocated by the supporters of the theory of natural rights. They are relative to the law of the land. The state formulates them, enforces them and can restrict their scope. It can, if it so desires, abolish some of the rights or add more to the list of the existing rights. An individual's right to life, liberty, property, etc., is determined by the state.

Further, the individual has no rights against the state. If an individual has rights against the state, it is tantamount to saying that the individual has no rights. In a nutshell, the state is the only source of rights and individuals have no rights against the state. The rights have legal force behind them. They are protected and enforced by the law of the state. If anybody tries to violate or take away the right of another individual, he is punished by the law of the state. That is why the exponents of the legal theory of rights maintain the rights can exist only within the state. Outside the state, there can be no rights.

The theory of legal rights in opposed to the theory of natural rights. Its advocates argue that the so-called natural laws either agree with the laws of the land or disagree with them. If they agree, they are superfluous, and if they disagree, they are futile. Therefore, in either case, they can be ignored. It was in this context that Bentham, who pleads for the legal theory of rights, considered the so-called natural rights as being "nonsense upon stilts".

We also find traces of the legal theory of rights in the 'Social Contract' of Thomas Hobbes also. According to him, the fundamental right of every individual is that of self-preservation. This right, he believes, can be better maintained by the state than by the individual. When the Social Contract is formed, people unconditionally surrender all their rights to the sovereign and whatever the sovereign gives them is their right. In short, the three important implications of the theory of legal rights can be summarised as follows :

(i) Since the state is the only source of rights, the rights are not prior or interior to the state;

(ii) the state provides a legal machinery to guarantee the enjoyment of the rights accorded by it and

(iii) Rights are dynamic. Whenever the content of law changes, the substance of rights also changes.

Criticism of the Legal Theory of Rights

The theory of legal rights has been strongly criticised by many writers — Laski, N. Wilde, Plamentaz, Hocking and others. Laski, who is a pluralist, opines that the state does not create the rights; it merely recognises, maintains and co-ordinates them, so that all may enjoy the benefits of rights. According to him, and the other pluralists the sovereignty of the state is not absolute, it is limited by customs, traditions, morality as well as by the realities of the situation. Also man enjoys rights not only as a member of the state but also as a member of other associations. He observes : "Where ever men are banded together to perform a task that is part of the common welfare the body so formed has rights as real, and as compelling, as the right of the state." To limit the rights of man to the single category which membership of the state involves, "is to destroy his personality".

Further, it cannot be accepted that a mere decree of the state can make anything right. The question may be asked : Can law make bribery or corruption a right? Or, can law re-establish 'Satee'? Laski goes so far as to say that rights are independent of state recognition. This is, undoubtedly, and extreme view. The views of Herbert Spencer and N. Wilde seems to be more balanced. Spencer opines that the state does not create rights; it exists in order to maintain right. N. Wilde remarks : "The law does not create our rights, but only recognises and protects them. The rights themselves exist whether they are thus legalised or not. They are enforced because they are rights, and are not rights because they are enforced." A typical right should combine legal and moral recognition. Thus, the legal theory of rights is not acceptable to the pluralists.

Secondly, to say that the state is the sole creator of rights is to make it absolute. Legally, the state is supreme internally as well as externally. But, as pointed out earlier, there are many limitations imposed upon the state by customs, traditions, morality, habits and the will of the people. Laski holds, "The maintenance of right is much more a question of habit and tradition than of the formality of written enactment." Therefore, to argue that all rights are in reality derived from law is not correct. Also as the law of every country is subject to constant revision, it cannot be final creator of rights. Higher than law is our conception of right and wrong. Prof. Hocking says: "There is a logical distinction between what the law is and what it ought to be." Rights, according to Plamentaz, must have a foundation of right.

Thirdly, the legal theory of rights is very limited in scope. It does not cover the whole range of rights. As Hocking points out : "The weakness of the legal theory of rights is that it does not cover the whole field of rights. It explains the nature of only those rights which have been given a legal recognition by the state. It is silent in respect of moral rights." Also, this theory does not enable us to decide whether the rights that are recognised are the rights that ought to be recognised. When we say that a deaf man has the right to marry, we mean that no church or registrar can, in normal circumstances, refuse the performance of the necessary ceremonies, but we do not mean that we think he ought to have the right.

Finally, if we accept, as the theory of legal rights implies, that the state is the only source of rights, it would mean that there can be no rights against the state. It is a fallacious view. Under certain circumstances, the individuals can have rights against the state. While Laski calls it the right of resistance, T.H. Green regards it as the 'duty of resistance'. According to Laski, our obedience to the state is limited and conditional. It is the obedience to right and not the might; to justice, not to authority; to the ideal, not to the actual state. Therefore, the individual can have rights against the state just as much as the state can have rights against the individual.

Value of Theory

In spite of the above criticism, the legal theory of rights cannot be easily brushed aside. Rights, not supported by the laws of the state are mere claims. And, the state will support only such rights as are sanctioned by it. Barker is right when he says that the state is the immediate source of right. Also we cannot say that rights are possible apart from the state. Claims which are essential to the moral development of man, and which are violated or ignored by the state, can at best be only potential rights. They are the raw material or ground of rights. Only the legal recognition would make them rights. Thus, rights have both legal and moral aspects. To quote Bosanquet : "A right...... has both a legal and moral reference. It is a claim which can be enforced at law, which no moral imperative can be; but it is also recognised to be a claim which ought to be capable of enforcement at law, and thus it has a moral aspect...... A typical 'right' unites the two sides. It both is, and ought to be, capable of being enforced at law." It is in this context that Laski maintained that, "Every state is known by the rights that it maintains." A state is thus both a moral and legal entity.

3. The Historical Theory of Rights

This theory lays emphasis on the fact that rights are the product of history. In other words, the theory holds that : "History makes rights." This theory was propounded by the thinkers of the historical school of philosophy in the nineteenth century — Edmund Burke, Sir Henry Maine, Burges, etc. These thinkers maintained that rights are the product of long historical, evolutionary processes in society. And, rights are not static but go on changing with the changing times and circumstances.

The theory holds that rights are the crystallisation of customs and traditions. They have their origin in customs which once found practical social utility and passed on from one generation to another. Such customs were ultimately recognised as rights. For instance, the right to way on a public road is nothing but a customary right. If a person has been receiving a birthday gift from a friend for a number of years; he begins to expect it as a matter of right. What is a pure gratuity becomes a custom, and one expects it as a matter of course. In this regard Ritchie remarks : "The rights which the people think they ought to have are just those rights which they have been accustomed to have, or which they have a tradition (whether true or false) of having one possessed. Custom is primitive law." He further says that many of the so-called natural rights are the claims which have "the sanction of the longest and the least broken custom."

It is maintained by Edmund Burke that while the French Revolution (1789) was based on the abstract rights of man, the English Revolution (1688) was based on the customary rights of Englishmen. This statement contains much truth. There is no denying the fact that the French Revolution was the outcome of the political, economic and social conditions which prevailed in France in the eighteenth century. It had for its battle-cry the abstract principles of liberty, equality and fraternity, applicable to all men. The English Revolution, on the other hand, was simply a reassertion of rights that Englishmen had enjoyed since the days of Anglo-Saxon rule and which had found expression in documents like the Magna Carta and the Petition of Rights.

Criticism of the Historical Theory of Rights

There is some truth in the historical theory of rights. Many of our rights are based on customs and traditions. However, it does not mean that the origin of all our rights can be traced back to ancient customs and traditions. Prof. Summer of the Yale University opined that the *mores* or customs of people can make anything right. However, this view is not acceptable. Prof. Hocking asks : "Was slavery right when it was lawful? Was infanticide right?" And, the answer obviously is in the negative. Although slavery was customary in most parts of the world, it was never right. Thus, says Prof. Hocking : "It is just as foolish to say that custom is always right as to say that law makes right." Rights are dynamic. When they are tied to customs alone, we altogether ignore the dynamic nature of society and, accordingly, the changing contents of rights. Rights change with the facts of time and place. History, as such, is not the only basis of rights and customs do not provide an absolute right or standard.

If the right is always in relation to custom, reforms in society would become impossible. Without reforms the society would stagnate. The abolition of *Satee;* prohibition of polygamy ; the enactment of the Sharda Act; temple entry for the Scheduled Castes in India, etc., were all contrary to the prevalent customs of the country. Yet, enlightened public opinion supported such reforms. Thus, the historical theory of rights gives only a partial explanation of rights.

It is also pointed out by the critics of the above theory that all rights are not based on customs. For example, the right to social security or the right to education or the right to work, which are of recent origin and which most of the welfare states provide, have no basis in customs. Hence, the historical theory of rights is not correct.

To conclude, we can say that history, as such, is not the only basis of rights and customs do not provide an absolute right or standard. Thus, Prof. Hocking says : "Historical theory either gives no guidance at all or else gives false guidance, it is a helpless method unless lighted up by independent sources of interpretation. History, of course, cannot he ignored, but history cannot he relied on alone."

4. The Idealist or Personality Theory of Rights

The Idealist Theory of Rights is also called the "Personality Theory of Rights". The chief exponents of this theory were the German idealist philosophers though T.H. Green, an idealist thinker of England, and some other writers also supported this theory. According to this theory, rights are the external conditions essential to man's internal and real development. Human beings need healthy and congenial external conditions for the development of their personality. These conditions can only be created by the state.

Krause describes the system of rights "as the organic whole of the outward conditions necessary to the rational life." Hencrici defines a right as "that which is really necessary for the maintenance of material conditions essential to the existence and perfection of human personality." Green says that rights are powers "necessary to the fulfilment of man's vocation as a moral being." In short, the Idealistic Theory of Rights lays emphasis on the creation of those conditions which help the individual to develop his personality to the highest possible extent.

The Idealist Theory of Rights considers that the supreme right of every man is the right of personality. Hence, the perfection of human personality is the end, and in order to achieve this end, all rights are directed and subordinated to it. In other words, the right to personality is man's fundamental right and all other rights are derived from it. Even such important rights as the right to life, the right to liberty and the right to property are not absolute rights. They are to be judged by their contribution towards the development of human personality. The moment an individual abuses any of these rights for self-development, the society is justified in taking it away from him.

The theory looks at rights from a highly moral point of view. Rights are powers which an individual can claim from society on a moral plane. They are rooted in the mind or soul of a man. Every time he claims a right, he must be able to establish two things. In the first place, he must be able to convince the society that the right which he claims is absolutely necessary for his self-development. Secondly, he must convince the society that in making such a claim, he is not in any way infringing or interfering with the similar claims of others.

The theory lays emphasis on the creation of external conditions for the moral development of man. Without these conditions, it is not possible for the individual to live and realise his full stature. However, they are to be understood in a social context. Just as an individual wants to develop his personality, others in society also have a similar aim and, therefore, it is implied that rights arise in a society and the rights of the individual should be in harmony with those of others. Rights are to be linked with the individual good and the common good of all in society.

The above explanation of the Idealist Theory of Rights discloses three important facts. They are as follows :

- (*i*) That rights arise in society; they are inherent in the nature of man, which is to will his own good. To will his own good implies the good of others also since an isolated good of the individual is not possible.
- (*ii*) Every right has a corresponding obligation, *i.e.,* an individual's right of self-development should not interfere with the right of development of others.
- (*iii*) Individual rights are subordinated to the fundamental right of man's perfection. The society should see that the enjoyment of a man's rights helps him to attain the perfection of his personality. If any one of these rights does not help him towards reaching that end, society can deprive him of the enjoyment of that right.

It is in the context of this explanation that Laski says : "Rights, in fact, are those conditions of social life without which no man can seek, in general, to be himself at his best." The system of rights is an organic whole which is moral in nature and helps to uplift the stature of man and society simultaneously.

Evaluation of the Idealist Theory of Rights

The Idealist Theory of Rights, in so far as it looks at rights from the moral or ethical angle, relates right to morality than legality. Its objective of the highest growth of the individual in a social context has greatly appealed to the moral and democratic mind of man. Its emphasis that no man is to be treated as a means to another's end has also rendered great service.

However, the theory is vague and ambiguous. It is very difficult either to fix the standards of moral freedom or the conditions necessary for each individual for his fullest self-development. Further, the problem of always reconciling the 'individual good' with the 'social good' remains insoluble. Moreover, as the principle of 'greatest happiness of the greatest number' as expounded by the utilitarians cannot be measured, similarly the conditions supposed to be aiming at the moral perfection of the individual cannot be assessed.

Nevertheless, the Idealist Theory of Rights is superior to the legal, historical and social welfare theories. It is because of its emphasis on the one absolute right of all human beings — the right of personality. This, undoubtedly, has been its monumental contribution in the realm of rights.

(5) The Social Welfare Theory of Rights

The Social Welfare Theory of Rights was popularised by the utilitarians, Bentham and Mill, during the later half of the nineteenth century. It came to be accepted because the philosophy of 'individualism' could not provide harmony in society or reconcile harmoniously 'self-interest' with the 'social interest'. It, thus, arose as a protest against the exploitation and dehumanisation of the 'social and moral man' and looked at right solely from the point of view of social welfare. It pointed out that rights are created by the society and are aimed at realising social welfare. And, since rights are conditions of social welfare, law, customs, usages, traditions and natural rights "should all yield to what is socially useful or socially desirable." What is socially useful should have for its test the greatest happiness of the greatest number. The right to speech, for instance, is not unlimited. It is to be determined by considerations of social expediency. Similarly, the right to property does not mean the right of the few to prosper at the cost of the many. In other words, the main thrust of the

Social Welfare Theory of Rights is that the rights of the individual are limited by considerations of social welfare and no individual can be given rights against the welfare of the society.

The exponents of the Social Welfare Theory of Rights set up the principle of the greatest happiness of the greatest number as the criterion by which to judge what ought to be Laski, too, accepted utility as the basis of rights and opined that "the utility of a right is, therefore, its value to all the members of the state." He further says that rights are not independent of society, but inherent in it. "We have them... for its protection as well as for our own...Rights, therefore, are correlative with functions." We have them so that we make our contribution to the social good. We have no right to act unsocially. We have no claim to receive without the attempt, at least, to pay for what we receive. Thus rights are the conditions of social life without which no man can seek, in general, to be himself at his best. We have rights so that we may contribute to the common good. Our rights are built upon our contribution to the well-being of society. And, to quote Laski again : "I cannot have rights against the public welfare, for that, ultimately, is to give me rights against a welfare which is intimately and inseparably associated with my own." Rights, as such, are built upon their utility to the individual and the community.

Evaluation of the Social Welfare Theory of Rights

The Social Welfare Theory of Rights has the great merit of upholding the principle of social justice. It lays emphasis on the social character of rights and the importance of social welfare. It is in tune with the concept of modern welfare states. The utilitarians who supported this theory provided a practical approach to the solution of the problems of rights. They advocated legislation in different fields to uphold the rights of individuals and, it was owing to the Social Welfare Theory of Rights that in many countries several political, social and economic rights were guaranteed to individuals and many reforms were introduced. Their pragmatic approach to rights yielded rich dividends for the common man.

At the same time it cannot be denied that the theory not only suffers from vagueness but can even prove dangerous for the individual. It is very difficult to say as to what exactly social welfare means or what precisely constitutes happiness. Does 'social welfare' means the greatest happiness of the greatest number, majority interest, public opinion or what the government of the day considers to be the common good? In fact, much political wrong has been done, during recent times, to the individuality of man in the name of social good. In the garb of social good, the governments are arming themselves with excessive powers and this has led to the erosion of the rights of the individual. Social welfare can be made a convenient excuse for trampling upon the rights of the individual. A social system which discounts individual personality and glorifies common interest of society cannot continue for long. It is bound to give rise to opposition from that section of society whose personality is crushed and whose rights are frustrated. Thus, the Social Welfare Theory of Rights, in spite of its merits, also suffers from serious handicaps.

3

The Universal Declaration of Human Rights

The Universal Declaration of Human Rights was adopted by United Nations General Assembly on 10 December 1948. It was proclaimed by the same Assembly Resolution 217 (iii) of 10 December 1948.

Preamble

Its Preamble reads,

Whereas recognition of the inherent dignity and of the equal and inalienable rights of all members of the human family is the foundation of freedom, justice and peace in the world.

Whereas disregard and contempt for the human rights have resulted barbarous acts which have outraged the conscience of mankind, and the advent of a world in which human beings shall enjoy freedom of speech and belief and freedom from fear and want has been proclaimed as the highest aspiration of the common people.

Whereas it is essential, if man is not to be compelled to have recourse, as a last resort, to rebellion against tyranny and oppression, that human rights should be protected by the rule of law.

Whereas it is essential to promote the development of friendly relations between nations.

Whereas the peoples of the United Nations have in the Charter reaffirmed their faith in fundamental human rights, in the dignity and worth of the human person and in the equal rights of men and women and have determined to promote social progress and better standards of life in larger freedom.

Whereas Member States have pledged themselves to achieve, in Co-operation with the United Nations, the promotion of universal respect for and observance of human rights and fundamental freedoms.

Whereas a common understanding of these rights and freedoms is of the greatest importance for the full realization of this pledge.

Now, therefore,

The General Assembly

Proclaims this Universal Declaration of Human Rights as a common standard of achievement for all peoples and all nations, to the end that every individual and every organ of society, keeping this Declaration constantly in mind, shall strive by teaching and education to promote respect for these rights and freedoms and by progressive measures, national and international to secure their universal and effective recognition and observance, both among the people of member States themselves and among the people of territories under their jurisdiction.

Provisions of the UDHR

The UDHR differs from the traditional and fundamental laws of the 18th and 19th centuries. The Declaration consists of 30 articles.

They are,

Article 1

All human beings are born free and equal in dignity and rights. They are endowed with reason and conscience and should act towards one another in a spirit of brotherhood.

Article 2

Every one is entitled to all the rights and freedoms setforth in this Declaration, without distinction of any kind, such as race, colour, sex, language, religion, political or other opinion, national or social origin, property, birth or other status.

Further more, no distinction shall be made on the basis of the political, jurisdictional or international status of the country or territory to which a person belongs, whether it be independent, trust, non-self governing or under any other limitation of sovereignty.

Article 3

Every one has the right to life, liberty and security of person.

Article 4

No one shall be held in slavery or servitude; slavery and the slave trade shall be prohibited in all their forms.

Article 5

No one shall be subjected to torture or to cruel, inhuman or degrading treatment or punishment.

Article 6

Every one has the right to recognition everywhere as a person before the law.

Article 7

All are equal before the law and are entitled without any discrimination to equal protection of the law. All are entitled to equal protection against any discrimination in violation of this Declaration and against any incitement to such discrimination.

Article 8

Every one has the right to an effective remedy by the competent national tribunals for acts violating the fundamental rights granted him by the constitution or by law.

Article 9

No one shall be subjected to arbitrary arrest, detention or exile.

Article 10

Every one is entitled in full equality to a fair and public hearing by an independent and impartial tribunal, in the determination of his rights and obligations and of any criminal charge against him.

Article 11

(1) Every one charged with a penal offence has the right to be presumed innocent until proved guilty according to law in a

public trial at which he has had all the guarantees necessary for his defence.

(2) No one shall be held guilty of any penal offence on account of any act or omission which did not constitute a penal offence, under national or international law, at the time when it was committed. Nor shall a heavier penalty be imposed than the one that was applicable at the time the penal offence was committed.

Article 12

No one shall be subjected to arbitrary interference with his privacy, family, home or correspondence, nor to attacks upon his honour and reputation. Every one has the right to protection of the law against such interference or attacks.

Article 13

(1) Every one has the right of freedom of movement and residence within the borders of each State.

(2) Everyone has the right to leave any country, including his own, and to return to his country.

Article 14

(1) Everyone has the right to seek and to enjoy in other countries asylum from persecution.

(2) This right may not be involved in the case of prosecutions genuinely arising from non-political crimes or from acts contrary to the purposes and principles of the United Nations.

Article 15

(1) Everyone has the right to a nationality.

(2) No one shall be arbitrarily deprived of his nationality nor denied the right to change his nationality.

Article 16

(1) Men and women of all age, without any limitation due to race, nationality or religion, have the right to marry and found a family. Then are entitled to equal rights as to marriage, during marriage and at its dissolution.

(2) Marriage shall be entered into only with the free and full consent of the intending spouses.

(3) The family is the natural and fundamental group unit of society and is entitled to protection by the society and the State.

Article 17

(1) Every one has the right to own property alone as well as in accosication with others.

(2) No one shall be arbitrarily deprived of his property.

Article 18

Every one has the right to freedom of thought, conscience and religion; this right includes freedom to change his religion or belief, and freedom, either alone or in community with others and in public or private, to manifest his religion or belief in teaching, practice, worship and observance.

Article 19

Every one has the right to freedom of opinion and expression; this right includes freedom to hold opinions without reference and to seek, receive and impart information an ideas through any media and regardless of frontiers.

Article 20

(1) Every one has the right to freedom of peaceful assembly and association.

(2) No one may be compelled to belong to an association.

Article 21

(1) Every one has the right to take part in the Government of his country, directly or through freely chosen representatives.

(2) Everyone has the right to equal access to public service in his country.

(3) The will of the people shall be the basis of the authority of Government; this will be expressed in periodic and genuine elections which shall be by universal and equal suffrage and shall be held by secret vote or by equivalent free voting procedures.

Article 22

Every one, as a member of society has the right to social security and is entitled to realisation, through national effort and international co-operation and in accordance with the organisation and resources of each State, of the economic, social and cultural rights indispensable for the dignity and the free development of his personality.

Article 23

(1) Every one has the right to work, to free choice of employment, to just and favourable conditions of work and to protection against unemployment.

(2) Every one, without any discrimination has the right to equal pay for equal work.

(3) Every one who works has the right to just and favourable remuneration ensuring for himself and his family an existence worthy of human dignity and supplemented, if necessary, by other means of social protection.

(4) Every one has the right to form and to join trade unions for the protection of his interests.

Article 24

Every one has the right to rest and leisure, including reasonable limitation of working hours and periodic holidays with pay.

Article 25

(1) Every one has the right to a standard of living adequate for the health and well-being of himself and of his family, including food, clothing, housing and medical care and necessary social services and the right to security in the event of unemployment, sickness, disability, widowhood, old age or other lack of livelihood in circumstances beyond his control.

(2) Motherhood and childhood are entitled to special care and assistance. All children, whether born in or out of wedlock shall enjoy the same social protection.

Article 26

(1) Every one has the right to education. Education shall be free, atleast in the elementary and fundamental stages. Elementary education shall be compulsory. Technical and professional

education shall be made generally available and higher education shall be equally accessible to all on the basis of merit.

(2) Education shall be directed to the full development of the human personality and to the strengthening of respect for human rights and fundamental freedoms. It shall promote understanding, tolerance and friendship among all nations, racial or religious groups and shall further the activities of the UN for the maintenance of peace.

(3) Parents have a prior right to chose the kind of education that shall be given to their children.

Article 27

(1) Every one has the right to freely participate in the cultural life of the community, to enjoy the arts and to share in scientific advancement and its benefits.

(2) Every one has the right to the protection of the moral and material interest resulting from any scientific, literary (or) artistic production of which he is the author.

Article 28

Every one is entitled to a social and international order in which the rights and freedoms set-forth in this Declaration can be fully realized.

Article 29

(1) Every one has duties to the community in which alone the free and full development of his personality is possible.

(2) In the exercise of his rights and freedoms every one shall be subject only to such limitations as are determined by law solely for the purpose of securing due recognition and respect for the rights and freedom of others and of meeting the just requirements of morality, public order and the general welfare in a democratic society.

(3) These rights and freedoms may in no case be exercised contrary to the purposes and principles of the United Nations.

Article 30

Nothing in this Declaration may be interpreted as implying for any State, group (or) person any right to engage in any activity or to perform any act aimed at the destruction of any of the rights and freedoms set forth herein.

Out of these 30 articles, 21 of them set forth civil and political rights; 6 cover economic, social and cultural rights and the rest deal with general direction, to be followed by the member States (For details Refer Last Chapter).

Importance

The UDHR sets a new International Standard.

According to Mrs. Roosevelt (The Chairperson of the Commission of Human Rights and the Principal representative of the U.S.A on the Third Committee), The Declaration was the first and foremost a declaration of the basic principles to serve as a common standard for all nations. She also added that, "It is the International Magna Carta of all Mankind".

No doubt it is the greatest effort made by mankind to give society new legal and moral foundations.

According to Prof. Humphery, "It is a part of the law of nations. It possesses the moral and political authority. It is sufficiently electric and flexible. The recent developments ensure its continuing relevance as a living instrument of incomparable importance in the field of human rights."

The Director General of UNESCO, Mr. T. Bodet called this Declaration as "The richest in promise of all the International texts to which the government have subscribed since 1945 in order to give life to the San Francisco Charter." The Declaration has changed the very nature of international law.

Impact of UDHR

The Tehran Proclamation (1968) and the Helsinki Declaration of 1975 endorsed by the General Assembly emphasis the Human Rights and Freedom of Status.

4

International Covenants on Human Rights

During the San Francisco Conference held in 1945, a proposal was put forward to embody an international Bill of Rights in the United Nations Charter. The General Assembly of the UN agreed it in January 1946.

In 1947, the Commission on Human Rights decided that the bill should consist of the 'Declaration', 'the Convention' (Covenant) and the 'Measures of Implementation'. This decision was again approved by the General Assembly in 1948. In 1952, it was decided that there shall be two great Covenants one on Civil and Political Rights and the other on Economic, Social and Cultural Rights. Following this, a separate instrument called the optional Protocol to the Civil and Political Right Covenant was adopted in 1966 to regulate the implementation arrangements. As such the two Covenants were adopted unanimously on 16, December 1966 but they came into force only in 1976.

The Covenants are to affirm legal obligations of States to respect human rights. The UDHR, the ICCPR and the ICESCR constitute a trinity, often referred as the *Magna Carta of Humanity.*

1. The International Covenant on Civil and Political Rights-1966

It came into force on 23, March 1976 together with its Optional Protocol. The major rights and freedoms provided by this Covenant are Right to Self Determination, right to life, abolition of slavery and suppression of slave trade, right to liberty, right of prisoners to be treated with humanity, right of not to be imprisoned arbitrarily, right of every one to leave any country, including his own and to return to his country, right to equality in the administration of justice, right to provide legal assistance, right against retroactive criminal legislation, right to privacy, right to freedom of thought, conscience and religion, right to freedom of opinion and expression, right to freedom of peaceful assembly, right to freedom of association, rights relating to marriage and family protection, right of the child, right to take part in the conduct of public affairs, and right to equality before law and equal protection of the law.

I. *The Right of Self Determination* : Article I of this Covenant provides for the peoples, right to exercise self-determination. By this, the signatory States freely determine their political status and pursue their economic, social and cultural development and freely dispose of their natural wealth and resources without prejudice to any obligations arising out of international economic co-operation based upon the principle of mutual benefits and international law. At the same time people should not be deprived of their means of subsistence.

II. *Right to life* : Article 6 of the Covenant provides that every one has the inherent right to life and this right shall be protected by law. No one has the right to interfere in the right of one's life.

III. *Prohibition of torture and inhuman treatment* : As per this right, no one shall be subjected to torture and inhuman treatment. Article 7 provides for this right.

IV. *Prohibition of Slavery and Slave Trade* : Article 8 provides for this right and as such no one shall be held in slavery. It also prohibits slave trade in all forms.

V. *Right to liberty* : Article 9 speaks about the right to liberty. It provides security to each and every one. It establishes that no one shall be arrested arbitrarily or put under detention. No one shall be deprived of his liberty except on the grounds of law.

VI. *Right of Prisoners :* Article 10 provides that the prisoners shall be treated with humanity and respect. It also stresses the need for respecting their inherent dignity.

VII. *Right of not to be imprisoned for inability to fulfil a contractual obligation :* Article 11 provides that no one shall be imprisoned just on the ground of inability to fulfil a contractual obligation.

VIII. *Right to freedom of Movement, to leave any country and to return to his country* : Article 12 provides that every one within the territory of a State shall have the right to freedom of movement and right to choose his residence. It also provides that every one is free to leave his country and go to any country and return to his own country.

IX. *Right to equality before the Courts* : Article 14 provides that all are equal before law. As such every one shall be entitled to a fair and public hearing by a competent, independent court or tribunal established by law.

X. *Right provide legal assistance* : Article 14 (3) (d) provides that every one shall be entitled to defend himself in person or through legal assistance of his choice.

XI. *Right against retroactive criminal legislation* : Article 15 provides that no one shall be held guilty of any criminal offence of any act which did not constitute a criminal offence, under national or international laws at that time when it was committed. It also provides that no heavy penalty shall be imposed rather than the one that was applicable at the time when the criminal committed that offence.

XII. *Right to privacy* : Article 17 provides that no one shall be subjected to unlawful interference with his private life, family, home etc. and it also provides that no unlawful attack shall be posed on any one so as to affect his reputation. If any one is affected by such interferences he shall have the right to seek the protection of law.

XIII. *Right to freedom of thought, conscience and religion* : Article 18 provides that every one shall have the right to freedom of thought, conscience and religion *i.e.*, one has the right to adopt any religious belief of his choice either individually or in union with others and either in public or private. One also has the freedom of worship, religious practice and teaching.

XIV. *Right to freedom of opinion & expression* : Article 19 provides that every one shall have the right to freedom of opinion without any interference and the right to freedom of expression. This includes freedom of speech, the right to receive and impart all sorts of information, regardless of frontier either orally or in writing or in print.

XV. *Right to freedom of peaceful assembly* : Article 21 provides for the recognition of peaceful assembly. Except law, no restrictions shall be imposed on this right. This right is to be enjoyed without any hindrance to the democratic society in the interests of national safety and security. At the same time it also stresses the need for the protection of public health and freedom of others. One's freedom should not affect the freedom of others.

XVI. *Right to freedom of association* : Article 22 provides the right to freedom of association with others. This includes the right to form trade unions and join in them for the protection of one's interests.

XVII. *Rights relating to marriage and family protection* : Article 23 provides the right relating to marriage and family protection. In recognises the right of men and women of marriageable age to marry and form a family. It also provides that no marriage shall be conducted without the full consent of the concerned intending spouses.

XVIII. *Right of the Child* : Article 24 provides that every child has the right of protection without any discrimination in the name of race, sex, colour, nation, language, origin, or birth. It also provides that every child shall be registered immediately after his/her birth and shall have a name and every child has the right to acquire a nationality.

XIX. *Right to take part in the conduct of public affairs* : Article 25 provides that each and every citizen has the right to take part in the conduct of public affairs directly or through freely chosen representatives. It also provides the right to vote and to be elected at elections by universal suffrage and shall be held by secret ballots. It further provides equality in public services in the country to which one belongs to.

XX. *Right to equality before law and equal protection of the law* : Article 26 provides that all are equal before law. All are entitled to the equal protection of the law of the land. Here, the law shall prohibit any discrimination and guarantee to all persons equal and effective protection against discrimination in the name of race, sex, colour, religion, language etc.

Implementation of the Covenant

This Covenant has the provision to check violation of human rights and implement human rights. In order to implement it, an international organ has been established by the Covenant. That is known as the "Human Rights Committee".

Constitution of the Human Rights Committee

This committee consists of 18 members of high calibre in the field of human rights. Among these members some are legal experts and others are interested experts in the field of human rights. As per rules, the members of Human Rights Committee should be elected by the International Court of Justice. But the Covenant envisages that the members shall be elected by the state parties to the covenant. At the same time due consideration shall be given to equitable geographical distribution of membership and to the representation of the different forms of civilizations and of the principal legal systems. Further the Committee shall not include more than one national of the same State. The elected member's term of office is for four years. However, the term of 9 of the elected members at the first instance shall expire at the end of 2 years. The names of these members shall be chosen by lot by the Chairman of the meeting. They are eligible for re-election if renominated. The elected members receive emoluments from the resources of UN. Accordingly 38 State parties to the Covenant met for the first time on 20, September 1976 and the elected members term began from 1, January 1977. The elected 18 members belonged to Bulgaria, Canada, Equador, Iran, Mauritius, Norway, Romania, Rwanda, Soviet Russia, Syria, Tunisia, UK and West Germany.

Measures of Implementation

The Human Rights Committee follows 4 different ways of procedure in implementing the human rights as provided in the Covenant. They are (1) Meetings, (2) Reporting, (3) Inter State Communication System and (4) Conciliation.

1. Meetings. The Committee's meetings usually held at Geneva. It elects its officers for a period of 2 years and they are eligible for re-election. It establishes its own rules and its decisions are to be made accordingly. It also adopts provisional rules of procedure as per the rules of the UN. organs.

2. Reporting. Article 40 (1) provides the State Parties to submit the reports with in one year of the entry into force of the Covenant and also whenever they are requested to do so by the Committee. All such reports are to be submitted to the Secretary General of the UN. He will transfer them to the Committee for further action. The Committee in turn scrutinises the sent reports and sends them to the State Parties with its comments. A copy of the report will be sent to ECOSOC by the Committee. Further the committee is required to submit an annual report on its activities to the General Assembly. The reports are divided into two parts. The first part contains the general legal framework within which the Civil and Political rights arc protected in the concerned State. It also includes whether the provisions of the Covenant can be directly enforced by the Courts or authorities concerned. If any of the human rights mentioned in the Covenant has been violated, the report should speak about the remedies that are available to the concerned and other measures that have been taken to implement the Covenant.

The second part of the report consists of the legislative, administrative or other measures that are in practice with regard to each right. It should also come out with any limitation or restriction imposed on the enjoyment of the right and should describe other problems or hurdles that affect the enjoyment of the rights by the people of the State. In addition, all other informations related to the rights referred to in the Covenant could also be sent. It will help the Committee to develop a suitable and constructive dialogue and discussion with the State Party in connection with the implementation of the Covenant. This helps for a better and peaceful understanding among nations. Some State Parties are not showing due interest in submitting the reports to the Committee. Out of 38 States that have required to submit their reports by the end of 1977, only 23 State Parties submitted their reports to the Committee in 1978. There were some States which sent their reports only after reminders from the Committee and there are other States which did not sent their reports even after reminders and there are other States which did not furnish the required information in their reports which stand as a hurdle to the successful functioning of the Committee.

3. Inter State Communication System. The Covenant on Civil and Political Rights acknowledges this system and expects that the State Parties should be keen on the treatment of citizens in other countries an complain the same to the Committee. But in practice, they are little interested in doing so. Rather they are interested in protecting and promoting their own countries interest. This sort of behaviour could not help the functioning of inter-state communication system in the expected level. Article 41 (1) (a) of the Covenant on Civil and Political Rights stresses the bilateral settlement between the concerned States. As such, if a State Party considers that another State Party is not giving effect to the provisions of the Covenant, it may draw the attention of that concerned State Party by sending a communication in writing. The State that have received the communication should respond it within three months after the receipt of the communication by sending a communication to the sender State. That should contain the explanation in writing and the clarification of the communicated matter and it should also include the remedies taken by the Government of the State to solve the referred matter.

Article 41 (1) (b) insists that if the matter is not adjusted to the fullest satisfaction of both the concerned States with in 6 months after the receipt of communication, they have the right to refer the matter to the Human Rights Committee. There are also provisions for domestic remedies. By this, it is clear that the Committee has the obligation to ascertain if all the domestic remedies have been exhausted in the matter in confirmity with the international law. If the matter is prolonged by a State without any reason, this principle is not applicable. The communication received by the Committee may call upon the concerned State Parties to find out a friendly solution of the referred matter on the basis of respect for human rights and fundamental freedoms as recognised in the Covenant. Sometimes the Committee may ask the State Parties concerned to furnish relevant informations, if needed. The concerned State Parties also have the right to represent and make their submissions either in writing or oral explanation. On receipt of information the committee should scrutinise it and shall submit its reports within 12 months and a copy of the report shall be communicated to the concerned State Parties. This process is optional and is applicable only to those States that have accepted it by a declaration. Such declarations are to be submitted to the Secretary General and may be withdrawn by the State Parties Whenever they want, after sending a notification to the Secretary General. It is to be observed that this will not affect the continuance of consideration of a matter which has been already referred by a State Party or Parties. In 1979, only ten States opted for the Inter-State Communication system, a discouraging response indeed.

4. Conciliation Procedure. When the Committee is not able to find out a solution for a referred matter, with the consent of the concerned State Parties, it may appoint an Adhoc Conciliation Commission. This will help the concerned State Parties to reach a suitable solution. This Commission shall consists of 5 members acceptable to the concerned State Parties. They shall not be the nationals of concerned State Parties. These members serve in their personal capacity. If the concerned State Parties fail to reach an amicable solution within 3 months after the composition of the said Commission, its members concerning are elected by secret ballot by a 2/3 majority of the Committee from among its members. Then the Commission elects its own Chairman and carry on its procedure. The meeting shall be held at Geneva or at the headquarters of the UN or at any other convenient place as determined by the Commission with the consultation of the Secretary General and the concerned State Parties. The Commission has the special right to consider the matter. Here the concerned State Parties representation is not sought.

After consideration, the Commission is required to submit its reports to the Chairman of the Committee. The time capsule is 12 months. If the solution is amicable, the Commission confines its report to a brief statement of the facts and of the solution reached. If a solution is not reached the Commission shall explain its 'findings' and its 'views' in its report. As a follow up, the concerned State Parties are required to notify the Chairman stating whether they accept the report of the Commission or not, within 3 months. The concerned State Parties are free to accept or reject the views submitted by the Commission. It is to be noted that there are certain limitations imposed upon the rights enumerated in the Covenant. They are subject to derogation at the time of public emergency.

Optional Protocol to the Covenant on Civil and Political Rights (16 December 1966)

The International Covenant on Civil and Political Rights and the Optional Protocol are separate instruments. But they are related to each other. Because, only the State Parties to the Covenant can become parties to the Protocol. Both the Covenant and the Protocol came into force simultaneously on 23, March 1976. This has provided the individuals a right to make petitions before the Human Rights Committee. It has proved that the individual is the nucleus of every human activity in the field of International Law. The Protocol provides a right to the State Parties to denounce it at any time by sending a notification to the Secretary General of the United Nations. Articles 1, 2, and 3 refer the sources, subject matter and admissibility of communications. The Human Rights Committee is competent to receive communications from individuals. Communications may be declared inadmissible by the Committee. Articles 4, 5 and 6 prescribe the action taken by the Committee on the individual communications. Article 5 (2) of the Protocol provides the conditions for admissibility of communication. The Optional Protocol speaks of only individuals. So, a group of individuals can also make communications. The activities of the Committee in protecting the rights of man is praise-worthy.

Details of the Optional Protocol

Optional protocol to the International Covenant on Civil and Political Rights.

Adopted and opened for signature, ratification and accession by General Assembly Resolution 2200 A (XXI) of 16 December 1966. Entry into force 23 March 1976, in accordance with Article 9 (For Details Refer Last Chapter)

The Covenant has flashed out the fundamental freedom and India has ratified it during 1977-79. Ratifying country undertakes to protect its people by law against cruel, inhuman or degrading treatment. It recognizes the right of every human being to life, liberty, privacy and security of a person. (For details refer the Chapter "India and Human Rights").

Right to Self-Determination

United Nations' concern for human rights begins with the right to self-determination. As per Article 1 of the International Covenant on Civil and Political Rights (1966), all, peoples, have the right of self determination. They freely determine their political status and pursue their economic, social and cultural development and may, for their own ends, freely prejudice to any obligations arising out of international economic co-operation, based upon the principle of mutual benefit and international law. People may not be deprived of their own means of subsistance.

The Universal human right-the Right to self-determination is within the frame-work of the UN Charter, and the two historical Covenants-1966. Equal rights and self-determination of peoples are the principles incorporated in the conventional law and customary International Law. The UN Charter lays down the self-determination and equality of nations as conventional rules of International Law. The General Assembly Declarations on the self-determination made under Articles 10, 13 and 14 of the UN Charter constitute a customary law of the UN on that. The self-determination right falls in the Article 38 of the International Court of Justice. The UN has provided the general principles of international law relating to the 'Right of the Nations' self-determination. The General Assembly of the UN made a declaration on 14, December 1960, *i.e.,* The Declaration on the granting of Independence to Colonial Countries and people. The General Assembly declares that all peoples have the right to self-determination, by virtue of the right they freely determine their political status and freely pursue their economic, social and cultural development. The subjection of people to alien subjection, domination and exploitation constitutes a denial of fundamental human rights in country to the Charter of UN and is an impediment to the promotion of world peace and co-operation. Inadequacy of political, economic, social or educational preparedness should never serve as a pretext for delaying independence. All armed action or repressive measures of all kinds directed against dependent peoples shall cease so as to enable them to exercise peacefully and freely their right to complete independence, and the integrity of their national territory shall be respected. Any attempt aimed at the partial or total disruption of the national unity and the territorial integrity of a country is incompatible with the purposes and principles of the Charter of the UN. All States shall observe faithfully and strictly the provisions of the UN Charter, the UDHR, and the present declaration on the basis of equality, non-interference in the internal affairs of all States and respect for the sovereign rights of all peoples and their territorial integrity.

The UN General Assembly further reaffirmed the right to self-determination by passing various Resolutions on various occasions between 1966 and 1974. They were :

(1) 2189 (XXI) of 13 December 1966.
(2) 2326 (XXII) of 10 December 1967.
(3) 2465 (XXIII) of 20 December 1968.
(4) 2545 (XXIV) of 11 December 1969.
(5) 2078 (XXV) of 14 December 1970.
(6) 2878 (XXVI) of 20 December 1971.
(7) 2910 (XXVII) of 2 November 1972.
(8) 3163 (XXVIII) of 14 December 1973.
(9) 3328 (XXIX) of December 1974. The resolutions warrant the peoples to exercise their right to self-determination and independence.

The sovereignty of the people including those who are struggling for their Right to self-determination and independence embodies sovereignty over their national resources. The General Assembly of the UN, adopted the principles of 'Permanent Sovereignty' over natural resources by the resolution 1803 (XVII) on 14 December 1962. The UN Charter provides the principle of non-use of force and non-intervention in its Article 2(4). The self-determination principle is further re-affirmed in the context of stability and growth of nations in Article 55 of the UN Charter. All these provisions make it clear that the dependent peoples have the inalienable Right to self determination. Colonisation in any form is illegal. The UN declarations urge the member States to fulfil decolonisation process in order to maintain equality of nations, peace and stability in the comity of nations. The General Assembly had urged the Colonial powers to stop military installations in colonies immediately. The Vienna Conference on Human Rights held in 1993 urged the States to remove reservations on the rights of the dependent peoples. The Rights of Nations to self-determination has been universally accepted. The Right to self-determinations has been firmly established within the decolonisation framework and its exercise is lawful and legitimate.

2. International Covenant on Economic, Social and Cultural Rights

The adoption of 'A Bill of Rights of Man' was desired by several delegations at the San Francisco Conference'. The General Assembly decided to adopt 2 Covenants in 1952. One was on the Civil and Political Rights and the other was on the Economic, Social and Cultural Rights. On 16 December 1966, the General Assembly unanimously adopted these covenants. They were put into practice on 23 March 1976. 175 States became the signatories of this Covenant. Almost all the UN member countries ratified this Covenant. India is also one among the signatories of the Covenant.

A country ratifying the Covenant on Economic, Social and Cultural Rights acknowledges its responsibility to promote better living conditions of its people. It recognises every one's right to work, to fair wages, to social security, to adequate standards of living and freedom from hunger and to health and education. It also undertakes to ensure the right of every one to form and join trade unions. For that, the State Parties are expected to adopt legislative measures. The rights affirmed by the Covenant contribute yet another milestone in the field of human rights in 20th century. Further it had helped for the development of freedom and human rights. All the State Parties have extended full support to the Covenant. It also helps the State Parties to develop friendly and prestigeous relationship among themselves. The Covenant also envisages the duties and responsibilities of man for himself and for the society too. The State Parties to the Covenant agree to take steps either individually or through international assistance and co-operation, especially economic and technical, to the maximum of its available resources, with a view to achieve progressively the full realisation of the rights recognised in the Covenant. The Covenant and its provisions are put in five different parts.

PART I

(1) Each individual has the right to establish his own status. Based on this, he may develop his economic, social, cultural and political rights.

(2) For the Welfare of the people one country in co-operation with the other should realise its responsibility.

(3) Self rule and security is assured to the people.

PART II

(1) All participating countries should make use of its available resources to provide the rights.

(2) No room for colour, caste, creed etc to enjoy these rights.

(3) Even the developing countries should make it as a point to provide these rights.

PART III

(1) All signatories to agree to implement these rights without any sex discrimination.

(2) Suitable control system to be implemented to these rights.

(3) No country should go beyond the conditions established in this Covenant.

(a) No fault should be found out in the existing and implemented rights — no ill-treatment to the people.

(4) Signatories should

(a) acknowledge the employment rights

(b) to safeguard employment rights — to find out and use technological ways and means to learn the new knowledge of fields, training, safeguards the social, economic and cultural rights — and also to see that it is on working.

(5) (i) Sincerity in job and guarantee this.

(ii) (a) Equal work to men and women.

(b) Equal pay to men and women.

(iii) To help their family members by providing prestigeous life — enough income to run life.

(iv) Security and hygiene in working conditions.

(v) Employment experience, skill-equal opportunity for promotion.

(vi) Rest, entertainment, right working hours, leave with salary, general holiday and pay for the same.

(6) (i) (a) Each one should work for the promotion of social and economic condition by abiding to the rules and

regulations of the Covenant. Each one has the right to start trade unions to join trade unions, right to run such unions (No other conditions that may harm the exercise of human right).

(b) Each one has the right to join with other trade unions on international level.

(c) Right to function independently.

(ii) Military, police and national administration should follow these rules.

(iii) To form associations, to mingle under one banner, International Labour Organisation and the countries participated in such conferences should not go against the Covenant.

(7) Every one has the right to undertake social insurance and the signatories should safeguard this right.

PART IV

As per this Covenant, the signatories acknowledge the rights :

(1) (a) to form family, take care of children, education, marriages etc.

(b) Mothers' security, leave during convalescence period, social security etc.

(c) to safeguard children and youth against social and economic, exploitation, guarantee peaceful life, to eradicate child labour and punish those who put the children and preventing children to get education are against law. Signatories are to follow these rules compulsorily.

(2) (a) All the signatory States should provide the right to get enough food, dress and shelter — to get all these to choose a job.

(b) States should strive for and provide scientific and technological development, agricultural development, production features, to conserve food, supply and distribution.

(c) States should solve the food and other problems through imports and exports.

(3) States should provide proper health and hygienic facilities to the people.

(b) To implement this, the signatories should give priority to

(i) reduce the rate of infant mortality, delinquencies and take care of prematured born babies.

(ii) to develop health and hygiene in working conditions.

(iii) to arrest the spread of contageous diseases, to prevent and proper treatment.

(iv) to provide medical aid and care.

(4) (i) All the signatories ratify the right to education. The have agreed to give priority to the development of education as education is a means to understand and safeguard human rights and fundamental freedom, to develop cordial relationship among nations and work for world peace.

(ii) For that the following are necessary :

(a) Compulsory education.

(b) To provide opportunities for all to get school and higher education, technical education and training.

(c) Equal opportunities to all to get education.

(d) Primary education and adult education.

(e) To improve the standard of students, to develop educational institutions by improving educational policies and to improve the conditions of teachers by increasing their pay and allowances.

(iii) Parents should give freedom to children in education — to give importance for primary education.

(iv) All subjects should be taught with freedom in the institutions like universities.

(5) (a) All to live a cultural way of life.

(b) To improve the standard of life through scientific development.

(c) Scientific inventions to be used for the benefit of making in a constructive way.

(d) Signatories to develop their relations by exchanging scientific and cultural findings.

(6) Signatories to submit a report to the UN about the functioning of these rights in their States.

(7) Signatories to conduct social and economic

(a) Conferences to implement and safeguard the said rights in the Covenant and the report should be based on these conferences.

- (b) All such reports to be sent to the Secretary General of the UN-copies of such reports to be sent to the ECOSOC.
- (c) If needed, a copy of the same may be sent to the UN agents.

(8) Signatories to agree to accept the action

- (a) taken by the UN over the reports sent by them.
- (b) signatories to include the problems faced by them in implementing the rights.

(9) The role of special agents of UN in this regard comes under this Article.

(10) To identify the States that violate human right and take proper action against them find a place in this Article.

(11) This speaks about the complaints of one State over the other, and the rights of UN in it.

(12) The role of ECOSOC in implementing these rights is put up in this Article.

(13) This Article explains the norms for conducting meetings.

PART V

(1) (a) The willing members of UN can sign and ratify this Covenant.

- (b) Ratification is a must.
- (c) This Covenant is open.
- (d) Details with the Secretary General.
- (e) Signatories to receive the details of the Covenant.

(2) The Covenant would be put into parties after 3 months from the date of ratification.

(3) The Covenant to be implemented in all parts of free states.

(4) Signatories, if they need any change in it, they may inform it to the Secretary General, 2/3 majority is needed for introducing amendments.

(5) Afterwards, the Signatories can include needed changes in their constitutions.

Measures of Implementation

The Covenant provides for a system of periodic reports by State Parties in its Article 16-25. The State Parties undertake to submit reports to the ECOSOC on the measures adopted and the progress made in this field.

The ECOSOC in turn sends the reports to the Commission on Human Rights for perusal and recommendation. Specialised Agencies of UN also have their contribution in these procedures. Article 21 lays down that the ECOSOC may submit the reports and of the measures taken to the General Assembly.

5

ECOSOC and Human Rights

One of the important organs of UN is Economic and Social Council *i.e.,* ECOSOC. It has been established to handle International Economic, Social, Cultural, Health and other related matters.

The functions of the ECOSOC are :

(1) To make or initiate studies and reports with respect to International economic, social, cultural, educational, health and related matters.

(2) To recommend measures to promote respect for the human rights and observance of human rights and fundamental freedom.

(3) To prepare draft conventions for the submission to the General Assembly with respect to matters falling with in its competence.

(4) To call international conferences on matters falling within its competence.

It also coordinates the activities of the specialised agencies of the UN.

It functions through 12 commissions-international and regional. The ECOSOC has three sessional committees — the economic, social and co-ordination committees.

The ECOSOC has set up the Commission on Human Rights in 1946 (Article 68). Both the ECOSOC and the HRC are composed of government representatives. The HRC adopted a report to the ECOSOC on the important question of the implementation of the Charter. It also stressed the need for an international agency of implementations entrusted with the task of watching over the general observance of human rights.

Of late, various governments in the world countries have urged the Secretary General to exercise his powers in the field of human rights. Besides, the policy making organs, the ECOSOC, the General Assembly and the Commission on Human Rights have also stressed the importance of the role of the Secretary General in the field of human rights. Much concern is being shown on the violation of human rights and how they are to be treated. The ECOSOC's resolution 75, provides the exact rules to be followed by the Secretariat in dealing with the matters related to human rights and their violations. The resolution underwent many amendments from time to time. As such in 1967, the ECOSOC authorised the HRC and the Sub Commission to examine the actual communications received. The HRC, recommended a new revolutionary course which was approved by the ECOSOC. That is the famous prevention of Discrimination and the Protection of Minorities. In 1967, the ECOSOC recommended for the establishment of a UN Right Commissioner's Office for the Human Rights. The ECOSOC also strives to strengthen international co-operation and to achieve it, the ECOSOC brings to the knowledge of the organs concerned by furnishing technical assistance. The ECOSOC is the controlling organ of the international Covenant on Economic, Social and Cultural Rights.

International Commission on Human Rights

It is the Commission that is referred to in UN Charter (Article 68). It was decided by the ECOSOC to set up a HRC, on 16 February 1946. In the beginning the Commission consisted of 9 members, appointed by the ECOSOC. Then it was increased to 18 members and at present it consists of 21 members. With its members, the Commission makes studies and recommendations either on its own initiative or at the request of the General Assembly or ECOSOC. It was to discharge matters regarding international declarations or conventions in civil liberties, the status of women and other similar matters, the protection of minorities, and the prevention of discrimination on the grounds of sex, race, language or religion. The HRC has the right to make recommendations to the ECOSOC regarding Sub Commission, that is to be needed. In this regard the HRC has the right to utilise the service of experts and to appoint and adhoc work group of non-governmental experts in specialised fields of individual experts. To carry on, the HRC needs the approval of the President of the ECOSOC and the Secretary General. As such, the HRC had its first session in February 1947 and the Second Session in December 1947. The HRC decided that International Bill on Human Rights consists of three parts, *i.e.*, (1) declaration, (2) convention and (3) measures of implementation. In the third session that held on 10 December 1948, it adopted the UDHR. In 1952, it was decided by the General Assembly to have two multilateral Covenants (conventions) on human rights. They were (1) The International Covenant on Civil and Political Rights and (2) The International Covenant on Economic, Social and Cultural Rights. The work was completed by the HRC in 1954 and they were approved by the General Assembly in 1966 and they came into practice in 1976.

The HRC in its area of powers have submitted certain conventions which are considered to be very important. They are :

(1) Declaration of the Rights of the child (1953).
(2) United Nations Declaration on the Elimination of All Forms of Racial Discrimination, 1963.
(3) Declaration on the Elimination of Religious Intolerance, 1964.
(4) International Convention on the Elimination of All forms of Racial Discrimination, 1965.
(5) Declaration on Territorial Asylum, 1967.
(6) International Convention on the suppression and punishment of the Crime of Apartheid, 1972.
(7) Declaration on the Protection of All Persons from being subjected to Torture and other Cruel, Inhuman or Degrading Treatment or Punishments, 1975, and
(8) The Convention on the Rights of the Child, 1989.

The HRC has 3 Sub-Commissions to assist it. They are :

(1) The sub-commission on freedom of information and of the press,
(2) The sub-commission on the prevention of discrimination and protection of minorities, and
(3) The one on the status of women.

Among these, the sub-commission on the status of women has done a laudable work. The function of the Commission shall be to prepare recommendations and reports to the ECOSOC on promoting women's rights in political, economic, civil, social and educational fields. It shall also make recommendations to the ECOSOC on urgent problems requiring immediate attention in the field of woman's rights with the object of implementing the principle that men and women shall have equal rights and to develop proposals to give effect to such recommendations.

The Commission has requested the ILO to promote the principle of equal work and to complete a convention on this subject. Following this, the ILO adopted special instruments to carry on these measures it has also requested the UNESCO to provide equal opportunities for women in education. It also made a declaration of the elimination of discrimination against women. It was adopted by the General Assembly on 7, November 1967. As per the request made by the commission, the General Assembly adopted the Convention on Political Rights of Women, in 1952. The status of women though education has increased enormously in connection with co-education and technical education. Special attention has been given for the advancement of education for boys and girls.

The year 1975, was declared as the International Women's year by the General Assembly of UN. Measures were introduced to promote equality between men and women and to ensure the integration of women in the development efforts. The importance of women was also recognised towards the development of friendly relations and co-operating among States to strengthen world peace. The International year was a call to men and women to exert all efforts to achieve its objectives.

The period 1976-1985 was declared as the 'UN Decade for Women. It aimed at the world plan of action to ensure women's equality in society. Its motto was 'Equality, Development and Peace'. The Commission on the Status of Women initiated (1) Declaration and Convention on the Elimination of the forms of Discrimination against Women, (2) Convention on the Political Rights of Women, (3) Convention on the Nationality of Married Women, (4) Convention on the Consent of Marriage and (5) Convention on the Protection of Women and Children during emergency and armed conflicts. All these contributed much to development of the status of women.

6

United Nations General Assembly and Human Rights

The General Assembly is one among the working organs of UN. It consists of the representatives of all member States. Each State has a right to send five delegates but has only one vote. The Assembly can discuss any matter within the scope of the Charter and any matter relating to peace and security brought to its attention. Applications for membership by the State recommended by the Security Council require the approval of the General Assembly. The approval is also needed for the appointment of the Secretary General. It elects its own President and Vice-President. It needs atleast once in a year. Special sessions may be summoned by the Secretary General. The Assembly adopts its own rules and procedures.

Questions concerned with human rights are mostly referred to one of the third Committees called Social, Humanitarian and Cultural Committee. The list of 'important question' contained in the UN Charter includes those concerned with the maintenance of international peace and security, admission of members, expulsion of members etc., but it does not include human rights as such. But the Assembly may determine additional questions to be decided by a two-third majority. The rights of people and nations of permanent sovereignty over their natural resources is a question which comes within the field of human rights. Usually, the decision in matters of human rights have been taken by the Assembly with two-third majority.

The General Assembly has two important obligations in matters of human rights. The Article 13 (1) (b) of the UN Charter provides this power to the General Assembly. They are, to initiate studies and to make recommendations for the purpose of assisting in the realization of human rights and fundamental freedoms for all without distinction as to race, sex, language or religion. The Assembly requests the ECOSOC, the Secretary General, specialized agencies, subsidiary organs and the member States in initiating studies. The annual report of the ECOSOC is the occasion for the General Assembly's initiation of the additional investigations and studies and for taking action too.

The Assembly's recommendations on matters of human rights are not legally binding on States. Article 55 and 56 of the UN Charter provide all members to take joint and separate action in co-operation with the Organization to promote human rights and fundamental freedoms. As per Article 62 (3) of the UN Charter, the ECOSOC has the right to prepare draft conventions for submission to the General Assembly. The Assembly has proclaimed certain standing declarations in matters of human rights. They are the UDHR (1948), ICCPR, ICESCR, (1966) etc.

Some subsidiary organs are established by the Assembly to discharge its duties. Almost all of them are concerned with human rights. Some such notable organs are :

(1) The UNICEF (1947);
(2) The UNHCR (1951);
(3) Commission to study the racial problems in South Africa (1952);
(4) The Special Committee on the Policies of Apartheid (1962) (this was renamed as the Special Committee on Apartheid in 1970 and again it was termed as the Special Committee against Apartheism in 1974);
(5) The Special Committee to implement the granting of Independence to Colonial Countries and People (1961) and
(6) UN Council for Namibia (1968).

All these subsidiary organs are either exclusively or largely concerned with human rights. But each one varies in their nature of work. Some are permanent organs while some are temporary.

7

Indian Constitution and Human Rights

Part III of the Constitution deals with the Fundamental Rights which borne the essential freedoms of the Indian people. A fundamental right may be defined as a privilege protected by the highest Law of the country. The Government may impose reasonable restrictions on their enjoyment and the President can suspend them during the period of national emergency. Yet, they are normally protected and guaranteed by the Constitution. These are called "Fundamental" because, an ordinary legal right is enforced by the ordinary law of the land and may be changed by the Legislature of the country, but a Fundamental Right cannot be altered in the same way. It can be changed only by amending the Constitution itself.

The aims and objectives of the Constitution are expressed in the Preamble in a nutshell. It can be described as the soul of the Constitution. It is a proper yardstick with which one can measure the worth of the Constitution. The text of the preamble runs as follows :

"We, the people of Indian, having solemnly resolved constitute India into a Sovereign, Socialist, Secular and Democratic Republic and to secure to all its citizens :

> Justice, Social, Economic and Political; Liberty of thought, expression, faith, belief and worship; Equality of status and opportunity; and to promote among them all;
>
> Fraternity, assuring the dignity of the individual and the unity and integrity of the nation.

In our Constituent Assembly, this twenty-sixth day of November 1949, we do hereby adopt, enact, and give to ourselves this Constitution."

The Preamble represents the spirit of the Constitution. The above expression indicates that it is a Constitution framed with the consent of the people of India. It is not a Constitution imposed by a foreign power. It is a Constitution enacted and adopted by the people through the Constituent Assembly.

1. Nature of the State. The very first line of the preamble explains the nature and purpose of the State of Indian Union. It is a Sovereign, Socialist, Secular, Democratic Republic. Therefore, emphasis is given to these five words.

Indian Union is a Sovereign State. It exercises freedom internally as well as in its relations with other countries. It is a socialist State. Thereby it is assumed that the Government would implement such policies that minimise the economic inequalities in the social and promote social ownership of the means of production. Thirdly, Indian Union is Secular State. It does not mean irreligious or atheistic state. By Secular we mean that no discrimination of citizens will be made on the basis of their religion. Freedom of worship is provided to all. Fourthly, ours is a democratic state. The form of Government we have opted is parliamentary democracy. It is based on universal adult suffrage and free and fair periodical elections. Fifthly, Indian is a Republic in which the head of the State shall be an elected President instead of a hereditary king. It also indicates that there will not be any privileged class and all offices are open to all citizens without any distinction of class, caste or creed.

2. Aims of the Constitution. In the second part of the preamble, the aims and objectives of the Constitution are spelled out. The constitution aims at securing Justice; Liberty, Equality and Fraternity to all citizens of India.

It wants to provide economic, social and political justice to all citizens. Thereby the state is expected to improve the lot of the downtrodden and weaker sections of the society. Economic exploitation should be prevented. State has to provide opportunities for free and fair participation of people in political field.

People should be provided liberty to develop their faculties. Healthy conditions should be created to develop the individual. Liberty implies freedom of thought, expression faith and worship.

Equality of status and opportunity has to be secured for all citizens. Economic disparities in the society ought to be minimised. Untouchability has to be eradicated to ensure social equality.

The idea of Fraternity implies a feeling of brotherhood among all citizens of India. It also points out the importance of maintaining the unity and integrity of nation and dignity of the individual.

Thus the preamble denotes the political, moral and religious values which the Constitution intends to promote.

1. Right to Equality

Article 14 to 18 of the Constitution guarantee the right to equality. Article 14 guarantees equality before law and equal protection of law. Article 15 prohibits discrimination on the grounds of religion, race, caste, or place of birth. Article 16 guarantees equality of opportunity in matters of public employment. Article 17 abolishes untouchability in the country and Article 18 abolishes titles other then military or academic distinctions.

(a) *Equality before law* (Article 14) : Article 14 of the Indian Constitution guarantees that the "State shall not deny to any person equality before the law or equal protection of the law" within the territory of India. Though the phrases "equality before the law" and "equal protection of the laws" look alike, they are different in meaning. Article 7 of the UDHR provides that "all are equal before the law and are entitled without any discrimination to equal protection of law". Both the expressions aim at establishing equality of Status. Equality before the law is a negative concept. In both the cases, equal justice is aimed at. Chief Justice Patanjali Sastri viewed that "the equal protection of laws" is corollary of the expression "equality before the law". But the violation of one leads to the violation of the other. Article 14 applies to any person and is not limited to citizens alone. Both individuals and Juristic persons are entitled to the benefit of Article 14. Article 10 of UDHR guarantees every one "full equality to a fair and public hearing by an independent and impartial tribunal, in the determination of his rights and obligations and of any criminal charge against him". So also the International Covenant on Civil and Political Rights in its article 14 directs that "All persons shall be equal before the courts and tribunals". The American and British Constitutions also provide these ideals. Similarly the Article 3 of the African Charter on Human and Peoples' Rights Provides that "Every individual shall be equal before the law and every individual is entitled to equal protection of the law".

Equality means that the same law is applicable to the specific class of people. So the Article 14 is to protect persons against discrimination among equals. Equality before law means that among equals the law should be equal and it should be equally administered. As such, Article

14 forbids class legislation but at the same time it permits reasonable classification. A reasonable classification is not only permitted but is necessary, if society is to progress.

There has been a definite change in the construction of Article 14 after the Judgement of the supreme court in Maneka Gandhi V Union of India case. After the judgement, the courts have held that the Article 14 is not to be equated with the principle of classification. It goes much beyond that. Justice Bhagwati said that "Equality is a dynamic concept with many aspects and dimentions and it cannot be imprisoned with in traditional and doctrinaire limits." Article 14 strikes at arbitrariness in State action and ensures fairness and equality of treatment.

In the case of Buddhan Choudhry *Vs.* State of Bihar, the Supreme Court observed that while Article 14 forbids class legislation, it does not forbid reasonable classification for purposes of legislation. Article 14 condemns discrimination not only by substantive law but also by the law of procedure.

(b) *Discrimination on the grounds of religion etc.* (Article 15) : Article 15 (1) provides that the State shall not discriminate against any citizen on grounds only or religion, race, caste, sex, place, of birth or any of them. Article 15 (2) provides that no citizen shall, on grounds only of religion, race, caste, sex, place of birth or any of them, be subjected to any disability, liability, restriction or condition with regard to access to shops, public restaurants, hotels and places of public entertainment or the use of wells, tanks, bathing ghats, roads and place of public resort maintained wholly or partly out of State funds or dedicated to use of the general public. Article lays down the nothing in this Article shall prevent, the State from making any special provision for women and children. Article 15 (4) provides that nothing in Article 15 shall prevent the State from making any special provision for the advancement of any socially and educationally backward classes of citizens or for the Scheduled Castes and Scheduled Tribes. The guarantee under this Article is available to all citizens and not to every persons. Article 15 (3) permits special protection to women and children and it is recognised universally. Article 15 (4) was added in the Constitution in 1951 as a result of the decision of the Supreme Court in the State of Madras V Champakam Dorairajam (AIR 1951 SC 226). In the State of Uttar Pradesh V Pradip Tandon case, the Government of Uttar Pradesh made reservations of seats in medical colleges in favour of rural areas, hill areas and Uttarakhand on the basis that reservations were for socially and educationally backward classes.

(c) *Equality of Opportunity in Matters of Public Employment* (Article 16) : Article 16 (1) provides that there shall be equality of opportunity for all citizens in matters relating to employment and appointment to any office under the State. Article 16 (2) provides that no citizen shall, on grounds only of religion, race, caste, sex, descent, place of birth residence or any of them, be ineligible for, or discriminated against in respect of any employment of office under the State. Article 16 (3), (4) and (5) are the exceptions to this general rule of equality of opportunity. Article 16 is an instance of the general rule of the equality before law laid down in Article 14 of the Constitution and the prohibition of discrimination guaranteed by Article 15 with special reference to the opportunity for employment or appointment to any office under the State. Equality of opportunity, need not be confused with absolute equality. Article 16 bars discrimination not only in the matter of initial appointment but also of promotion and termination of service. It is a safeguard not only against communal discrimination but also against local discrimination or discrimination against the weaker sects.

In General Manager, Southern Railway V, Rangachari case, the Supreme Court has held that equality of opportunity of employment does apply not only to initial appointments but subsequent promotions or dismissals as well. Article 16(4) permits the State to make provisions for reservation of some appointment in favour of backward classes who, in the opinion of the State, are not adequately represented in the service. The power of reservation which is conferred on the State as per this Article can be exercised by the State not only for providing reservation in appointments but also providing reservation in selection posts.

(d) *Abolition of Untouchability* (Article 17) : Article 17 provides that untouchability is abolished and its practice in any form is forbidden. Article 17 must be read with Article 35 (a) ii. which confers upon Parliament the exclusive power to make laws prescribing punishment for those acts which are declared to be offences under Part III of the Constitution. This led to the enactment of the Untouchability (offences) Act in 1955 by the Parliament of India. This Act was amended in 1976 and the amended Act has been given the name of Protection of Civil Rights Act, which came into force on 19 November 1976.

(e) *Abolition of Titles* (Article 18) : Article 18 provides that on title, not being a military or academic distinction, shall be conferred by the State. No citizen of India shall accept any title from any foreign State. No person who is not a citizen of India shall, while he holds any office of profit or trust under the State, accept without the concent of the President, any title from any foreign State. The ban under Article 18 operates only against the State. Military and academic distinctions are exempted under Article 18. The Government confer such honours as Asoka Chakra. Vir Chakra, Param Vir Chakra etc. In fact, it is not a right at all, but a restriction on executive and legislative power.

II. Right to Freedom

Article 19 to 22 deal with the right to freedom. Article 19 lays down that all citizens shall have the right to freedom of speech and expression, to assemble peacefully and without arms, to form associations or unions, to move freely throughout the territory of India, to reside and settle in any part of the territory of India and to practice any profession or to carry on any occupation trade or business.

Article 20 lays down that no person shall be convicted of any offence except for violation of law in force at the time of the commission of the offence. No person shall be prosecuted and punished more than once. No person accused of an offence shall be compelled to be a witness against himself.

Article 21 provides that no person shall be deprived of his life or personal liberty except according to procedure established by law.

Article 22 provides protection against arrest and detention in certain cases.

Article 19 was amended in 1951, 1963 and 1978. By the Amendment in 1978, the right to acquire, hold and dispose of property was taken over from the Fundamental Right and is now provided in Article 300A of the Constitution.

Indian Constitution provides freedom of speech and expression in Article 19 (1) (a) and 19 (2); freedom of assembly in Article 19 (1) (b) and 19 (3); freedom to form association in Article 19 (1) (c) and 19 (4); freedom of movement in Article 19 (1) (d); freedom of residence in Article 19 (1) (e) (5), freedom of profession, occupation, trade of business in Article 19 (1) (g) and 19 (6).

The UDHR (Articles, 19, 20, 23); The International Covenant on Civil and Political Rights (Articles 19, 21); The American Declaration of the Rights and Duties of Man (Articles IV, XXII); The European Convention of Human Rights (Articles 10, 11). The American Convention of Human Rights (Article 13); and the African Charter on Human and Peoples' Rights (Article 9, 10) indicate that the Indian Constitution has fulfilled the International obligations by incorporating various rights under Article

19. The rights under Article 19 of the Indian Constitution are exhaustive of all the right of a free man. Article 358 provides for the suspension of Article 19 during emergency.

III. Right Against Exploitation

Articles 23 and 24 deal with the right against exploitation. Article 23 prohibits forced labour. Article 23 is designed to protect the individual not only against the State but also other private citizens. Article 23 embodies two declarations. The first declaration is that the traffic in human beings, beggar and other similar forms of forced labour are prohibited. The second declaration is that any contravention of the provision shall be an offence punishable according to the law. Nothing in this Article shall prevent the State from imposing compulsory service for public purposes, and in imposing such service the State shall not make any discrimination on grounds only of religion, race, caste, or class or any of them. Article 24 provides that no child below the age of 14 years shall be employed to work in any factory or mind or engaged in any other hazardous employment.

The UDHR (Article 4); ICCPR Article (8), The EHR (Article 5) etc prescribe the right against exploitation. They cover the various kinds of exploitation such as slavery, the slave trade, servitude and forced labour. Articles 23 and 24 of the Indian Constitution fulfil the obligations of the above said international provisions. The Indian Factories Act and Mines act 1952, The Plantation Labour Act 1951, The Bidi and Cigar Workers Act 1966 etc. prohibit employment of child labour below 14 years of age.

IV. Right to Freedom of Religion

Articles 25, 26, 27 and 28 provide the right to freedom of religion. Article 25 deals with freedom of conscience and free profession, practice and propagation of religion. Article 26 deals with freedom to manage religious affairs. Article 27 deals with freedom as to payment to taxes for promotion of any particular religion. Article 28 deals with freedom as to attendance at religious instruction or religious worship in certain educational institutions. As a result of the above provisions Indian is a secular state.

Article 25 (1) provides that all persons are equally entitled to freedom of conscience and the right to profess, practice and propagate religion. Article 25 (2) provides that nothing in Article 25 shall affect the operation of any existing law. A person has a right to practice his belief by practical expression in any manner he likes. The Constitution puts certain restrictions on the freedom of religion.

(1) Freedom of religion is subject to public order, morality and other provisions of Part III of the Constitution.

(2) The freedom of speech and expression in matters of religion is subject to reasonable restrictions under Article 19 (2).

(3) Article 25 (2) (a) provides that the State can make any law regulating or restricting any economic, financial, political or other secular activities which may be associated with religious practice.

Article 26 deals with freedom to manage religious affairs. It provides the right to establish and maintain institutions for religious and charitable purposes, to manage its own affairs in matters of religion, to own and acquire moveable and immovable property and to administer such property in accordance with law.

Article 27 provides that no person shall be compelled to pay any taxes the proceeds of which are specifically appropriated in payment of expenses for the promotion or maintenance of any particular religion or religious denomination.

Article 28 provides that no religious instruction shall be provided in any educational institution wholly maintained out of State fund. Article 28 makes a distinction between educational institutions wholly maintained out of State funds and those recognised by the state receiving aid out of State fund. Article 28 speaks about four types of educational institutions. They are (1) Institutions wholly maintained by the State, (2) Institutions recognised by the State, (3) Institutions that are receiving aid out of the State fund and (4) Institutions that are administered by the state but are established under any trust or endowment. In the first type of institutions, no religious instructions can be imparted. In the second and third category of institutions instructions may be imparted only with the consent of the individuals. In the last type of institutions, there is no restriction on religious instructions.

The UDHR (Article 18), the ICCPR (Article 18), The EHR (Article 9), the AMR (Article 12), and the ADRD (Article III) provide similar provisions to safeguard freedom of conscience and religion.

V. Cultural and Educational Rights

Articles 29 and 30 provide cultural and educational rights. Article 29 protects the interests of the minorities regarding their language, script and culture. Article 29 (1) provides that any section of the citizens residing in the territory of India or any part there of, having a distinct language, script or culture of its own, shall have the right to conserve the same. Article 29 (a) provides that no citizen shall be denied admission into any educational institution maintained by the State or receiving aid out of State funds on grounds of religion, race, caste, language or any of them.

Article 30 (1) provides that all minorities whether based on religion or language, shall have the right to establish and administer educational institutions of their choice. This right is in absolute terms,. Article 30 (2) provides that the State shall not, in granting aid to educational institutions, discriminate against any educational institution on the ground that it is under the management of a minority, whether based on religion or language.

Articles 29 and 30 confer four district rights. They are, any section of citizens has the right to conserve its own language, script or culture. All religious and linguistic minorities have the right to establish and administer educational institutions of their own choice. Every such institution has the right not to be discriminated in matters of state aid on the ground that it is managed by a religious or linguistic minority. Every citizen has a right not to be denied admission into any State maintained or State-aided institution on the ground of religion, caste, race or language. The provisions of Articles 29 and 30 are unique in their thoroughness. They are in conformity with the right to religious freedom.

The UDHR (Article 29), the ICCPR (Article 27), the ICESCR (Article 15) and the ADRD (Article XIII) provide similar rights. The Indian Constitution fulfils the spirit of the UNESCO Declaration of principles of International Co-operation by providing cultural and educational right in it. These rights are essential to the relationship between people and their society. Above all, these rights are interdependent and closely connected to other economic and social rights.

VI. Protection of Life and Personal Liberty

Article 21 provides that no person shall be deprived of his life or personal liberty except according to the procedure established by law. These rights are the most fundamental of all the rights. Other rights will lose their value in the absence of protection of life and personal liberty. Bhagwati. J. held the view that Article 21 confers the fundamental right to life and liberty. It does not exclude Article 19.

The UDHR in its Article 21 speaks that every one has the right to life, liberty and security. So also the ICCPR's Article 6. Undoubtedly the right to life is a paramount one. It means not only the right to exist but also the right to exert. It is the duty of the courts to express the real meaning of the concept of life and personal liberty as explained in Article 21 of the Indian Constitution. Therefore, the Constitutional provision is only of evidentiary value. "Even in the absence of Article 21, the State has no power to deprive a person of his life and liberty without the authority of law," viewed Justice H.R. Khanna.

VII. Protection Against Arrest and Detention

Article 22 provides protection against arrest and detention in certain cases. Article 21 has been read as supplemented by Article 22. One can not be arrested or detained unless there is some charge against him or he is suspected to be involved in anti-social or anti-national activities. Article 22(1) provides that no person who is arrested shall be detained in custody without being informed; as soon as he may, of the grounds for such arrest, nor shall be denied the right to consult and to be defended by a legal practitioner of his choice. Article 22(2) provides that every person who is arrested and detained in custody shall be produced before the nearest Magistrate within a period of 24 hours of such arrest excluding the time necessary for the journey from the place of arrest to the court of the Magistrate and no such person shall be detained in custody beyond the said period without the authority of a Magistrate.

The UDHR (Article 9), the ICCPR (Articles 9 and 10), the EHR (Article 5), the ADRD (Article XXV) and the AMR (Article 7) also provide the safeguards that no one shall be subjected to arbitrary arrest and detention.

VIII. Right to Constitutional Remedies

Dr. Ambedkar, the father and architect of Indian Constitution emphasised the importance of Article 32 and referred it as the very soul of the Indian Constitution and the very heart of it. Chief Justice Patanjali regarded the Supreme Court as 'the protector and guarantor of fundamental rights. Article 32 provides the right to move the Supreme Court by appropriate proceedings for the enforcement of the fundamental rights conferred by Part III of the Constitution. It also guarantees that the rights provided by this Article shall not be suspended except as otherwise provided by this Constitution. The Supreme Court shall have the power to issue directions or orders or writs. Including writs in the nature of habeas corpus, mandamus, prohibition, quo warrant and certiorari, which ever may be appropriate, for the enforcement of any of the rights conferred by this part. Without prejudice to the powers conferred on the Supreme Court by clauses (1) and (2), Parliament may by law empower any other

Court to exercise within local units of its jurisdiction all, or any of the powers exerciseable by the Supreme Court and the right guaranteed by this Article shall not be suspended except as otherwise provided for by the Constitution.

The UDHR (Article 10), the ICCPR [Article 14 (1)], the EHR [Article 6 (1)], the ADRD (Article XXVI) and the AMR [Article 8 (1)] also provide the right to fair trial.

IX. Other Rights

There are some other rights which do not find place in the fundamental rights in the Indian Constitution. They are the right to citizenship and the right to franchise. By virtue of citizenship, a person becomes subject of the State. Article 5 provides that every person has his domicile in India. Article 6 lays down the rights of citizenship of specified persons. Article 15 of the UDHR speaks that every one has the right to nationality. No one shall be arbitrarily deprived of his nationality nor denied the right to change his nationality. This right helps a person to become attached to the State. One is recognised only through his nationality. Every State is expected to protect its nationals abroad.

In a democracy, right to franchise is a must. Articles 325 and 326 provide the right to franchise. Every person who is a citizen of India and who is not less than 18 years of age has a right to be registered as a voter.

The UDHR [Article 21 (iii)] and the ICCPR [Article 25 (b)] provide the right of universal and equal suffrage.

X. Directive Principles of State Policy

The Directive Principles of State Policy are a novel feature of the Indian constitution. The idea seems to have been borrowed from the Irish Constitution. Part IV of our Constitution deals with these Directive Principles.

(1) According to Article 39, the State shall direct its policy towards securing that the citizens, men and women equally, have the right to an adequate means of livelihood. The ownership and control of the material resources of the community should be so distributed as best of subserve the common good. The operation of the economic system must not result in the concentration of wealth and means of production to the common detriment. There should be equal pay for equal work for both men and women. The health and strength of the workers should not be abused and

the citizens should not be forced by economic necessity to enter those professions which are unsuited to their age or strength. Childhood and youth should be protected from exploitation and moral and material abandonment.

(2) According to Article 40, the State shall take steps to organise village Panchayats and endow them with such powers and authority as may be necessary to enable them to function as units of self-government.

(3) Article 41, States that the State shall, within the limits of its economic capacity and development, make effective provision for securing the right to work, to education and to public assistance in cases of unemployment, old age, sickness and disablement, and any other case of undeserved want.

(4) Article 42, provides that the State shall make provision for securing just and humane conditions of work and for material relief.

(5) Article 43 provides that the State shall endeavour to secure, by suitable legislation or economic organisation or in any other way, to all workers, agricultural or industrial, a living wage, conditions of work ensuring a decent standard of living and full enjoyment of leisure and social and cultural opportunities. The State shall also endeavour to promote village industries on an individual or co-operative basis in the rural areas.

(6) Article 44, urges the State shall endeavour to secure for the citizens a uniform civil code throughout the territory of India. When this Article was on the legislative anvil, both the Hindus and the Muslims attacked it on the ground that it was likely to destroy the personal law of the Hindus and the Muslims. However, it was pointed out that the perpetuation of separate personal laws for the various communities in India was not in the higher interests of the nation as a whole. It was bound to stand in the way of the development of the common ideal of nationality. If India was to maintain her independence and not become a slave to any foreign power in the future, no better, sensible or safer method of achieving that end could be conceived than that of a universal civil code for the whole country. There was no substance in the objection that a uniform civil code would infringe the Fundamental Right of freedom of religion. Undoubtedly, laws could be passed by the Government regulating secular activity

for social reform and welfare. The adoption of a uniform civil code was not to be tyrannical to the minority.

(7) According to Article 45, the State shall endeavour to provide, within a period of ten years from the commencement of the Constitution, for free and compulsory education for all children up to the age of 14.

(8) Article 46, sets down that the State shall promote with special care the educational and economic interests of the weaker sections of the people, and particularly of the Scheduled Castes and the Scheduled Tribes, and shall protect them from social injustice in all forms of exploitation.

(9) Article 47 provides that the State shall regard the raising of the level of the nutrition and the standard of living of its people and the improvement of public health as among its primary duties and particularly the State shall endeavour to bring about prohibition of consumption except for medicinal purposes, of intoxicating drugs and of drags which are injurious to health.

(10) According to Article 48, the State shall endeavour to organise agricultural and animal husbandry on modern and scientific lines and shall particularly take steps for preserving and improving their breeds, and prohibiting the slaughter of cows and calves and other milch and draught cattle.

(11) It shall be the obligation of the State to protect every monument or place or object of artistic or historic interest, declared by Parliament by law to be of national importance, from disfigurement, destruction, removal, disposal or export, (Article 49)

(12) Article 50 specifically lays down that the State shall take steps to separate the judiciary from the executive in the public services. It is to be noted that something is being done in this direction practically in every State.

(13) Article 51 declares that the State shall endeavour to promote international peace and security, maintain just and honourable relations between nations, foster respect for international law and treaty obligations in the dealings of organised people with one another and encourage settlement of international disputes by arbitration.

8

Rights — Civil, Political, Economic, Social and Cultural

The UN Charter refers to human rights in its Preamble as, the people of the UN expressed their determination "to reaffirm faith in fundamental human rights, in the dignity and worth of human person, in the equal rights of men and women . . . . freedom."

The UDHR is the basic international pronouncement if inalienable and inviolable rights of all members of the human family. The UN General Assembly adopted it on 10, December 1948. The International Covenant on Civil and Political Rights was adopted by the General Assembly in 1966. India ratified it on 10, April 1979 and it came to effect on 10, July 1979. So also the International Covenant on Economic, Social and Cultural Rights was adopted by the General Assembly in 1966. The Covenant came into force on 3, January 1977. An Optional Protocal to the Covenant on Civil and Political Rights was adopted in 1966 and it came to effect on 23, March 1976.

As we have seen already, rights are divided into civil, political, economic, social and cultural rights. Each and every individual is enjoying these rights without any discrimination in the name of race, religion, colour, creed, sex or place of birth.

Civil Rights

Civil Rights include right to self determination, right to live, right to liberty and security, right to equality, right to privacy, right to freedom of thought, conscience and religion, right to freedom of opinion and expression, right to freedom of peaceful assembly, right to freedom of association, right to marry and family protection, rights of the child, right to take part in the conduct of public affairs, right to equality before law and equal protection of the law, prohibition of slavery and slave trade, right to freedom of movement to leave any country and return to his country.

Political Rights

Political rights include right to compete and contest in elections, right to take part in government, right to criticise government, and the right to individual petition, and the right to take part in administration.

Economic, Social and Cultural Rights

Economic rights are right to self-determination, right to work, right to just and favourable conditions of work, right to form and join trade unions, right to equal wages and remunerations for equal work.

Social rights include right to social security, rights relating to motherhood, childhood etc, right to adequately standard of living, right to physical and mental health.

Cultural rights include right to education, rights relating to science, art, music, and culture.

The International Covenant on Civil and Political rights, in its Article 1 provides that all peoples have the right of self-determination.

Article 6 lays down that all human beings have the inherent right to life and this right shall be protected by law (Indian Constitution Article 21); (UDHR, Article 3).

Article 7 provides that no one shall be subjected to torture or to cruel, inhuman or degrading treatment or punishment.

Article 8 provides that no one shall be held in slavery and the slave trade in all forms shall be prohibited.

Article 9 provides that everyone has the right to liberty and security.

Article 10 provides that even the prisoners are to be treated with humanity.

Article 11 provides that every one has the right to freedom of movement to leave any country and to return to his country.

Article 14 speaks about the right to equality before the courts and the right to provide legal assistance (Indian Constitution Article 7)

Article 15 speaks about the right against retroactive criminal legislation.

Article 17 provides the right to privacy.

Article 18 provides that every one shall have the right to freedom of thought, conscience and religion (Indian Constitution Article 25-25. UDHR- Article 18).

Article 19 lays down that every one shall have the right to hold opinions without interference *i.e.,* freedom of opinion and expression.

Article 21 provides the right to freedom of peaceful assembly.

Article 22 provides for the right to freedom of association [Indian Constitution, Article 20 (1) (2), UDHR, Article 19 (1) (4)].

Article 23 provides for the rights relating to marriage and family protection.

Article 24 speaks about the right of the child.

Article 25 provides for the right to take part in the conduct of public affairs.

Article 26 provides for the right to equal protection of the law. All are equal in front of law and are entitled to equal protection of law without any discrimination.

The International Covenant on Economic, Social and Cultural rights provides economic rights in its various Articles.

As per the Article I, all people have the right to self determination. As such, each and every one can freely determine and pursue his/her economic, social and cultural rights. This right also includes disposal of natural resources without prejudice.

Article 6 provides the right to work and take necessary steps to safeguard this right. [UDHR, Article 23 (1); Indian Constitution, Article 41].

Article 7 provides the right to just and favourable conditions of work, fair wages, a decent life, healthy living conditions, equal opportunity of promotion and rest, leisure and reasonable limitation of working hours and periodic holidays with pay and remuneration for public holidays. [UDHR Article 23 (2) (3); Indian Constitution Article 30 (d)].

Article 8 lays down the right to form and join Trade Unions of his choice, for the promotion and protection of his economic and social interest. Right to establish federations and confederations also comes under this Article.

Article 9 provides the right to social security and social insurance.

Article 10 provides the right relating to motherhood and childhood. It stresses that marriage must be entered into with the free consent of the intended spouses; special protection for mothers during and after child birth; leave with adequate benefits and children should be protected from exploitation of any kind [UDHR-Article 25 (2), Indian Constitution, Article 23, 24],

Article 11 speaks about the right to adequate standard of living for himself and his family. Food, clothing, housing and other living conditions are recognised as the fundamental rights of every one.

Article 12 lays down the right to physical and mental health. All the signatories of the Covenant are required to provide steps for the improvement of physical and mental health. [Indian Constitution, Article 47; UDHR, Article 25 (1)].

Article 13 provides the right to education. All kinds of education should aim at strengthening the respect for human rights and fundamental freedoms. As such primary education is freely available to all [Indian Constitution-Article 45, UDHR-Article 26 (1)].

Article 15, speaks about the right relating to science and culture. Everyone has the right to take part in cultural life, to enjoy the advantages of scientific, literary or artistic production of which he/she is the author.

Having analysed the importance of the rights mentioned in both the International Covenant, the General Assembly of the UN passed a resolution in 1977 affirming "All human rights and fundamental freedoms are indivisible and inter-dependent and equal attention and urgent consideration should be given to the implementation, promotion and protection of both civil, political, economic, social and cultural rights (In context with India, refer the chapter on Indian Constitution and Human Rights).

9

Children's Rights

The importance of Children's Rights cannot be ignored. Their rights should be given special attention. So the world body has taken serious views on them. The UDHR (1948) in its Article 25 (2) provides for the protection of children. It is stated that special protection, care and assistance are needed for the motherhood and childhood.

The ICESCR (1966) lays down in its Article 10(2) and (3) special measures of protection to children and youth without any discrimination. They are to be protected from exploitation.

The ICCPR (1966) in its Article 24 provides that every child shall have the right of protection.

Indian Constitution in its Article 39(1) states, "The State shall, in particular direct its policy towards seeing that children are given opportunities and facilities to develop in a healthy manner and conditions of freedom and dignity and that childhood and youth are protected against exploitation and against moral and material abandonment".

Article 23 of the Indian Constitution prohibits traffic in human beings including children and Article 24 prohibits engagement of children below the age of 14 in hazardous jobs.

Despite all these provisions, we find that most of the children in India and in other countries too, are being neglected both by the parents and government. As soon as a child is born, proper steps must be taken by the parents to register the birth of that child, to give it a name, look after the child with proper care, educated him and maintain him in a proper way so as to make him as a useful citizen of the country. If proper care is not taken to maintain the children, they become abandoned children and in future they are either street children, beggars, criminals, smugglers etc. It is estimated that in India, every year nearly a million children are being abandoned either due to social or economic conditions of the parents. Protection of children against moral and material abandonment is a must. All children are to be given the right to live with human dignity. Children should be provided with opportunities and facilities to grow in a healthy manner. It is also the duty of the State to protect and promote children's rights with a view to ensuring full development of their personality and with human dignity. Or else, the right to life and liberty would become meaningless. Some children are forced to become bonded labourers and even they are held as slaves. Millions of children in the developing nations work in mines, match factories, knit wear companies, carpet industries, quarries and other hazardous industries. Thousands of children are forced to undertake prostitution and drug addicts. Children are misused only on account of poverty. A study in South America revealted that thousands of teenaged children in Brazil live in abandoned condition and prostitution. It is officially estimated that more than 20 million children are employed as labours in the developing countries, 25 crores child labourers in the world over, and 12 crores in the age group of 5-14 years.

Recently, the press (The Hindu 24 April 1998) brought into light the need to protect the rights of children. A 15 year old girl was raped by armed guards after her father was killed for allowing her to go to school. A 14 year old rap picker was tortured by piercing pins through his finger nails. A two year old was killed in indiscriminate bombing. Young children are held captive in private jails as bonded labourers and 10 year old are repeatedly raped by the landlords. A 12 year old boy serves in chains held continuously in leg chains for a robbery conviction. Dozens of children disappear after being picked up by security forces. An estimated 9,000 girls are brought from Nepal and Bangladesh to India and Pakistan destined for life as sex workers each year.

Such revelation could not be put in words. It is quite shocking, disgusting and cruel. All the governments in Asian region have committed to uphold the Convention on the Rights of the child and have strengthened this commitment through the SAARC. But still, children continue to be ill-treated in the custody of the States as it administers juvenile justice. Children are left unprotected in the family and community and suffer the consequences of living in the midst of armed conflict.

Neglected children turn into thieves and live an unfair life. No one is a born criminal. Only the circumstances that exist in society convert the abandoned children into criminals. In order to reform the young offenders, the government of India has passed the probation of offenders Act in 1958. As per this Act, if persons below the age group of 21 years are found guilty of committing an offence punishable with imprisonment, they would be considered as Juveniles. But it is surprising that often police arrest children without mentioning their age and imprison them. The Supreme Court viewed that children should not be confined in jails and exploited in jails. In Sheela Barse V Union of India case, a writ petition by way of PIL was filed under Article 32 of the Constitution by a social worker seeking the release of children below the age of 16 years of age, detained in jails in different states of the country, production of complete information of children in jails. Information as to the existence of Juvenile Courts, homes and schools and for a direction that the District Judges should visit jails or sub-jails within their jurisdiction to ensure that children are properly looked after when in custody as also for a direction to the State Legal Aid Boards to appoint duty Counsel to ensure availability of legal protection for children as and when they are involved in criminal cases and are proceeded against. The Supreme Court with a view to protect children from exploitation in jails pointed out that "It is an elementary requirement of any civilized society — children should not be confined in jail — it is harmful to the growth and development of children".

The Government of India took interest in children and made an attempt to protect the children from exploitation and to give opportunity to develop the children in a healthy way by introducing the Children's Act in 1960. Despite, children still are exploited and ill-treated in one way or the other. A National policy for Children was developed in 1974, by the Government and it provided different disciplines for the protection of children. The year 1979, was declared by the UN as the International Year of the Children. In 1985, the UN adopted Standard Minimum Rules for administration of Juvenile Justice System. The Government of India promulgated the Juvenile Justice Act in 1986 to provide special protection to the children, who commit crimes at the tender age. Large number of criminals i.e. about 50% of them belong to the neglected group. Poor parents neglect their children as they find it difficult to pull on their life and lead their families. Such neglected children are abused, exploited, placed under prostitution and forced to become criminals. Instead of learning at schools, they are compelled to learn crimes and become delinquent Juveniles. These children have no home to rest, no care, no education, and have no hope about their future. This pathetic situation makes them to indulge in beggary, thieving and committing crimes that are punishable. There is a Juvenile Board which enquires the child, finds out the reasons for the Juvenile delinquency and sends him to the observation home (Juvenile Training Home.) He is mended there through education, and training so as to train himself for a better future. Proper employment facilities for such children are to be provided to help them further in a right path. As today's children are the tomorrows nation builders, they should be cared, educated and trained in such a way to make them to realise their duties and responsibilities. Parents should come forward to put it into practice honestly and wholeheartedly.

Amnesty International is working on securing the rights of children and appealed for an intensive action that would ensure the protection of children's rights. An official campaign highlighting children's rights in South Asia and other public activities was launched in Karachi and Dhaka. Representatives of India, Sri Lanka and Non-Governmental Organisations took part and stressed the need to protect rights of children. Still, children in custody are cruelly treated, detained arbitrarily and punished inhumanly. This shows that the State's failure to protect the children from abuses at various levels. Some governments have taken worthy initiatives to protect the rights of children, curb bonded labour etc., through human rights education programmes and passing special legislations to protect the rights of children. In reality, they are not implemented properly and children's sufferings continue to prevail.

It is our bounden duty to protect the rights of children in a better and fitter manner in every nook and corner of India and the world.

10

Refugees and their Rights

The problem of refugees is one of the most important problems in the world today. The UN has taken series of successful steps to protect their rights.

The UN's 1951 Convention relating to the status of refugees defines a "refugee" as a person who "........ owing to well founded fear of persecution for reasons of race, religion, nationality, membership of a particular social group or political opinion, is outside the country of his/her nationality .... and unable or unwilling to avail the protection of his/her country".

No South Asian nation has laws or policies on refugees. Nor any of them has ratified the 1951 Convention of the UN or the Protocol of 1967, which is the Magna Carta of International Refugee protection. In India also people often confuse with economic migrants as refugees. Economic migrants' are different from refugees. A refugee flees persecution to save his/her life and liberty; whereas economic migrant leaves his/her country voluntarily, in order to improve his standard of living. A refugee enjoys no state protection. Migration of people from poor countries to poorer countries is becoming quite common in recent years.

The refugee crisis has become an important aspect of human rights activists. The changing nature of the crises is the rising concept of the nation state which has forced the people to move from their known habitates to unknown lands. It leads to the destruction of social and cultural harmony of the region, besides generating mistrust and suspicion among the people. Refugees are minorities and stateless, and the development policies are not fulfilling the needs of the uprooted millions.

They have no proper dwellings, roads, electrification, education and other needs. Every year millions of people are displaced as refugees, creating a sort of insecurity about their future. Their story is pitiable. They are exploited by politicians, police and others. The local people view refugees as a threat to employment.

The UDHR of 1948 deals with the refugees problems too. Article 3 of the UDHR provides that "every one has the right to life, liberty and security of person", It also states that "Every one has the right to seek and to enjoy in other countries asylum from persecution".

The United Nations High Commission for Refugees was established in January 1951 by the General Assembly of UN. The high Commission is not a part of the UN Secretariat. It is a subsidiary organ of the General Assembly. The High Commissioner is elected by the General Assembly. He is to report annually to the General Assembly through ECOSOC. The UNHCR is to protect refugees at the international level as per the Statute framed by the Commission in 1951 and the Protocol in 1967. According to the Statute of the UNHCR, 'refugee' is a person who is outside the country of his nationality, the country of his former habitual residence, because he had well founded fear of persecution by reasons of his race, religion, nationality or political opinion and is unable or, because of such fear, is unwilling to avail himself of the protection of the government of the country of his nationality, or if he has no nationality, to return to the country, of his former habitual residence. Here 'Protection' of refugees means legal protection. Material assistance does not come under the 'Protection' referred here. All the administrative expenses of the office of the UNHCR are met from the regular UN budget. The other expenses of the Commission are financed by Voluntary Organisations.

As the size of the refugee problem is bulging day by day all over the world, the responsibilities of the High Commissioner have increased in its volume. The Commission has taken efforts to grant asylum, on a temporary basis atleast, to rescue the refugees from distress. The High Commissioner has reported in 1979 that there are instances where lack of respect for the fundamental human rights of refugees that met with difficulties and that have led to tragic consequences.

The main functions of the Commission are :

(1) To promote the conclusion and ratification of International conventions for the protection of refugees.

(2) To supervise the application of such Conventions.

(3) To propose amendments in the said Conventions.

(4) To promote in signatory States, the execution of measures to improve the position of refugees.

(5) To reduce the number of refugees.

(6) To assist governments to promote voluntary repatriation or assimilation within new national communities.

(7) To promote the admission of refugees to the territories of State.

(8) To strive to obtain permission for refugees to transfer their assets that are essential for their resettlement.

(9) To obtain from the States reports concerning the number of refugees and legislative measures meant for refugees.

(10) To have always a close contact with the States.

(11) To have contact with other private organisations that deal with refugees and to work for the welfare of refugees in co-ordination with such private organisations.

Problem Solving

The UNHCR concentrates much on its aim of helping States in the solution for refugees and other displaced persons. It also supports the refugees to return to their country of origin or farmer habitual residence by means of voluntary repatriation. Resettlement also is given due consideration wherever necessary. The major refugee problems are form Bangladesh, South Africa, Sri Lanka, Afghanistan, Burma, (Myanmar) Nicaragua, Cuba and Bosnia. Millions of people have left their homes and accumulated in Third World countries. At present there are more than 20 million refugees all over the world and it is growing further. The brutal treatment of the Somali government made the Somalis (About 400,000) to flee to Ethiopia and Djibouti. Due to the war between Serbs and Crotians more than four million people were driven out of their native land. Due to the war between Iraq and Kuwait in 1990, more than 300,000 Kuwaits vacated their native land and moved to other areas. In 1991, about 270,000 Rohingyas, the Myanmar Muslims took refuge in Bangladesh. India has more than 500,000 refugees at present. They are from Bangladesh, Tibet, Sri Lanka, Afghanistan and Burma. These refugees are not only victims of persecution but also of desperate social, political, economic and environmental circumstances. They lost their possessions, position, kith and kin and even hopes in life. For the welfare of refugees there are treaties and conventions at the International level and national level. The International level conventions we have already dealt with.

At the national and regional level, there are various conventions that work towards the protection of refugees. The Inter-American Convention on Human Rights (1969) lays down provisions relevant to the protection or refugees. As such every person has the right to asylum in a foreign territory in accordance with the legislation of the State and International Conventions. In no case may in aline he be deported to a country regardless of whether or not it is his country of origin, if in that country his right to life or personal freedom is in danger of being violated because of his race, religion, social status or political opinion. The Cartagena Declaration (1984) is meant for the Latin American Countries, to deal with the problem of refugees. For the Asian-African region there exists the Bangkok Principles (1966). The OAU Convention (1969) is for the African Continent as a whole.

Ms. Sadako Ogata, the UNH Commissioner for refugees says, "Today refugees situation requires a comprehensive approach : encouraging the search for solutions which addressing the underlying causes of mass movements. This approach is rooted deeply in the promotion of human rights, as violation of human rights are major cause of refugee flows. The protection of refugees is based on respect for human rights. The restoration of human rights in the country of origin is often a pre-condition for refugees to return home in safety and dignity".

The problem before the States is how to protect the individual who is unable to defend himself. His individual interests are in danger. His own State finds it difficult to defend him. If the protection of human rights can be achieved the question of refugees would automatically be resolved. Refugee problem comes under the problem of protection of human rights. Both the problems are inter related. The laws related to human rights and refugees aim at human well-being and progress.

India

Mr. Brain Gorlick, the Law Officer of UNHCR said that India has been kind and generous to refugees. India had neither signed the UN Conventions relating to refugees nor enacted a common law to deal with refugees at the national level. The signing of UN Convention assumes significance, as it would be followed by the signatory States passing domestic laws on the subject of refugees. "India should take the lead among the South Asian Nations in ratifying the UN Convention relating to the refugees", suggested Mr. Gorlick.

At present about 2,60,000 refugees are in India with Tibetians comprising the largest group (1 lakh) followed by Sri Lankan Tamils

(64,000), Chankmas from Bangladesh (44,500), Afghans (19,000) and others mainly from Iran, Iraq, Somalia, Sudan and Myanmar (1,000). While the Government of India recognises the refugees from Tibet, Bangladesh and Sri Lanka, other groups are not recognised and considered as foreign nationals temporarily residing in India. Those who were not recognised by the Government of India, were being assisted by the UNHCR and provided international protection and assistance. It is expected that the number of refugees seeking refuge in India will continue to increase and hence the need for a law to deal with refugees.

Gandhiji once wrote to the Governor General of Pakistan Qaid-e-Azam Jinnah that "Each state will induce the refugees to return and occupy their respective homes". It is applicable in modern context too. For that, like mind, like word and like action is wanted between the States. The spirit of brotherhood of man was needed vigourously. Unfailing power of love is also the need of the hour in dealing with refugees.

Since April 1986, thousands of Chakma refugees had crossed the International border and taken refuge in South Tripura District aggravating the problems of the State Government. The Chakma insurgency in the Chittagong Hill Tracts also created new problems. The Pambatta Chattagram Jana Sanghati Samity and Shanti Bahini have adopted a draft unanimously, paving the way for a peaceful resolution of long pending issues of refugees found in Tripura Camps. As per the talk held in 1996, a gesture of goodwill was arrived at. The Bangladesh government even disbanded some camps of the security forces from the sensitive border areas. But it paved no solution. India has reluctantly sheltered about 50,000 CHT refugees in half a dozen Tripura camps and had been using its good offices with Bangladesh for a peaceful settlement so that the unfortunate Chakmas could be repatriated to their original homeland. Under the 20 points agreement, the repatriation process was expected to pick up momentum but in vain. Then due to further dealings, the Bangladesh government expressed its willingness to settle the Chakma refugees in Chittagong area. So far 11,900 Chakmas have gone back. About 12,300 refugees had returned to Bangladesh in the earlier 3 phases in February and June 1994 and March 1997. About 49,000 refugees are still left in six camps in Tripura.

In Tamil Nadu, Mandampam, Rameswaram and Chennai are some of the important centres where the Sri Lankan Tamil Refugees are sheltered. These refugees belong to EPRLF, the PLOT and the TELO and thousands of them are put up in a special refugee camp *i.e.* the proposed central jail at Red Hills area. Here Gandhiji's dictum is quite applicable and admirable that "No one should rest till proper arrangements are made for looking after all refugees".

Refugees have the right to fight for their rights and establish them. In November, 1997, The Committee for citizenship Rights of Chakma refugees requested the NHRC to intervence in their matter and urged the NHRC to send a team to probe the continuous violation of human rights of the tribals and direct the Government of India to take effective steps to withdraw economic blockade and investigate the misuse of public money by the State government.

World Scenario

Of the thousands of thousands of Afghan refugees who entered Pakistan from 1979 onwards, about half of them returned to their native home after the fall of the communist government. But thousand more refugees have come since the fall of Kabul to the Taliban and the bulk of the women had fled Kabul. So many are destined to suffer and all possible help should be extended to these refugees.

It is to be noted that the Palestine refugees do not fall within the competence of the UNHCR. The Statute lays down that this competence does not extend to persons who receive help from other organs of UN. In Palestine the UN Relief and works Agency is the relevant body that works for the welfare of Palestine refugees.

Thousands of Rwandan Hutu refugees emerged from the jungles or eastern Zaire in April 1997. Their hunger was more powerful than the fear of Zairian mobs. Peter Kessler, a spokesman of the UN refugee agency said in Nairobi that 100,000 of them drove from their homeland and they seemed nervous and frightened. Many of them were sick and exhausted. About 20 rebels beat three hospital workers and berated others for carring the refugees. These refugees were either lost or abandoned during the refugees flight from camps along the Rwandan borders. Kabila's forces have over-run more than half of Zaire in their months long war to topple president Mobutu. Bill Richardson, US Ambassador to the UN held talks with Mobutu and Kabila and it may help to improve the condition of the refugees.

The recent problems dealt with the UNHCR show that the number of refugees are increasing day by day an average of 2000 per day. In 1995, it was estimated that there were 27.4 million refugees. Adding to the spurt in the influx of refugees, of late (22 March 1998) 127 Sri Lankan Tamils have reached the Rameswaram Coast in four batches. It so happens in Burundi, Rwanda, Somalia and other parts of the world.

In spite of the bright hope, the problem of refugees is assuming an unprecedented dimension at the international level. It was expected that the end of cold war between America and USSR may provide ample chance of bringing the refugees' problem to an end but in vain. By 1990, the number of refugees at the world level was estimated as 15 millions. In 1994, it touched 18 millions and it was 21 million in 1995 and 24.3 million in 1997. As the number of refuges increase the problem of refugees are touching their peak in almost all refugee camps. When there is a possibility and hope in implementing the provisions of the UDHR, it becomes clear that the problems of refugees also could be dealt with special care and be solved amicably. The laws meant for refugees should be treated as a part of the laws on human rights. Human become refugees only due to the violation of human rights. Human rights protection in its real sense is the need of the hour. This may surely help the refugees to return to their native homes and live with security and prestige too.

Overall Problems of Refugees

People fleeing for their lives has become a common feature. Those seeking refugee status face ever so many restrictions and they are put in desperation. Sometimes they are even prevented from entering other territories to seek asylum. For that frontiers are closed. Refugees are forced to return. They are rather driven to Third World countries as these countries are believed to be the safer places for refugees. Their human rights are abused. Men, women and even children are not spared. There is no guarantee for their protection. When there is no protection in their homeland, no wonder, protection is questioned in other countries too. They are always at risk. All these stand as challenges to the International system set up for the protection of refugees.

Amnesty International had reported that millions of refugees fled from massacre in Rwanda and Burundi to the other neighbouring territories and they were forcibly returned to Rwanda and Burundi. Many families got separated during their flee. Young children are separated from their parents. They lost their relatives, friends etc. Their property is looted and destroyed. This makes them to remain and suffer without food. Shelter and other needs, Forced return in turn leads to further violence and human rights abuses. Individual rights are not respected. Rather, the refugees are not considered as human beings. Sometimes, deadlines are fixed for the return of refugees to their homeland. At the end of the period, they are forcibly expelled form the country in which they have sought asylum. Such incident had happened in Zair in 1995. This is nothing but a breach of international and regional treaties.

The poor refugees are illtreated, beaten and women are raped. In some cases, refugees are killed by the army. It is yet another grave human rights abuse.

The countries which give asylum to refugees also undergo a huge burden and they find it difficult to deal with the problem of refugees. Millions of refugees have been forced to flee the conflicts during the break up of Yugoslavia. Thousands of people fled and even forcibly expelled from Boania and Serbia. Surprisingly, most of the refugees are sent back directly to the place of fighting. This affects the refugees from resettlement. Usage of restrictive asylum procedures by countries also affect the rights of refugees. This bluntly deprive asylum seekers of their right to claim asylum *e.g.*, Turkey expelled the asylum seekers from Iran and Iraq. Such forcible return of asylum seekers in nothing but a violation of International standards. The asylum seekers from Afghanistan were detained in Latvia in 1995 and they were ill-treated in detention.

There is a new development called 'White List' that has emerged in certain countries to deal with refugees. As such, a list of countries (*e.g.*, Denmark, UK etc.) where the risk of human rights abuses was deemed to be insufficient to justify individuals fleeing to seek protection abroad. By this, the asylum seekers are put under greater risk. Further, indiscriminate attacks also cause people to seek temporary safety in the nearest places. For example, during the attacks on Kabul in 1995 thousands of people have sought temporary safety at Sar-Sharhi camp inside Afghanistan. Some countries consider that seeking asylum itself is an offence punishable by death (Iraq and North Korea). Such countries forget that they are the law breakers and violate human rights. Around the world, the refugees are made to face enormous problems by the countries in which they seek asylum. One cannot disagree that the problem of refugees is not a separate unit, but a part of human rights by and large.

A group of illegal immigrants drove into the Kulalumpur Office of the UNHCR seeking political refuge on 29, March 1998. These immigrants escaped from a detention camp in Indonesia, where violent clashes broke out some days back. These immigrants claim 'political refuge' from the UNHCR. It is believed that this could spark a fresh crisis for Malaysia, which was always opposing a stranger present or role of human rights groups and agencies. The Malaysian foreign Minister Mr. Abdullah Ahmad Badani, maintained that all illegal immigrants from Indonesia were only "economic refugees" and there was no case of "Political refuge" for them.

Over 500 Tibetian refugees from Bylaklappe organised a rally and hunger strike in Chennai (Madras), in support of their demands. The demand included to appoint a special rapporteur to investigate the human rights violations in Chinese occupied Tibet. They followed the true spirit of a Gandhian movement to create awareness throughout the world about their problem. It was learnt that the situation of the minorities in Tibet is a critical one. Hundreds of Nepalese fled from Kathmandu to India due to starvation. The Humlis were abandoning their homes and migrating to India.

The number of UN registered refugees in the world has risen consistently on an average of more than 12 per cent a year since 1976. If this continues, the world refugee population will have doubled to 46 millions by 2000 AD. In the mid seventies, there were only 2.5 million refugees. It rose to 15 million by 1989. In 1997 it reached the height of 23 million. This numbers reflect the strict standard established by the 1951 UN Convention on Refugees. There are about 27 millions of displaced people at the world level. These do not include people who leave their homes for economic reasons Besides there are illegal immigrants, who constitute around 10 million. In 1985, 100 million migrants moved from their homeland to improve their livelihood. In 1995, it was estimated that 107 million migrants moved out from their native land in search of livelihood. Every now and then various incidents in different States create hopeless conditions in the minds of the people due to the violation of human rights, especially the right to life. Human rights are under threat and people are forced to face unbearable problems and challenges.

11

Indigenous People and their Rights

The question arises who are the indigenous people of India. For this it is realised that any definition of indigenous people will be controversial because of the social and political consequences of such definitions. However, the ILO Convention No. 107 of 1957 has defined the indigenous people as "Those which having a historical continuity with pre-invasion and pre-colonial societies — consider themselves distinct from other sectors of societies now prevailing in those territories — The form at present non-dominant sectors of society".

A special UN Report (E/CN4) Sub 2/1566, (p. 10) emphasised that "Indigenous populations are composed of the existing descendants of the people who inhabited the present territory of a country wholly or partially at the time when persons of a different culture or ethnic origin aimed there from other parts of the world, overcome them and by conquest, settlement or other means, reduced them to a non-dominant or colonial action."

The representatives of Indian Tribals at the meeting of the UN Working Group on Indigenous Populations in August 1987 stated "From historical, anthropological and sociological point of view we know that we are the indigenous people of India from pre-historic times with distinct social, economic, political and territorial identities. But the Adivasis (Original settlers) *i.e.,* indigenous tribals people, we still maintain our distinct identity".

The history of the indigenous people has been the history of their constant struggle for existence as a different cultural entry against the civilization of the colonisers. The indigenous peoples' historical consciousness of their cultural identity and individuality of every community is based on the notion of the "Small is beautiful". It stands for a social value of respecting each other's way of life, mutual co-operation and peaceful co-existence. The struggles of the indigenous and tribal peoples centre around the issues of land, forests, water, resources, culture, transport and communication, health and hygiene, nutrition, education, identity etc., directed towards their self-determination and finding a rightful place in the social, cultural, economic and political spheres of life in India. The thrust is also for the due recognition of the indigenous peoples by the Government of India which would establish their long denied rights and employment of their traditional habitat, and community life and will prevent their cultural subjugation, economic exploitation and politico-social marginalisation.

The identity of the indigenous peoples of India consists of their geographical, historical, ethnological, linguistic and other features which give them district characters, distinguish them from the other peoples of the country. The indigenous people are facing a number of oppressing forces through the ages. Present day sufferings of them have a historical background. A well thoughtout solidarity is necessary on the part of the strategy of the liberation struggle of the indigenous people.

Land is an important ingredient of the indigenous people's identity not only for the economic usage but also for the spiritual and emotional quality. Economic dispossession has an extremely adverse effect on the cultural life of the indigenous people. The process of Sanskritisation forces them to emulate Hindu norms, rituals and rites and also to accept their language. Displacement, land alienation, loss of forest, economic exploitation and impoverishment, cultural and identity crises etc have marked the recent history of the indigenous people of India. In the face of centuries old oppression the indigenous peoples have rebelled from time to time to establish their rights. Some of the movements of the indigenous people of India like the Narmada Bachao Andolan, Koel-Karo, antiland alienation and forest protection agitation in Telengana, Singbhum, Gujarat, some tribal areas of Maharashtra, movement of extra garden labourers for the governmental recognition of their scheduled tribe status and that the Kurnis in West Bengal, coal mines and industrial workers movement in Chattisgarh and Jharkand, autonomy movements in Uttar Khand, Bhilkhand, Vidarba, Tripura, Andhara, Tamil Nadu agitation against non-tribal treaders, money lenders and usherers, contractors, governmental officials etc have brought into focus the improverishment of the indigenous communities through displacement and other types of dispossession and powerlessness and their search for self-reliance. But, unfortunately these movements have been condemned as anti-national and anti developmental too.

A demand was made by the indigenous people during the UN year of indigenous people that tribals and semi-tribals be recognised as the indigenous peoples of India. But the Government of India refused to accept this demand saying that India has long been a 'melting pot' of culture and that in India hardly any of the tribes exist as a separate society and that they have all be absorbed in varying degrees into the wider society of India. Yet, it is to be noted that the autonomy that is demanded by these people is around their life support system.

There are about 60 million Adivasi Communities in India. In principle, the State has a number of provisions for the protection of the Adivasis/indigenous people. Article 46 of the Directive Principles of the State Policy (Part IV) of Indian Constitution provides for the promotion of the interests of the indigenous people. But these people attempt to claim their rights, they meet with hostile, violent and repressive measures of the entire State machinery. The indigenous people still wage many struggles to retain their birth rights *i.e.* human rights. The more recent struggle of the less organised adivasis of South India, is just coming into focus. Under the banner of the South Zone Adivasi Forum, they have set out an agenda to reclaim their rights, including dispossessed lands. Deforestation results in impoverishment of the local indigenous population and estabilisation of adivasi culture and economy. Since tribal and forest economy is essentially a women's economy, the impact of deforestation is felt more by tribal women. It also leads to the deterioration in health and nutritional status too. Having all these in mind, the Vienna Declaration on Human Rights enjoyed the governments with regard to the right of the indigenous people. The conference also recognised the inherent dignity and the unique contribution of indigenous people to the development and plurality of society as a whole.

Of late, these people are not allowed to enjoy their human rights. The Narmada Valley has been a territory of protest and has become synonymous with human rights struggles the world over. They undergo cheating, ill treatment, torture, etc. The tribals of the Narmada Valley have chosen to die rather live without their identity. That has made them to raise the slogan "We shall drown but we refuse to move out". These people's struggle to control access and utilization of their resources is waged on behalf of all toiling people. These people are struggling in almost all spheres. In Tamil Nadu, the tribals are at the verge of losing their rights on lands. Their rights are being neglected. Even in education, employment opportunities, empowerment etc, injustice prevails. All these prove that their human rights are being neglected and violated.

Vienna World Conference on Human Rights (1993) has given a global programme of action for Human Rights Setting. India has set up a NHRC and India Parliament has enacted Human Rights Bill on 22 December 1993. The wretched of the earth — the suppressed and the oppressed of the world would get their legitimate dues, as a matter of right and not as a gift from the ruling elites. Even after 50 years of India's Independence the indigenous people are rightless groups such as the suppressed and oppressed dalits. They are landless, unapproachable, homeless and are denied those constitutional inputs of India. Their women are allowed to die without health or safety. They are illiterate, indigent, disorganised forest dwellers, easily deceived and fragmented and so scattered in mountain enclaves that constitutional freedoms are the vanishing point of tribal justice. Courts to them are alien, laws their enemy and human justice their despair. The fact is that the battle for the cause of indigenous people is long, hard and a tough one. The most sin towards our fellow creatures is not to hate them, but to be indifferent to them; that's the essence of inhumanity. It is better to act by remembering humanity has a commitment to make human rights a viable reality.

12

Educational Rights

Education plays a prominent part in the society and hence its need and necessity is realised by every one in the world. Particularly the countries of the world and the UN have done yeoman service in the field of education.

Education is a liberating force in our age. It is also a democratic force cutting across the barriers of class and caste. It helps to erase the irregularities imposed by birth and other circumstances. The UDHR guarantees cultural rights in its Article 27. It provides :

(1) "Every one has the right freely to participate in the cultural community; to enjoy the arts and to share in scientific advancement and its benefits" and

(2) "Every one has the right to the protection of the moral and material interests resulting from any scientific, literary or artistic production of which he is the author".

The ICCPR speaks in its Article 27 "In those States in which ethnic, religious or linguistic minorities exist, persons belonging to such minorities shall not be denied the right, in community with the other members of their group, to enjoy their own culture, to profess and practice their own religion or to use their own language".

The ICESCR Provides in its Article 15 :

(1) The State parties to the present Covenant recognise the right of every one,

   (a) to take part in cultural life,

   (b) to enjoy the benefit of scientific progress and its applications,

(c) to benefit from the protection of the moral and material interests resulting from any scientific, literary or artistic production of which he is the author.

(2) The steps to be taken by the State Parties to the present Covenant to achieve the full realization of this right shall include those necessary for the conservation, the development and the diffusion of science and culture.

(3) The State parties to the present Covenant undertake to respect the freedom indispensable for scientific research and creative activity.

(4) The State parties of the present Covenant recognise the benefit to be derived from the encouragement and development of international contacts and co-operation in the scientific and cultural field.

The Indian Constitution in its Articles 29 and 30 speak about the cultural and educational rights.

Article 29 (1) protects the interests of the minorities regarding their language, script and culture. Article 29 (2) lays down that no citizen shall be denied admission into any educational institution maintained by the State or receiving aid out of State funds on the grounds only of religion, race, caste, language or any of these.

Article 30 gives minorities the right to establish and administer educational institutions. The rights of the minorities cannot be absolute. They are subject to restrictions in the interest of education and in pursuance of socio-economic objective embodied in the Directive Principles of State Policy.

The purpose of Articles 29 and 30 was not to create vested interests in separateness of the minorities. The Constitution gives cultural and educational rights with a view to enable the religious and linguistic minorities to maintain their individuality and distinct identity of their language and culture but that should not result in the minorities remaining isolated from the main stream of national life.

The Directive Principles of State Policy — Part IV of the Indian Constitution in its Article 46 provides that the State shall promote with special care the educational and economic interests of the weaker sections of the people and, in particular of the Scheduled Castes and Scheduled Tribes and shall protect them from social injustice and all forms of exploitation.

The Government of India is striving hard to provide free and compulsory primary education and to promote educational and economic interests of weaker sections and to protect that from social injustice.

The proposed 83rd amendment of the Constitution provides opportunities and thereby to make education a fundamental right. Today, the minorities and the depressed classes in the world are at the lowest ebb of society and they are to be improved at any cost so as to bring them on par with that of the mainstream. The basic need to achieve this aim is no doubt, education. International human rights law also has provisions for the same. All world countries have realised the need for and the importance of education. Indian government has made necessary provisions in the Constitution by providing 15 per cent reservation in educational institutions and at the same time special provisions are also made for free and compulsory education for all upto the age of 16 years. The NHRC's ex-president Justice Ranganatha Mishra also has recommended for the free and compulsory education for all. This is also quite encouraging to hear that provisions are also there to get education either through the medium of regional language or through Hindi or through English.

International instruments also provide for the safety and security of the minorities' language and culture. Even the countries like America, Austria, Africa and India necessary Constitutional arrangements are in existence in order to protect minorities are their welfare. As the world is standing on the threshold of 21st century, an unified world should be aimed at forgetting the racial, linguistic, religious, territorial and other discriminations. All the signatories of the UDHR have come forward to build up and develop the status of minorities in almost all spheres. Hopes are pinned on the functioning of constitutional frame work of the concerned States in building up the poor condition of minorities in all possible ways.

13

Women's Rights

Today women's rights are given more importance than any other rights in the society. Women's rights are integral to Human rights. In ancient scriptures like Vedas, Epics, Manu Smirtis, Dharmasastras etc. refer the position of women and restrictions on their rights and privileges in India.

If we turn the pages of Indian History we come across the position of women in the society at various stages. The Greek invasion and the coming of Arabs and Turks further reduced the position of women in society. The medieval period witnessed the heart burning social evils like sati, child marriage, female infanticide, dowry system, prohibition of widow remarriage etc., and all these exhibited the pitiable position of women in society. Above all the Devadasi system and polygamy aggravated the women's position to the background.

The social and religious movements of 19th century provided an opportunity for the rehabilitation of Women. Yet their position was not improved satisfactorily. In 20th century series of steps were taken to create a sort of awareness of women and providing equal opportunities to them.

Notable ladies like Mrs. Annie Besant, Mrs. Sarojini Naidu, Durgabhai Deshmukh, Kasturiba Gandhi and Sister Nivedita became prominent in this sphere.

Besides independent Indian Constitution, Western system of education and the development of education in India helped a lot for the elevation of handful of women in various fields like administration, legislature etc.

Sex determination test that prevailed in India created a havoc leading to female foeticide.

A number of women's movements took place in India after 1975 to create awareness in the minds of all. So a sweeping change takes place in this field.

World Scenario

It is estimated that 80 million women world wide have undergone the female genetal mutilation. It is practiced in one form or another in 40 countries, mostly in East, West Africa, some parts of Arabian Peninsula, North America and in some European countries too. Several countries have enacted laws forbidding this practice. Even in India in certain states like Bihar, Gujarat, Madhya Pradesh, Uttar Pradesh, Maharastra and Gujarat such tests have been popular.

The UDHR provides general action against discrimination on the ground of sex and in matter relating to the status of women in general. The General Assembly of UN at its 9th session, dealt with the status of women in private law, customs, ancient laws and practices affecting the human dignity of women. Article 26 of the International Covenant on Civil and Political Rights provides that all persons are equal before the law and are entitled without any discrimination of the equal protection of the law.

The ECOSOC established a sub-commission on the status of women.

The International Women's Year (1975) was a call to men and women everywhere to government and non-governmental organisations to exert every effort to promote equality of men and women, the integration of women in the development of their countries and the strengthening of world peace.

The Decade of women (1975-1985) denoted to the world plan of action to ensure their equality in society. Women are entitled to vote in elections, eligible for election to all publicly elected bodies and entitled to hold public office and exercise all public functions on equal terms with men.

India and other world countries have passed various Acts and enacted Rules with a view to mould the rights of women. Despite, society and almost all governments are male dominated.

Indian Context

Despite the growth of education and the other notable changes that had taken place in society, Indian women are still in darkness. The Sati

Prevention Act, 1829 prohibited the custom of burning Hindu widow alive in the funeral pyre of her husband. But unfortunately the practice is still in vogue among some orthodox Hindus. To put an end to this crime, the Commission of Sati Prevention Act was passed by the Government of India in 1987. During the British rule itself the Child Marriage Restraint Act was passed in 1929 to prevent the early marriage of girls in their tender age, but the system of child marriage still persists in India.

Article 38 of the Indian Constitution provides for the welfare of women in matters relating to justice. This includes social, political and economic justice. Article 39 provides the citizens, men and women equally have the right to an adequate means of livelihood. It also provides for equal pay for equal work for both men and women. The Hindu Marriage Act of 1995, had brought for the first time, the right of divorce of women-folk. Prior to this, normally a Hindu Woman could not even imagine about divorce from her husband.

The right of widow remarriage is also provided in this Act. Though there was already an act called the Hindu Widow Remarriage Act (1856), this could not stop the social humiliation faced by the Hindu widows.

The most remarkable Act that is welcome by the women folk and the rest in India is the Dowry Prohibition Act of 1961. This Act prohibits giving dowry in any form. This practice is considered as a social evil and a burning problem in our society. As Dowry deaths and problems connected with dowry are increasing day by day, the government of India felt the need for amending the Criminal law in 1986. As such an amendment was made in Section 304-B of IPC by the Act 43 of 1986.

The property of women was divided in to two heads (a) stridhan, and (b) women's estate. Literally the word 'stridhan' means woman's property. In the entire history of Indian Law, women's right to hold and dispose of property has been recognised. Stridhan includes mostly movable property such as ornaments, jewellery, dresses etc. Gift and bequests from relative, gift and bequests from strangers, property acquired by self-exertion and mechanical arts, property purchased with stridhan, property acquired by compromise, property by adverse possession, property obtained in lieu of maintenance, property obtained by inheritance and share obtained on partition enumerate woman's property. Dowry and traditional presents made to wife at the time of the marriage constitute her stridhan, and if the husband or her in-law refuse to give it back to her, on her demand, they would be guilty of criminal breach of trust. The Hindu Woman's Right to Property Act, 1937 which has been repealed by the Hindu Succession Act 1956, recognized the widow's rights to property. For instance, if a

Hindu dies leaving behind his separate property and his own widow, son's widow and grandson's widow, each of the widows will take one-third share in the property.

Any woman victim of suppression of immoral traffic can seek justice in the court against the offender under Immoral Traffic (Prevention) Act 1956 and also by the Act 44 of 1986. Further to protect the women and their dignity. Indecent Representation of Women (Prohibition) Act was passed in 1986. India Constitution also provides special consideration for certain category of people-citizens, which reflected in the laws regarding Muslims. A Muslim divorcee is entitled to claim maintenance only for Iddat period — three months after pronouncing Talaque. This right is provided under Muslim Women Protection of Rights on Divorce Act of 1986.

Until 1929, Hindu females have no right of inheritance or property right as per law. The Hindu Law of Inheritance Act, 1929 for the first time recognised the right of inheritance. The Hindu Women's Right to Property Act of 1937, introduced certain notable changes in the law of succession. The Hindu Succession Act introduced in 1956, recognised the right of Hindu daughters' property right. As such a daughter is legally entitled to get equal share of property left by her father. This Act also paved the way for a Hindu widow to become the sole owner of the property left by her deceased husband. Muslim Law also provides wife and daughter, the right to own property and inherit the share off husband's as well as father's property.

Problems of Women

Women face a number of problems at political, economic, social, religious and educational level. Such problems are not only in India but in other world countries too. Some of the problems that are to be given top most priority to be dealt with are the female infanticide, child marriage, compulsory marriage, dowry deaths, sex harassment, raping, bonded labour, poverty, illiteracy, illtreatment, wage disparities in agricultural and industrial sectors, child labour, police atrocities, slavery, orphans, neglected women, subordination at home and outside, torture, murder and the like.

Female Infanticide

It is nothing but killing of a female child, soon after its birth, especially with mother's consent. This custom of killing new born babies is prevalent all over India. Parents, being afraid of the future problems they have to face in connection with that female baby they decide to nip it in the bud. Traditional social norms and processes have continued from time to time, and from generation to generation. In India, in certain states like Bihar, Gujarat, Uttar Pradesh, Madhya Pradesh, Maharastra and Tamil Nadu, the practice has become popular since it brings relief to the parents from the problems of paying dowry and spending a lot at the time of marriage.

The Tamil Nadu government has proposed to implement a project to improve the status of girl children from financially backward families. Tamil Nadu government's plan of 'Cradle Babies' was a step towards curbing this problem. Female infanticide which had come into focus, after reports about it appeared in the main stream press in 1985 and later in 1992 is one of the major factors which kept the IMR in districts like Dharmapuri, Salem, Namakkal, Theni, Madurai and Dindgul exceptionally high.

Child Marriage, Compulsory and Conditional Marriage

During British regime, child marriage was made illegal in India and special acts were in force to safeguard it. Girls and boys at the age of 7 and 9 were found married. It was and is mostly a voluntary practice. The public life of a nation is but the elaboration of its family life. The Child Marriage Restraint Act (1929) and the Sharda Act did much to solve this problem. Yet it is heartening to note that, in some parts of India (Rajasthan, Chidambaram in Tamil Nadu etc.) this customary habit is still lingering. Educated parents are no exception from this, as they prefer to conduct the marriage of their daughters put up at the high school level itself. This leads to the breakage of law in force. But things go on smoothly, with a simple nod of the parents concerned. No doubt, in a way it is compulsory marriage. There are other incidents where, the girl is given compulsorily to marriage, due to certain family tie-ups as there was no escapism at all. So also, the conditional marriages that take place in a number of families where the girl has no role at all. She has to simply give up her personal right just to satisfy the elders in the family. Undoubtedly the very right to marry is nullified here.

Raping

Raping and group raping occur everywhere in India and abroad as well. This proves that women are the weaker section in society. In India, according to the official records, around 1000 women get raped every year, who generally belonged to dalit groups inhabited area. In several areas of UP and Bihar, frequent reports are published about women's molestation, resorted to by the powerful and influential landholders in retaliation for refusal of the depressed classes on the use of bullocks and the like by landholders. Police personnels are also involved in raping and the guilty officials get transferred with the help of the powerful political leaders. Out of the total number of women kept in police custody, 70 per cent had been subjected to physical and sexual abuse (Childambaram Padmini's Case). Some years back; one Bhanwari Devi of Rajasthan was gang raped just because she took up the risk of reporting an incident of child marriage in her place. Frequent cases of violence against women and sex discrimination by the law-enforcing authorities, had been reported by the 'Asia Watch' and 'Women's Rights Project Division of US Human Rights Organisation'.

Police Torture

Police torture to women is yet another problem to be given top priority. Severe beatings, hanging upside down, inserting pins and nails in the sensitive parts of the body etc. had been some of the methods used by the police against women prisoners in custody. Applying electric shock and burning the skin with cigars etc had also been reported. In some causes, the victims were found to be paralysed. Custodial deaths are common in almost all states and cities of India. Reports of such incidents appear regularly in the press but the police are never convicted.

Dowry

"Dowry" is defined as any property or valuable security given or agreed to be given, directly or indirectly by one party to the marriage to the other party to marriage, or by parents of either party to the marriage, or by any person to either party to the marriage or to any other person at or before or at any time, after the marriage "in connection with the marriage of said parties". Taking or giving dowry or abetting to give dowry or abetting to take dowry continue to be offences. Demanding of dowry by any person is a dowry offence. The offence relating to dowry are non-bailable.

The Dowry Prohibition Act, (1961) confers jurisdiction to try dowry offences only on the Metropolitan Magistrate or the Magistrate of the First Class. This Act was again amended in 1984 and 1986 to enforce it effectively. Despite, it is now a notorious fact that a bride who fails to bring the desired dowry is subjected to physical and mental torture, and suspension of marital rights, which ultimately leads to bride burning or bride-suicide.

Dowry has been identified as one of the most killing problems of women in India. Bride burning for insufficient dowry is a field in which India can claim to be the undisputed champion. It was established at the International Women's Conference held at Beijing in August 1996. Numberless women die in India, as a by-product of the system in which a bride's parents have to provide gifts to the groom as a part of marriage settlement.

According to official records, within a period of 3-1/2 years, that is from 1988 to 1992 as many as 1049 cases of dowry deaths took place and among these cases only 312 husbands faced trials and others simply escaped. During the said period, in Delhi alone 122 dowry deaths had been enlightened by the press. (*e.g.*) The Hindu, Junior Vikatan etc. In developing countries it is a unique paradox that social progress lags behind the law. Dowry is a deep rooted social evil and legilation alone cannot eradicate it and safeguard women from this acute problem. Legislation can only help the social movement for the eradication of dowry. The Dowry Prohibition Acts should not merely bark, but should be able to bite. It is heart burning to note that the Dowry Prohibition Law does not appear as a biting law.

Torture

Torture is one way or other caused to housewives is a targeting problem of women in India. Both in rural and urban areas women were not spared from torture either by their husbands or by the family members. Indian women in foreign countries also undergo torture and other inhuman treatment by their men. A survey of Indian residents in America conducted by the Asian-Indian Women of America (AIWA) in 1989, showed that out of an estimated 160,000 Indian families 20-25 per cent of Indian women residents in USA faced marital abuse and torture from their husbands. An organisation by name 'World in Action' conducted a survey on married women in Britain and revealed that 28 per cent of women had been hit or threatened with physical violence by their spouses. Women seldom reported such cases, as they were either too hurt or frightened and demoralised to report. Very often, women were found retracting their statements for fear of further humiliation. Alcoholism, poverty and male-chauvinism lead to such sort of activities against women, especially in rural areas.

Disparities in Wage

Women play a significant role in agricultural development and allied fields. Most of the rural agricultural women have to work from dawn to dusk *i.e.*, from sun rise to sun set without rest. Besides domestic work, women do all kinds of agricultural work like sowing seeds, weeding, harvesting, thrashing, husking, drying, storage etc. They work for long hours but they are paid poor wages. But for the same work, men are given more wages than that of the women.

It is also seen from the analysis conducted by the ILO.

Apart from the low wages, women workers face many other problems. They carry their infants with them and expose them in the hot sun and this affects the health of children. The behaviour of the landlords is another problem. They assault, abuse and shout at the women workers even at the slightest provocation.

Women including girls are put up as bonded labourers in beedi factories, match factories, brick industries, weaving industries, quarries etc. This sort of inequality of women is mainly due to greater consentration of poverty, backwordness, illiteracy and low level of technical know how.

Women earn fifty to eighty per cent of what men earn for the same kind of work. The lower end is seen among women workers in Korea, Japan, Singapore, and India. It is somewhat better in developed countries. It is further improved in developing countries *e.g.*, Sri Lanka.

Gender Bias

It is very essential in the male dominated society. It has been highlighted by the Human Development Report 1995 brought out by the UNDP. In India the 30 per cent reservation of women have got opportunities in Punchayat Raj elections. It is really a welcoming one. According to Robert Ingersol, "There will never be a generation of great men until there has been a generation of free women of free mothers". Gandhiji and Dr. Ambedkar tried very much to eradicate legal discrimination. Gandhiji, the Father of our Nation appreciated the qualities of Indian women and said, "To call women the weaker sex is a libel, it is men's injustice to women".

So the need of the hour is the progress without any gender bias. The Secretary General of the UN is also pushing for 50 per cent top UN jobs for women. The deadline to achieve the target is 2000 AD. Let us hope for the best. Now India is also working hard for this.

To solve those problems it is better and fitter to follow the ideals of Gandhiji regarding women.

Crimes Against Women

Crimes against Women are increasing day by day in India. While the number of dowry deaths rose from 50 in 1991 to 104 in 1996, the number of rape cases increased from 43 in 1992 to 148 in 1996. In 1996, 20 incidents of rape cases were reported in Hoshiarpur district of Punjab, 15 in Ludhiana, 11 each in Amritsar and Jullendur, 8 in Ferozhpur and 6 in Tamil Nadu. Cases like eve-teasing, molestation and domestic violence against women have shown an alarming increase since 1996. Similarly the number of rape cases also increased from 26 in 1996, to 148 in 1997.

To contain and curtail those crimes the government should appoint women's Rights Commission with powers to enforce decisions and punish those found guilty of offence against women.

Gender bias, exploitation and discrimination are other forms of crimes that exist against women in almost all states of India. Men should change their attitude towards women.

The supreme court's decision in 'Vishaka' 1997 penalises sexual misconduct on a broad basis. The criminal law should be tightened against those criminals. It should be in support of and not at the cost of women's rights.

Childhood and Motherhood

The UN Commission on the States of Women's meet in New York between March 2nd and 13, 1998 assumes important to improve the condition of girl child. The same stand was taken by the Asia Pacific Watch Conference held in Chandigarh in India in January 1998 and the National Commission for Women.

It is the duty of the mothers to take care of their children in general and girls in particular. Mothers are always to care, to learn, to love, to guide, to sacrifice, to boost, to feel, to tender, to support and the like. Mother gets the children to learn, to debate, to art, to sing and to express themselves without fear or bias. No doubt mother is a collection of wisdom. Women are 'credle of civilisation' and so that women are responsible for producing and rearing responsible children.

Protection of Rural Women Workers

Special legislations are needed to protect the rural women workers in India. Among the women workers 66 per cent belong either to the S.Cs. or S.Ts. and vast majority of them are landless. In most of the states they are paid low wages. At the same time their conditions are more pitiable and pathetic. For *e.g.*, in Vaishali district of Bihar, the Dalit women were beaten and raped as they refused to work for too low wages. Hence, special legislations are essential to improve their conditions.

Empowerment of Women

Empowerment implies a state of mind and attitude of a person. Empowerment emerges in the form of an awareness in the women. 'By empowerment' women face challenges boldly and overcome barriers in their life through which they increase their ability to shape their own lives and environment. For the progress and prosperity of India women's progress is essential. The role of women can be summed up in 4 M's — Match, Mother, Manager and Mover. The following are the means of empowerment :

(1) Education
(2) Health and Nutrition
(3) Economic Independence
(4) Legal Awareness
(5) Organisational support and
(6) Intervention Programmes

In short women should be given equal representation in all fields.

International Women's Day, 3 March 1998

It is better to see the condition of women on the eve of International women's day. Women's campaigns have managed to effect some changes in the laws relating to violence against women. But at the same time there is no law to deal with many forms and levels of domestic violence, hidden within the four walls of the house. Recently various studies show that the domestic violence reveals the male superiority and female inferiority. We have to work towards the rights of women more and more to promote peace and property in their life.

Dual Role

In this connection the dual role of women cannot be ignored or minimised. They are managing quite successfully to balance the responsibilities at the office and at home. This is applicable to Indian women too. There are some problems for working women. Yet they are happy over with their dual roles.

Role of Organisations in Solving Women's Problems

The UNO is committed to the principle of equality of men and women, meaning equality in their dignity and work as human beings as well as equality in their rights, opportunities and representations. There are a number of UN instruments which deal with problems of women, including the Convention for the Suppression of the Traffic in persons and of the Prostitution of Others (1949), the Convention of the Political Rights of Women (1952) the Supplementary Convention to the Abolition of Slavery, the Slave Trade.....Slavery (1956) etc. The ILO's Convention concerning the Employment of Women and Equal Remuneration for Men and Women Workers for work of equal value (1951) and the Convention concerning Discrimination in Respect of Employment and Occupation (1958) and UNESCO'S Convention against Discrimination in Education (1960) and the Mexico Declaration all emphasized the equality of women.

India began to feel since 1975, the need of organising public opinion regard to the problems of women. As a result, Indian women got the incorporation of a new Ministry relating to the matters of women as a whole. To mention some significant laws relating to women are :

1. Child Marriage Restraint Act 1929,
2. Prohibition of Sati Act 1829, Sati Prevention Act (1987),
3. The Hindu Marriage Act 1955,
4. Hindu Adoption and Maintenance Act 1956,
5. Immoral Traffic Prevention Act 1956,
6. Hindu Succession Act 1956,
7. The Dowry Prohibition Act 1961,
8. The Maternity Benefit Act 1961,
9. Muslim Protection of Rights on Divorce Act 1986 etc.

Indian Constitution provides equality before the law (Article 14), shall not discriminate any citizen on the ground of sex (Article 15), equal opportunity for all (Article 16), equal justice (Article 38), equal pay for equal work for both men and women (Article 39), property right (Article 300A) etc.

The Australian Bill of Rights (1986) is designed to secure the basic Civil and Political Rights and freedoms of all Australians.

Canada has Bill of Rights since 1960 and later introduced the Constitution the **Canadian Charter of Rights and freedom** in 1982, which speaks about equality of men and women.

The Federal Constitution of Malaysia provides equality in all respects for men and women.

The African Charter on Human and Peoples Rights contribution in this regard is laudable.

In England there are no laws against discrimination because her law do not discriminate.

The American Bill of Rights put emphasis on the personal liberties of its citizens.

The role of NGOs in dealing with the problems of women is highly notable. International level NGOs like the International Court of Justice, International Amnesty, UNICEF, UNESCO, Asia-Watch, America Watch, Africa Watch etc contribute a lot to the promotion of women's status. No government on earth has ever admitted its atrocities against women and violation to their rights and hence the burden has been borne by the people themselves or the NGOs on their behalf. Peoples Union of Democratic Rights and Peoples Union for Civil Rights also take earnest efforts in safeguarding human rights.

Besides these, there are certain other organisations, that function at the national and regional level which have constant touch with women's problems and committed to safeguard women from all sorts of atrocities and uplift them to the maximum, *e.g.*, Naga Peoples Movement for Human Rights, Women's Rights Project Division, Dalits women Forum, Punjab Women's Association, Akhil Banga Mahila Samiti and Public Society, National Commission for Women (India) etc. Since independence the problem has become very acute and the NGOs canvas the need for putting an end to the problems of women and contribute their best than that of the government machinery.

Violation of women's rights has been a world wide phenomenon. Almost all the countries of the world have not been free from this crime. Every organisation, both private and public must have a complaint cell that would sympathetically examine complaints of economic disparities. Equality in all stages must be installed without any bias and discrimination. Though the position of Indian women had improved since independence, it was not up to the level of expectations. Because we live in a sick society, which leads to the problems which we have seen in the supra. Yet, the only hope is pinned on the role of NGOs. These NGOs use all available techniques to influence the deliberations of world bodies and campaign to mobilise public opinion. Judicial decisions, reports of various international and national NGO, News paper reports and public opinion are indicative of the fact that atrocities against women in India are on the increase and the women due to their problems face unwanted tests. The battle for women's cause is long and tough. It is not enough to provide and guarantee rights. Effective action and achievement should be the aim, goal and target in a democracy. Every one should realise it in reality and work for integrity.

14

Contemporary Issues in Human Rights

The burning contemporary issues in human rights are (1) Female Infanticide, (2) Child Labour, (3) Illiteracy, (4) Bonded Labour and (5) Dalits and Human Rights. Let us see them one by one in detail.

(1) Female Infanticide

Female infanticide means nothing but killing of a female infant, soon after its birth, especially with the consent of parents. This custom of killing new born female babies is prevalent in almost all parts of India. Ancient history speaks that the position of women in society was at the lowest ebb. No wonder in the modern world, despite development in all sectors, the birth of a female baby is considered as a burden to the family. Because the female child undergoes a number of unforeseen tests in society, that too the girl children born in poor families face lot of hardships. When the girl grows up, the parents find it very difficult to fulfil her needs and conduct the marriage of the girl. They have to spend a lot in the name of dowry and presentations. That does not end there. Even after the marriage, the girl is forced by her husband and in-laws to bring valuables on and on from her parental home. As such, the parents are driven into debts. When the parents fail to provide with the demands, surprisingly the dowry deaths take place. Sometimes the girl would be neglected by her husband and she will lose her social status and her life itself will become a challenging one. Further girls undergo sex harassment, rape, slavery, bonded labour, prostitution, torture, ill-treatment, teasing, scolding, suffering etc. To put an end to all these hardships, it is believed by the people to kill the female infant soon after its birth. Traditional social norms and processes have continued from generation to generation.

The cases and methods of sex determination test, and the medical termination of pregnancy have played havoc with the girl child, since these methods loom large as the Damocle's sword on their very chance of coming to the outside world. At a Mumbai (Bombay) clinic alone, out of 8000 abortions, most of the foetuses were found to be of female. However, no suitable legislation, banning such tests, had come into force till now. In India, in states like Bihar, Gujarat, Uttar Pradesh, Madhya Pradesh, Maharastra and Tamil Nadu, the practice has become popular since they bring relief to the parents from the problems of paying dowry, and spending a lot at the time of marriage ot their girls. The rate of female infanticide and child mortality is increasing day by day in India. The Tamil Nadu government has proposed to implement a project to improve the status of girl children from financially backward families. Tamil Nadu Government's plan of 'cradle babies' was a step towards curbing this problem.

A workshop on "Infant Mortality Rate in Tamil Nadu" organised by the Danida Health Care Project revealed that the IMR dropped from 113 in 1971 to 54 in 1995. It was found out by October 1997 that female mortality rate had surpassed in Dharmapuri District.

The circumstances that lead to female infanticide are quite clear and it is understood that poverty and illiteracy are the main root causes for this shameful practice. It was also found out by the study initiated by women's Policy Research and Advocacy (WOPRA) in 1994, that the ratio of the female child is on the decline in Karnataka.

Let us hope that the government will actively consider passing a 'Special Female Infanticide Act' to take criminal action against both the parents who kill their new born female child.

With regard to female infanticide, criminal cases should be filed against the husband involved in it. The government should come forward to put such people behind the bars. Special programmes should be launched to enlighten the rural masses, especially the women regarding health and safe motherhood.

(2) Child Labour

The UN General Assembly adopted the Declaration of the Rights of the Child in 1959. It was based on the basic principles of UN Charter. It recognised the need for the safeguards and legal protections of children. The SAARC, in its first summit (1986) emphasised the need to safeguard the children, fulfil their requirements and help them to grow into useful citizens of future. The Stockholm Conference (1989) focussed on the necessity of making UN Conventions on the right of the children a reality. The UN Convention on the Rights of the Child included 3 important principles. They are : (1) the children need special safeguards beyond those provided to the adults, (2) the children need better environment for survival and development and (3) the adults should act in the best possible interests of children. Children are the valuable assets of a nation in general and a home in particular. Today's children are the citizens of tomorrow and their role in nation building should not be underestimated.

Persons under 14 years are classified as children. There are 18.56 crore children in India in the age group of 5-14. When we analyse the general condition of children in India, we can come to a decision that the rights of the children approved by the UN and reflected in the Constitution are just mere prescriptions. Millions of children are either tortured or imputed.

Child labour is a nation wide phenomenon. In the year 1981, the number of child labourers in India were 13.64 millions and in 1990 it went upto 18.18 millions and by 2000 A.D. it is believed that it may cross 20 millions.

Children mew the cattle, take care of the young ones at home, gather firewood and other forest products and sometimes work in the fields along with the elders. Some children work in hotels and road side restaurants, automobile workshops, hosieries, tailoring houses, brick industry, match factories and fire works too. Some are employed as rag pickers, beggars and collect unused bottles and iron pieces, meant for resale. All these help to substitute their family income. But at the same time they fail to realise that they are not provided with the opportunity of enjoying their childhood nor they have no opportunity to attend schools and get education.

The reasons for the child labour are many and varied. Some of the main reasons are poverty, ill-treatment by the parents, neglected by the family members, frustration, compulsion, and above all illiteracy. Poverty drives a child to indulge in unwanted laboured. Poverty is not only a cause for child labour but also a consequence of child labour. The Director General of ILO Mr. Michel Hansenae, observed that as many as 250 million children are toiling around the world, (India, Pakistan, Bangladesh, Afghanistan, African countries etc.) to survive or to overcome poverty.

According to the 1991 census, 86 per cent of Indian child labour force is employed in the primary sector, that includes agriculture, forestry, fishing, animal husbandry, mining and quarrying. The child labour legislations do not apply in most of these areas of work. About 8 per cent of the child labour force is employed in the secondary sector which includes manufacturing industries (power loom, carpet making, gem cutting) processing and construction. Besides, a substantial number of child labourers are involved in rag picking, shoe polishing, vending, doing household word etc. These occupations are not covered by the law.

(3) Illiteracy

Illitaracy is the main cause for the child labour. Recently (1997) the Government of India has proposed the 83rd amendment to the Constitution to make education a fundamental right. In the recent International Conference of Child Labour held in Oslo, the UNICEF's Executive Director M.S. Carol Bellary, emphasised primary education as the only long term solution to the problem of child labour, thus echoing the new ILO Convention that all forms of work that keep children out of school should be construed as extremely exploitative labour. All those who are out of schools are either child labourers or potential victims of child labour. Hence, the importance of primary education in this context could not be underestimated. Article 32 of the Convention of Rights of Child recognises the rights of the child to be protected from economic exploitation and from performing any work that is likely to be hazardous or to interfere with the child's education or to be harmful to the child's health or physical, mental, moral, spiritual or social development. Despite the Government's emphasis on universalisation of primary health and education, millions of children mostly dalits, are being deprived of their fair share of education and nutrition. Trapped in hazardous work situation, most of them do not even dream of a better future.

Steps Towards Elimination of Child Labour

The Supreme Court of India in "the abolition of the Child Labour in the carpet and other hazardous industries matter" directed the Government of India to convene a meeting of the Ministry concerned in the respective States and the Principal Secretaries holding the department concerned to evolve the principles and policies for progressive elimination of the children below the age of 14 years in all employment governed by the respective enactments. The State government of Tamil Nadu is doing its best the deadline set by the Supreme Court for submitting the report relating to the survey on child labour. In Tamil Nadu, a Joint Committee comprising of certain knitwear garment factories of Tirupur and non-governmental organisations has been formed with the aim of eliminating child labour.

The ILO has entered into a memorandum of understanding (MOU) with the Indian Government to extend the International Programme on Elimination of Child Labour (IPECL) in the country. The thrust would be on promoting an awareness of the problem. Social Awareness and Voluntary Education (SAVE) recommended that 'Child Labour Literature' could contribute to quicker eradication of child labour and rehabilitation. All Trade Unions and employers as a whole should come forward to ensure that no child labour was encouraged.

Appraisal

Today India faces the prospect of entering the 21 century with crores of child labourers and illiterate children. Some of the basic facts are :

(1) There are 18.56 crore children in the age group of 5-14.

(2) 5.7 crores are not in school.

(3) Of 10 Children who start schooling in Standard I, only 4 manage to survive till Standard 8.

(4) Despite regular attendance in schools, achievement levels are low. It is a clear picture of the children's accessibility of education.

In India, all the NGOs joined the "Global March", to highlight the problem of children. The rally had the coverage at Geneva on 1 June 1998 to coincide with the meeting of the ILO. The Asian segment of the March had begun from Manila on 17, January 1998 and entered India *via* Bongkok and Singapore. It moved through Patna, Danbad, Howrah, Bhuvaneswar, Guntur and Nellore and came to Chennai on 27, March 1998. So also the March started from South American, and African continents. Its action includes increasing the minimum age of employment to 18. It also aimed at raising awareness about children and urged the Governments to ratify and enforce laws that protect children, provide education, mobilise greater national and International funding to support education for all children and also arouse public opinion and action against the injustices caused to children.

Children taking part in the Global March against child labour demanded compulsory and free education. The Asia leg of the March covered Cambodia, Vietnam, Thailand, Malaysia, Bangladesh, Napal and India. This March demanded for their rights and it reached Geneva in June 1998, when the ILO held its meeting on most intolerable forms of child labour there.

The Global March Against child labour passed through Jaipur before entering the capital city in the second week of April 1998 on the last leg of its month — long 13 state passage through India. According to Kailash Satyarthi of the South Asian Coalition on Child Servitude (SACCS), the international coordinator of this initiative, similar Marches were on in Latin America and Africa, while an European one began in May 1998. Representatives of the four pronged Global March had coverage in June, in Geneva, where this year's (1998) International Labour Conference adopted a new convention designed to eliminate the most extreme and intolerable forms of child labour.

SAARC nations also have decided to improve children's lot. According to the Joint Secretary of Department of Women and Child Development, Ms. Rekha Bhargava, the member countries would have to combat immediately on the priority problems related to children and their education. It also aimed at arriving at a common *status quo* in promoting the cause of the neglected, abused and delinquent children. The SAARC countries have also understood the need for a universal formulation of strategies for promoting children's participation. The SAARC Member States have also rectified the Convention on Rights of Children which aimed at survival, development, protection and participation.

The year 1996 was particularly eventful. It was declared the "International year for the Eradication of Child Labour". Towards the end of the year there were, coincidentally, at least three other important developments related to child labour. One of them was a landmark judgment by the Supreme Court. Now, nearly one and a half years later, perhaps it is time to take stock of what actually happened as a result of the order.

UNICEF's report on the state of the World's Children 1997, and an international meeting in India of working children from Africa, Latin America and other parts of Asia, under the auspices of the International Working Group on Child Labour give details about child labour. Of these the Supreme Court's judgment delivered on 10 December 1996 and its immediate aftermath received the maximum official, media and public attention here. Now, nearly one and a half years later, perhaps it is time to take stock of what actually happened as a result of the Apex Court's order (which, contrary to some media reported, did not ban child labour but sought to force the state to atleast implement the Child Labour (Prohibition and Regulation Act, 1986).

The schools should provide calm atmosphere so as to enlighten the children. But the way in which children are treated in schools reminds of little David Copper-field who was mentally and physically abused at school as detailed by Charles Dickens. Today's society is cruel to children at school. They treat children brutally. Such brutality is unpardonable. Violence against the young should be stopped as it could lead to serious repercussions.

In India not only parents, even certain teachers are guilty in ill-treating young children. In 1995, it was highlighted that a 13 years old Rakesh was 'manhandled' by his teachers in a Rajasthan School. The end resulted in his death. The crime committed by him was that he had written an objectionale letter to a girl of his class. There was an incident in Chennai, that 2 teenaged children committed suicide as their teachers humiliated at them. In another incident, a boy who had sprinkled ink on a girl, was beaten with iron pipe by the teachers and he was wounded seriously. Indeed it is quite sad that teachers who have the responsibility of moulding the future citizens indulge in such brutal attitude. Further, teachers though not all, do not have and find time to develop a friendly and genuine relationship with the students. This sort of surroundings make children to lead a life of frustration. They are frightened and grow up into insecure humans.

Suggestions to Eradicate Child Labour

(1) No country has ended child labour without first making education compulsory and free. A study had revealed that India has the largest number of urban and rural children in the world. It is a must the proper education facilities may attract the attention of the children towards school.

(2) Stringent laws against the employment of children should be enforced. Legislations on the abolition of child labour need more teeth especially in the case of children employed in more hazardous industries.

(3) Parents should be made to realise the mistakes committed from their side in sending the children in their tender age to work. Special measures should be put in practice to deter parents from sending their young ones to work.

(4) Film Industry could play a laudable role in eradicating child labour by producing documentary films depicting the consequences of child labour.

(5) Children prefer to earn by undergoing child labour must be made to realise the importance of education through proper teaching

and providing guidance, which may help them to escape from exploitation and construct their future in a better way and shine as bright citizens.

(6) Concerned governments should take steps to emphasise more on universalisation of primary health and education. Without health it is quite difficult to implement plans and policies on them. Primary education is the only long term solution to the problem of child labour. Total literacy campaign should be identified and transit schools are a must for child labours.

(7) No sort of economic exploitation should be imposed on the children and at the same time they should not be treated as slaves nor put into physical torture, on account of poverty or any other such problems. Children should be provided with the opportunities of enjoying love and affection both from family and outside.

(8) Children should be given full mental freedom. Darkness should not haunt the lives of children. Majority of children in developing countries are deprived of their basic fundamental rights, *i.e.,* right from their birth.

(9) Articles 24 and 35 of the Indian Constitution and other legislations that were meant for the eradication of child labour must be implemented in its real sense.

(10) This problem has to be tackled from various angles. For that both government and non-governmental organisations should contribute their best to protect children and provide social security and social justice.

(11) Individual's role in this regard is quite warranted as it is quite reliable and encouraging in solving the problem of child labour.

(12) Every school should have the right philosophy of education. Minimum and Standard norms should be established. The curriculum should aim at the physical, social, economic and cognitive development of children. Learning becomes a joyful task and the children will see a bright, colourful and enjoyable childhood and foundation for their bright future.

The most practical way to generate more genuine and useful information on the actual prevalence of child labour in India may be to prompt the census authorities to ensure that the next decennial exercise, due to begin in March 2001 A.D. yields more reliable data through the incorporation of a realistic definition of child labour and a better and understanding of its many manifestations.

Juvenile Delinquency and Juvenile Act-1986

Crime among children may not be a new phenomenon. If a boy or a girl commits a murder, it is almost beyond the realm of human imagination. The victims are often the neglected ones. Juvenile crime thus becomes the last world in treachery and brutality. Society is not willing to pardon them or take them back in the usual and normal fold. This amounts to a child criminal to grow into an adult criminal.

No doubt, there is an angel even in a satan. In Japan, a 14 year old boy confessed to killing and then decapitating an 11 year old school mate. He also told that he had killed the girl by beating with a steel pipe. It was learnt that he was bright and popular too. The Japanese Society was shocked to see his savagery and wondered why this sort of youth murders sprang up in numbers. In Tokya, a teen age girl was strangled by three boys in 1985. In 1988, there was an incident in Tokya again, that a 14 year boy used a knife to kill his parents. In 1996, another boy killed a bookshop owner. Not only in Japan but even in the developed country US (Michigan) three white teenagers were assaulted by a black youth and a white teenager died on the spot. In India, crime among children is quite horrifying. In 1996, a student in Tamil Nadu State lost his life by an act of ragging. States like West Bengal also witness the incidents of Juvenile violence. The main reason for this trend is the pressure that children face both at home and school. A Tokya scholar expresses that children are not growing normally because unreasonable demands are being placed on them. In India mostly frustration develops into juvenile tendencies. Sociologists feel that only frustration urges children to become a delinquent. More often films and T.V. serials promote a sort of sadism among children and they develop a sort of aggressive behaviour. In toto, all depends on the way in which the adults are going to exert on the young ones.

The General Assembly of the UN adopted the Declaration of the Rights of the Child in 1959. Following this The Convention on the Rights of the Child was adopted by consensus of the States in 1989. As such every State has taken special measures to care for the children because the future of any State depends fully upon its healthy children. The National Policy that was developed by the Government of India stressed the importance of children at the national level. The UN declared the year 1979 as the International Year of the Child. It was also realised by the UN to tackle the problem of Juvenile delinquency. Some children due to one reason or other, sometimes without their sense, commit certain offences. Such children are referred as juvenile delinquencies. In 1985, UN adopted Standard Minimum Rules for dealing with the juveniles. A Juvenile Justice

System also was evolved. The Government of India introduced a Child Act to deal with the child offenders in the light of the UN Scheme. This led to the passage of Juvenile Justice Act in 1986 by the Government of India. It was put into force in October 1987. Various reasons were found out as a cause for Juvenile delinquency. Either due to the neglect of parents, or due to some inducement, or due to compulsion or due to frustration and the like, the child commits offences. Here the child feels that as if it has lost the chance of getting sympathy from others. The child is totally ignorant of having committed an offence. Thus, a child becomes an offender and his name is enrolled in the list of criminals by the police.

In India, there are hundreds of criminal children and they have no opportunity to escape from committing crimes. As a self contained Act, The Juvenile Justice Act of 1986 in India, provided for looking after the children as well as the juveniles. All sorts of uncared and unwanted children get protection under this Act. This Act provides for the constitution of a 'Juvenile Welfare Board' which in turn shall have the power of a magistrate under the Code of Criminal Procedure. Children under the age of 16 years in the case of boys and 18 years in the case of girls are brought under this Act. If these children indulge in prostitution they will be considered as neglected ones. So also if they become drug addicts during this age group, they are considered as neglected juveniles. This Act also provides for the imprisonment of persons who may be responsible for the suffering of the child. The Board has also committed to find out the parents of neglected Juveniles and hand over them to the parents, such parents are advised to report to the Juvenile Board about the progress of the child.

Before the enquiry about the Juveniles is undertaken, the Board is expected to send the child to the Juvenile Home where the child is put under observation. He is given education, vocational and other training to rebuild his life and conduct himself in a better way in future. For that the major responsibility rests with the society in finding out the Juveniles in order to provide rehabilitation.

The Juvenile Act also provides for the constitution of Juvenile Courts in each and every State. This court exercises the powers conferred by the Code of Criminal Procedure, 1974. The speciality of this court is that among the members of the Court, there should be one woman member also. As per this Act, there are four kinds of Juvenile Homes, that work for the rehabilitation of the Juveniles. They are (1) Observation Home, (2) Juvenile Home, (3) Special Home and (4) After care organisation.

The Juvenile children are sent to the observation Homes for enquiry. These are temporary homes. Until the enquiries are over, special care is taken, their activities are observed so as to find out solutions for the problems. But the police torture the children in the name of enquiry. The neglected Juvenile children are accommodated in the Juvenile Homes and rehabilitation programmes are provided to develop their abilities and build up their character. Special Homes help to develop their mental and physical personalities so as to make them as responsible citizens.

The After Care Organisations enable the juveniles to mend themselves and lead an honest life. Though the provisions of the Act are quite encouraging in solving the problems of Juveniles, it is quite unfortunate that they are not strictly implemented in all the States.

(4) Bonded Labour

'Bonded' means put into bond or a tie or an agreement. 'Labour' means one works or labours. The labour may either be physical or mental. By this, one, toils under his employer. Bonded labourers are the persons who are bound to perform certain forced labour. A bond is between two persons. One is a master and the other is worker/labourer. Serfdom also is brought under this system. Here, the labourer or the tenant is bound to live and labour on the land belonging to another person. They have no freedom of movement. From serfdom came the forced labour, especially in agriculture. Here the landlords or the money lenders are the masters. Poverty makes them to borrow. The debt in turn makes them to become bonded men. The landlords or the money lenders force the underpriviledged people to work free or for very meagre wages on their lands. The rate of interest is abnormal. The debtor could not repay the borrowed amount with interest and it is compounded in due course. This makes him to work only for clearing the interest. As the debtors are illiterates, they are cheated by the money lenders. The debt is not cleared during his life time.

So his whole family enters into compulsory or forced labour, on the lender's land. Under these circumstances they lost their freedom of seeking other employment. Low wages also pose a threat to the labourers. They are not treated like humans. They are treated as commodities. This paved the way for selling or mortgaging the bonded labourers.

Bonded Labour in India before and since Independence

The system of bonded labour existed in India in various names such as slavery, serfs, bondage, forced labour, exploited labour etc. In India, its existence could be traced from the period of Indus Civilization. Due to the coming of Aryans in India, the caste system came into force. Sudras, the last cadre of society, were treated as slaves and untouchables. In the Buddha Jataka stories, we find evidences that speak about slavery. So also in Epics. Kautilya, in his Arthasasthra mentions that a man could be a slave either by birth or by profession. We get further evidences of forced labour during the period of Guptas, Harsha etc. The Chola period in South India, speaks about 'Vettian' a sort of forced labour. Domestic slaves also were in existence. Quidbuddin-Aibek himself was a slave. During wars, slaves were utilised at the maximum level by the rulers and commanders of army. During the period of moghuls slavery increased. Though Akbar tried to abolish slavery, he could not succeed in his attempt. The bondage of agrestic slaves originated in Bengal and Bihar during 18th century. Many, in order to survive during the famines in various parts of India, borrowed from the money lenders zamindars. When they failed to repay the loans, they were sold as slaves. Trafficking slaves had become a profitable task in India. The slave trade was intensified in the latter part of the 18th century. During the British period the Slavery Abolition Act was passed in 1843. Then came the forced labour. Indian Penal Code prohibited forced labour in 1860. On the abolition of slavery, the vested interests called it in a new name to evade the provisions of the above said Acts. Thus came the name of bonded labour. These bonded labourers are called in different names in different states of India. In Tamil Nadu they are referred as Velaikaran (Paniyal), in Kerala Cherumar, in Orissa Halios, in Andhra Pradesh Jassigula, in Gujarat Hali, in Karnataka Jeetha and the like. These bonded labourers were mostly poor, dalits and tribals.

At one stage Zamindari System was abolished in India. The Annual Report of the Commission for Scheduled Castes and Scheduled Tribes give a complete picture of bonded labour. As per the survey conducted by the National Labour Institute (1978) it was estimated that there were about 13 lakh bonded labourers in India. Almost every state in India has bonded labourers. In 1984, more than one lakh bonded — labourers were set free from the clutches of landlords or other well off leaders in society. Various studies reveal that in many parts of India, the practice of bonded labour still continues. It was reported in *The Hindustan Times* (8 February, 1991) that about 3000 bonded labourers are subject to exploitation. There is no reliable data available about the exact number of bonded labours in India.

The Right to live with human dignity is once for all forgotten. Neither the Government of India nor the state governments have the right to take any action that may deprive a person from enjoying the basic rights as envisaged in the Directive Principles of State Policy (Articles 39, 41 and 42). Bonded labourers, even after 50 years of independence are found in various occupations *e.g.*, agriculture, industries, stone quarries, brick industries, building construction sites, powerloom centres, match industries, knit wear industries, mines, jewel manufacturing centres, diamond and gem cutting industries, carpet industry, hotels and other establishments.

Steps taken by the Government to abolish bonded labour since Independence

(1) Article 23 (1) of the Indian Constitution provides that "Traffic in human beings and beggar and other similar forms of forced labour are prohibited and any contravention of this portion shall be an offence punishable in accordance with law."

(2) Mines Act of 1952.

(3) Contract Labour Abolition Act 1970.

(4) Contract Labour (Regulation and Abolition) Act 1970.

(5) Bonded Labour System Abolition 1976.

(6) Equal Remuneration Act 1976.

(7) The Inter-State Migrant Workmen (Regulation of Employment and Conditions of Services) Act 1979.

(8) Child Labour Prohibition Act 1981.

The Supreme Court of India is doing yeoman service to liberate the bonded labourers. It has directed the Central and State governments for the release of bonded labourers and rehabilitation.

As per the direction of Supreme Court, the Tamil Nadu Government planned to rehabilitate about 10,000 bonded labourers in 1997.

The judiciary has shown deep concern for the basic rights of the bonded labourers and issue the suitable directions for ensuring the protection and promotion of the human rights of the bonded labourers so as to help them to live with human dignity.

Rehabilitation Measures

In April 1998, as many as 851 bonded labourers have been identified in Salem district, Tamil Nadu, India. Efforts were taken to find out whether the elimination of bonded labourers was going on properly as per the Act of 1976 and whether the released bonded labourers were given immediate relief and assistance for rehabilitation. An official press release stated that among 881 bonded labourers 106, were from other states. NGOs and other interested personnels were appealed to make intense efforts to eradicate the bonded labour system in the country.

Identify cards were issued to 474 bonded labourers who were rescued from different parts of Tamil Nadu. The cards entitled the former bonded labourers to claim benefits under the various rehabilitation measures to be initiated for them. They need not repay the money that they had borrowed from their former employers. If they were harassed by their former employers, they could report to the nearest police station. Each one of the rescued was eligible for a financial grant of Rs. 10,000 Housing facilities also are arranged for them through the Block Development Officers. Arrangements are also made to provide jobs under the Employment Assurance Scheme. Priority would be given in all training schools under TRYSEM — (Training Youth for Self Employment), besides the arrangements made for the enrolment of their children in schools.

While rehabilitation measures were taken for the benefit of the former bonded labourers, on the legal form, the administration also launched action against the agents who employed the bonded labourers by filing cases against them. 212 persons were arrested under the Bonded Labour Abolition Act. The rescued ones should earn their livelihood without getting into debts again and failing into the hands of unscrupulous money — lender employers.

It was poverty which drove people to bonded labourers. In poor families, the men were addicted to liquor, smoking and films which took away a sizeable chunk of their earnings and force them to enter into bond. Unless they cut down their expenditure on such evil practices, they could not build up their future on the right path and lead a honourable life.

The enactment of the Bonded Labour Abolition Act in 1976 had not solved the problem because of the failure of the authorities to invoke the provisions of the Act to put down the evil practice. Steps should be taken to identify the bonded labourers in various parts of the country and initiate legal action against the culprits who kept the innocents in bondage. The role of NGOs is superb in identifying the bonded labourers.

A beedi worker who was a bond, said he was working as a bonded labourer for the last five years to repay a loan of Rs. 4000/- which he had taken from his employer, who cut 50 per cent of his wages by way of recovery of the loan dues and added that the employer asked him to work till he repaid the loan. It is a surprise that some bonded labourers did not keep track of the wages cut by the employer and were unaware of the balance amount they owed or whether they continued to work even after their employer had fully recovered the dues with interest.

Another case reveals that his employer charged a 5 per cent interest for the loan he had taken and he had been working for the last 5 years to clear the loan. The poor labourers was getting only Rs. 3700/- as his annual wage. It is quite unfortunate that most employers did not know that bonded labour was a crime while the bonded labourers also did not know they need not repay the amount to the employer as per the Bonded Labour Abolition Act.

The Supreme Court also directed the states of Tamil Nadu, Orissa, Karnataka and Andhra to take immediate steps for the rehabilitation of one thousand four hundred (1400) bonded labourers. This shows that the Courts are not only for the rich and well to do but also for the poor and downtrodden. It is also the duty of Courts to help the distressed people.

But the various legistations to abolish bonded labour are not successful put into force. The reason is quite simple *i.e.,* The bond master dominates over others and influences the executive. Thus, the system of the bonded continues to persist. To curb this proper and necessary amendments must be introduced in the existing Bonded Labour Abolition Act. Bonded labourers must be made to realise their rights, for which education is the only means. The loopholes in the Minimum Wages Act should be removed. Social conscience also could help to eradicate bonded labour.

(5) Dalits and Human Rights

Meaning : 'Dalit' means oppressed or suppressed or ground down. There are nearly 156 million dalits or members of the SCs and STs in India; that is more than Pakistan's population. Communities formerly considered "untouchable" under the caste system increasingly describe themselves as dalits. Whether in employment, literary or any other indicators, dalits are worse of than most. Thus, there are signs and symptoms of restlessness and change within these groups.

Dalits are mostly landless or marginal farmers. Most of the dalits opt out of the agricultural labour force. They seek food, firewood and other things in the forest. They even pick up wasted or damaged crops in the fields. They indulge in all sorts of hard work. Economically, they are at the bottom of the heap. They are poor and drowntrodden. They have no permanent shelters, nor cattle of their own. They live in one room hutments. The roof of such huts are even damaged and unfit to live. Yet they stick on in their hamlets.

History

The traditional social system in India has been divided into four varnas *i.e.* Brahmin, Kshatriya, Vaishya and Sudra. This class division is not peculiar to India. This type of social stratification has existed in all organised societies. Conforming to this fourfold classification of the India society there was the system of privileges, rights, duties etc. Among these four categories, the Sudras are the depressed and suppressed humans and untouchables belong to the lowest rang of the Sudras and these dalits are in despair.

Justice is denied to them for long. Ambedkar was angry against this caste system. Gandhiji was firm on the abolition of the caste system. He called the low caste people as 'Harijans'. Vivekananda hurled secular missiles against the malpractices followed against this downtrodden people. Nehru condemned the terrible injustices against this humble people. Many social and religious reformers strove hard for the uplift of these depressed brethren equal in the eyes of God. Ambedkar was more fierce in his annihilative antagonism to this inhumanity of man to man.

Dalits are noted as Scheduled Castes and Scheduled Tribes. The major political pathology threatening the integrity, solidarity and stability of India is the die-hard caste system. The most incurable wound is the exclusion of that depressed and desperate Dalit sector which is a substantial number. Nehru in his 'Discovery of India' has perceptively observed thus :

"But the ultimate weakness and failing of the caste system and the Indian social structure were that they degraded a mass of human beings and gave them no opportunities to get out of that condition educationally, culturally or economically."

Although the nation has advanced in material development and democratic conscience, the fact remains that the untouchables are drowned in illiteracy and grinding poverty. Every sixth man in the world is an Indian. Every fourth of five men in India is a Harijan. The Indian Constitution has emphasised the unity and integrity of the nation as a paramount value and insisted upon equality and dignity as a constitutional fundamental. In a powerful endeavour to produce a casteless society and Constitution has promised equal protection of the laws to the lowest and the last forbidden untouchability and made free access to all places of public resort.

Dr. Ambedker argued that "we must make our political democracy a social democracy as well. Political democracy cannot last unless there lies at the base of it social democracy. What does social democracy mean?

It means a way of life which recognises liberty, equality and fraternity as the principles of life. These principles of liberty, equality and fraternity are not to be treated as separate items in a Trinity. They form a union of Trinity in the sense that to divorce one from the other is to defeat the very purpose of democracy. Liberty cannot be divorced from equality; nor can liberty and equality be divorced from fraternity. With equality liberty would produce the supremacy of the few over the many. Equality without liberty would kill individual initiative. Without fraternity liberty and equality could not become a natural course of things."

The most creative contribution made by Dr. Ambedkar was an uncompromising fighter for Indian humanity, particularly the humble "usually described as the dalits or Scheduled Castes and Scheduled Tribes". Dr. Ambedkar was not a mere depressed class leader but a defender of human rights of weaker and exploited people.

Dr. Ambedkar said that "the Hindus wanted the Vedas and they sent for Veda Vyasa who was not a caste Hindu. The Hindus wanted an epic and they sent for Valmiki who was an untouchable. The Hindus wanted a Constitution and they sent for me" Rabindranath Tagore has stressed equality in his literature Geethanjali. Gandhiji, Nehru, Anna, Periyar and a number of others had contributed a lot to eradicate casteism from society. So also different personalities on different occasions have committed to improve the condition of dalits so as to provide equality in society.

Max Rodin has said that it is difficult to define equality. According to Mathew Arnold it is to be observed that elulity is to be praised at all levels. Edmund Burke says, "fight against Autocracy". Prof. Laski says, "There can not be any liberty without equality". Human Rights must triumph over in-human wrongs.

Reasons for their backwardness

The backwardness of Dalits is attributed to many reasons. They are (1) ignorance (2) illiteracy (3) landless people (4) untouchables (5) could not approach others easily (6) homeless (7) bonded labourers (8) poverty (9) highlandedness of the upper caste people (10) exploitation by others (11) serfs (12) no proper care takers (13) domination of tribalism (14) unwillingness to develop awareness among themselves.

Measures for their Upliftment

If at all the dalits are to be uplifted, primary importance should be bestowed on their education with basic needs. Basic and compulsory education could surely help to elevate their standard and position in society. It may even to societal recognition. As they are minorities special legislations should be put into force to provide opportunities for them in job oriented education and vocational groups. Special and individual attention should be paid for their higher education. Preference should be given to dalits in employment and vocational groups. Preference should be given to dalits in employment opportunities. If the Indian Democracy is really aiming at improving the standards of dalits at all levels, all these must be exercised in a fullfledged manner.

We often hear about rape, group rape, exploitation, sexual harassment, wage discrimination etc. in society, that too among the minorities. All developmental programmes are not reaching the dalits. Incidents of 'Melavalavu' — Tamil Nadu, portrays the violence that has surfaced in Tamil Nadu in the last couple of years (1996, 1997) due to rigid caste hierarchies and the growing assertiveness of the Dalits. At the Melavalavu, seven were murdered in June 1997. They were killed because they were dalits who had dared to stand for public office. One Mr. Raja, a Dalit, who was elected as Panchayat President has not been able to function because he is too terrified to visit his office as it is located in the upper caste locality. The Dalits in the village are too scared to take the main road out of Melavalavu, because it passes through the centre of the village. The village is known for its rigid caste hierarchies. He sit on the floor to eat. The caste Hindus expect the dalits to be servile and beat them when they ask for higher wages. The Caste Hindus are opposed to Dalit empowerment of any kind.

Indian Forest Department is fastly moving in creating social forests. Deforestation leads the Dalits to shift their dwellings from one place to another. This makes them to become helpless and hopeless. Their rights are denied here. About 200 million Dalits face this sort of harassment. The legislations meant for Dalits are not properly executed.

Not only in India, but even at the International level tribals called Scheduled Tribes are spread in various centres. They are minorities. They are socially, educationally and economically backward. Yet their culture and civilization are great with high calibre. All the other differences laugh at us. Justice Chinnappa Reddi observed that "they need help; they need protection in life; they need developmental plans; they need amelioration". He further added that "they demand only their needs, rather all their demands are their rights only. Instead they never expect nor ask any gift *i.e.,* they ask for their rights guaranteed in the Indian Constitution".

Untouchability is to be once for all eradicated in order to make democracy a successful one.

As per the census report of 1991 it was calculated that there were 450 sectors of Scheduled Tribes in India. Subdivisions in each sector also comes under this data. They speak different languages. India government has introduced integrated Tribal Development Programmes, Tribal sub-plans and special plans for the tribals in North Eastern Territories.

Indian Constitution has provided following safeguards to Dalits and Scheduled Tribes:-

1. Education — Article 15(4), 29
2. Employment — Articles 16(4); 320 (4); 333
3. Social Security — Articles 17, 25
4. Economic guarantee — Article 19
5. To abolish forced labour — Article 23
6. Security from social injustice and exploitation — Article 46
7. Tribal area administration — Articles 244, 339
8. Political Security — Articles 320, 332, 334
9. Tribal Welfare Ministry — Article 164
10. Nagaland, Assam, Manipur special concessions — Article 37(1) (b), (c)
11. Development measures, education and economy — Article 46
12. Tribal Welfare Fund — Article 275
13. Free aid — Article 39(a)

Despite, the number of atrocities committed on Dalits increase year by year. Nearly 73 per cent of cases were reported from the Northern and North — Eastern states. Mostly the Dalits suffered from physical violence, arson, rape, murder, ill-treatment, exploitation, etc.

In recent years, Dalit power is finding its hour and they are fighting for their rights as envisaged in the Constitution. Today, India struggles to maintain its integrity as a nation due to challenges from within and without. Only equality, liberty, fraternity and social justice can weave people into a strong garment of nationhood. The Indian caste system is anti-national and it brings about separation in social life. It generates jealousy and antipathy between castes. The Dalits are treated as nonpersons. Dalits are an unfortunate lot. They require a different kind of protection from the Constitution to preserve their identity, integrity and elimination of disability. No, doubt the policy of protection of Scheduled Tribes (Dalits) demands special treatment.

The need of the hour is to create a casteless society. For that, efforts are to be taken to adopt constant vigilance to monitor projects for the welfare of dalits. A special reservation policy in the areas of education and public services is enshrined in the Constitution. A general diffusion of literacy, a pervasive awareness of rights, a broad economic development and better ability to use the democracy of opportunities will make the meaning so far as the Dalits and their well being are concerned. Of course, the problem of reservations raises highly inflammable issues. Utilisation of human resources insists on the best talent, regardless of caste and community consideration.

The Constitution reserves and promises equality of status and opportunity hitherto denied to the vast majority of its members. Part III of the Indian Constitution provides enormous rights to 'the people of India'. The Directive Principles (Part IV) reinforced the thrust of the objective of Constitution-Article 14 speaks about equal protection of law. The Supreme Court has held that equality as a rule of law. It includes reservation for caste and community. Aristotle says, "Equality consists in treating equals and uneqals unequally". Redistributive justice to dalits insists on effective reforms. Reservation of posts and all other measures designed to promote the participation of the Scheduled Castes and the Scheduled Tribes in the public services at all levels are in our opinion necessary consequences flowing from the Fundamental Rights guaranteed by Article 16(1). This is again emphasised by Article 46 provides the State to promote with special care the educational and economic interest of the weaker sections of the people, especially the Scheduled Castes and Scheduled Tribes and shall protect them from social injustice and all forms of exploitation. It may help reservation and preferences. The Directive Principles embody a commitment which was imposed by the Constitution makers on the State to bring about economic and social regeneration of the teeming millions who are steeped in poverty and backwardness.

It is to be noted that the Fundamental Rights are justifiable and the Directive Principles are not. The Constitution is not a mere lawyer's document, it is a vehicle of life and its spirit is always the spirit of the age. There arises a question that how should elimination of social backwardness be assessed? A periodic review of the policy of reservation in the employment, education and legislative institutions has also been suggested by the Supreme Court with a view to a national debate and consequential correction. Poverty is the bane of Indian society. It is observed by Justice Desai that reservation in favour of Scheduled Castes and Scheduled Tribes must continue. Justice Chinnappa Reddy traces the complexity of the dynamic issue of socially and educationally backward classes — *vis-a-vis* social and economic justice. All the weaker sections of the people in society have long journeys to make. He further says, "They need aid; they need facility; they need launching; they need propulsion. Their needs are their demands. The demands are matters of right and not of philanthrophy. They ask for parity and not charity".

Poverty is the basic root cause for the social and educational backwardness of dalits. The government may provide for them liberal grants of scholarships, free studentship, free boarding and lodging facilities, free uniforms, free mid-day meals, free books and stationery, free special coaching etc. Many a projects to lift them have met with failure. Today, the Dalits; hunger for dynamic development is reflected in Dr. Ambedkar's demand for a new order, *i.e.,* not mere political freedom for the country but social liberation of the people. Dr. Ambedkar found untouchable India more or less like apartheid Africa.

Untouchability was a unique phenomenon unknown to humanity except the Hindus. Dalits are treated as permanent and hereditary slaves by the so called upper caste people. Dr. Ambedkar insisted that every Indian including every untouchable and unapproachable shall be equal. He was afraid that human rights had to be guaranteed if the downtrodden were to have a fair deal. Equality is the activist principles of democracy. The Constitutional philosophy of equality has been expounded by Justice. Bhagwati is in a different context. He argues that, "the concept of equality under the Constitution is a dynamic concept. It takes within its sweep every process of equalisation and protective discrimination......Equality of Opportunity is not simply a matter of legal equality. Its existence depends not merely on the absence of disabilities but on the presence of abilities...... Equality in law must produce real equality". India is a country of great economic, social and cultural diversity. The cultural diversity adds to the splendour of India. But others create problems. So the underprivileged, the deprived and exploited ones are to be protected and nourished so as to take their place in an egalitarian society.

Legally, untouchability is forbidden. But is persists traditionally. Article 15(4) of the Indian Constitution lays down the advancement of socially and educationally backward classes and of the Scheduled Castes and Scheduled Tribes. Article 46 refers to the weaker section of the people and in particular, the Scheduled Castes and Scheduled Tribes. They have Constitutional credentials for reservations. Dealing with the contention that the major benefits of reservation will be cornered by the more advanced section of the backward communities. The Mandal Commission dismisses it by saying that this vice is but a Universal Phenomenon among all classes and may be ignored as inevitable. The sluggish course of Scheduled Castes and Scheduled Tribes progress is disappointing in one way or other. Thus, proper steps are to be taken to integrate the dalits with the rest of the mainstream of the nation through the processes of education and public employment and empowerment.

15

Prisoners and Human Rights

Our Indian Constitution guarantees our Fundamental Rights. It provides safety and security to the rights of every individual in India. Even prisoners are not exempted.

Article 21 of the Indian constitution guarantees the rights of 'Personal Liberty' and prohibits any inhuman, cruel or degrading treatment to any person whether he is a national or a foreigner. Article 14 provides the right to equality and equal protection of laws. So prisoners too have their own rights. Any excesses committed on a prisoner, by the police is considered as a violation of rights and it warrants the attention of the legislature and judiciary.

In recent years, the Supreme Court of India has been very vigilant about the atrocities committed against the prisoners. The judiciary protects the right of prisoners and recognises their rights. They are protected from torture. Solitary confinement is also not recognised by the Government. Further, the Apex Court considers the prisoner's right to bail, right to meet friends, relatives and lawyers. The courts also allow the rights to medical examination to the prisoners. The torture inflicted on the prisoners may make them hardened criminals. The prisoners are provided with these rights, as they are also human beings and are entitled to enjoy their rights.

When one undergoes imprisonment, it doesn't mean that he has to bid farewell to his fundamental rights and freedom. In Sunil Batra V Delhi Administration case, the Supreme Court stated that, "in our Constitutional order it is axiomatic that the prison laws do not swallow up the fundamental rights of the legally unfree and as sentinels on the *qui vive,* courts will guard freedom behind bars, tempered, of course by environmental realism but intolerant of torture by executive echelons. The policy of the law is beyond purchase by authoritarians gribly invoking "dangerness" of inmates and peace in prisons. Human dignity is a dear value of our Constitution not to be battered away for mere apprehensions entertained by jail officials."

1. Bar Fetters and Head-cuffing

Justice Krishna Iyer observed that handcuffing in *prima facie* inhuman and, therefore, unreasonable, is over harsh and at the first flush, arbitrary. Absent fair procedure and objective monitoring to inflict 'irons' is to resort too zoological strategies repugnant to Article 21. He also observed that handcuffs were to be used only when the person was desperate, rowdy or the one who was involved in non-bailable offence.

2. Protection from Inhuman Torture

Prisoners also face inhuman torture at the hands of police. Supreme Court has protected the prisoners from all types of torture. In Kishore Singh V Rajasthan State case, the Supreme Court brought home the deep concern for human rights by observing against police cruelty as "Nothing is more cowardly and unconscionable than a person in police custody being beaten up and nothing inflicts a deeper wound on our Constitutional culture than a state official running berserk regardless of human rights". Thus, the Supreme Court has made it clear that any form of torture, inhuman or degrading treatment is offensive to human dignity and constitutes and inroad into the life.

3. Right to meet Friends and Relatives

The Supreme Court has recognised the rights of the prisoners to be visited by their relatives and friends. Here, the court held that the prisoner could not move about freely by going outside the jail and could not socialise with persons outside the jail. As such it was rightly stated that personal liberty would include the right to socialise with members of the family and friends subject, to any valid prison regulations and under Articles 14 and 21 such prison regulations must be reasonable and non-arbitrary. Prison regulations also recognise the right of prisoners to have interview with a legal adviser, in a reasonable manner.

4. Right to Bail

Indiscriminate arrests are notable examples for the violation of human rights. The prisoners also have the right to bail. The court recognised the right to bail as a part of personal liberty (Article 21 of the Indian Constitution). The court observed that a man on bail had a better chance to prepare or present his case than the one remanded in custody. Mostly, poor people do not have the chance of awailing bail due to poverty and illiteracy. The judiciary must be sympathetic towards poor, in this regard. The Directive principles of Indian Constitution (Part IV) provides the right to bail.

5. Speedy Trial

Article 21 of the Indian Constitution speaks about the right to speedy trial. It is one of the fundamental rights of a prisoner. It ensures "just, fair and reasonable" procedure. It is often noticed that a large number of men, women and children were put behind the bars for years together awaiting trial in courts of law. It is quite a discouraging fact from the side of judiciary. The Supreme Court as a protector of human rights has given warning which speaks, "the time has come and the legal and judicial system have to be revamped and restructured so that such injustice do not occur and disfigure the fair and otherwise luminous face of our nascent democracy".

6. Right to Legal Aid

Right to legal aid is also one of the rights of prisoners. It enables them to have access to justice in case of violation of their human rights. Legal aid is one of the Constitutional rights and the legal machinery is expected to deal with specifically. But in practice, the poor people are not aware of this right, due to poverty and illiteracy. Menaka Gandhi V Union of India case, made the "Procedure established by law" in Article 21 of the Indian Constitution as "Just, fair and reasonable". It has its impact in the cases dealt with legal aid. The court made it clear that the right to free legal services was clearly an essential ingredient of reasonable, fair and just procedure for a person accused of an offence.

In a democracy the rights and liberties of an individual are as important as the power of the state of regulate them in the interests of society and a balance maintained between them with the help of the judiciary. In India the rights of prisoners have been on many occasions under heavy strain. The justification of the stringent measures undertaken during the emergency in 1975 was beyond the purview of the court. The Indian Constitution visualises and attempts to usher in a society in which justice is equally and even-handed administered to all. No doubt, the Constitution enjoins on the citizen and the government to strive towards the ideal of full and equal justice to all. Speedy justice is in the interest of both the rich and the poor. So also legal aid should not be limited to a particular group but should be available to all those who are poor and needy. The Supreme Court has also emphasised the role of people and other social groups and voluntary organisations as a must in making legal aid meaningful, effective and purposeful. The legal Services Authority Act, 1987, provides free and competent legal services to the weaker sections.

Capital Punishment

The ICCPR in its Article 6(2) speaks that the countries may impose death sentence for the most serious crimes in arrogance with the law in force at that time of the final judgement of the court. It also says that any one sentenced to death shall have the right to seek pardon or commutation of the sentence. The second optional Protocol to the ICCPR, aimed at abolishing death sentence. The Indian Penal Code provides for death sentence for seven types of offences Though India has retained the death sentence in certain cases, it is clear that the basic human right to 'life' is protected in India.

Capital punishment is considered as cruel, inhuman, uncivilised and barbaric one. Despite, this practice is still in existence. There is difference of opinion among the juries and other eminent politicians about the imposition of capital punishment. So the question arises whether it should be abolished or retained? Here the very right to life, as guaranteed by Constitution and UN Declaration is violated. But if we analyse the IPC in detail, we can find, the provision for capital punishment if a person's life is liable to be extinguished any time after he has extinguished the life of another. Of course every one has the right to live. But none can divest anyone of his 'right to life'. If one does indulge so, it has to be at the cost of his own life. Certain learned jurists have undermined the fact that even right to life is not an absolute right. The question is how can one enjoy life at the cost of another man's life. The international trend is in favour of abolition of death penalty. The UDHR in its Articles 3 and 5 provide, "Every one has the right of life, liberty and security of person" and "No one shall be subjected to torture or to cruel, inhuman or degrading treatment or punishment". The International Covenant on Civil and Political Rights (1966) in its Article 6 provides, "Any one sentenced to death shall have the right to seek pardon or commutation of the sentence amnesty, pardon or commutation of the sentence of death may be granted in all cases. It also provides that Sentence of death shall not be imposed for crimes committed by persons below 18 years of age and shall not be carried on pregnant women."

The world level trend is in favour of abolition of capital punishment. In U.S.A. capital sentence was challenged in Furman's case on the ground of its violating the 8 and 14th Amendments. Some judges of U.S. declared the capital punishment as unconstitutional.

As far as India is concerned, the death sentence stands constitutionally valid till now. In India there is no 8th Amendment as in USA. Still, the constitutionality of death sentence was challenged in several occasions, in pursuance of Articles 14 and 21.

The Law Commission of India was given the task of examining the law regarding capital punishment in India and recommend the measures for abolishing, retaining or modifying it. A resolution was moved in the Lok Sabha, to abolish death sentence and this was taken to the notice of Law Commission. The Law Commission under the Chairmanship of Mr. J.L. Kapur, examined it in detail, and its recommendations revealed that it was not in favour of abolition of death sentence in India because of the inherent risks involved in such abolition. The summary of its recommendations is "Having regard; however, to the conditions in India, to the variety of the social upbringing of its inhabitants, to the disparity in the level of morality and education in the country, to the vastness of its area, to the diversity of its population and to the paramount need for maintaining law and order in the country at the present juncture, India cannot risk the experiment of abolition of capital punishment".

The Law Commission stressed that the Court should state the reasons as to why it chooses life imprisonment or death, as the case may be in a given situation. While the Commission recommended an amendment in the Criminal Procedure Code, it stated that "Thus, there appears to be sufficient justification for a provision requiring the court to state its reasons, whenever it awards either of the two sentence in a capital case". The Commission also favoured for the retention of the power of the President and the Governors to grant mercy.

The modifications made in the Criminal Procedure Code are quite encouraging and give a sigh of relief as the death sentence pronounced by a Sessions Court is required to be submitted to High Court for confirmation. But the confirmation should be signed by atleast two judges of the court. Thus, it is clear that the death sentence has to be awarded at the rarest.

Justice Bhagwati observed that "there can be no doubt that death penalty in its actual operation is discriminatory for it strikes mostly against the poor and deprived sections of the community and the right and the affluent usually escape from its clutches."

16

Human Rights Development

The development of human rights began only in the early 19th century. The most important problems that attracted the attention of the international law were related to the abolition of slavery, humanitarian law of warfare and the protection of minorities.

Slavery

Much concern was given to the problem of slavery and slave trade. It has been realised as a must to protect the human rights. There was no serious opposition to slavery till 19th century as the slavery existed in almost all the countries of the world. The first step was taken against slavery in 1807. It is only during this period that the Great Britain abolished slave traffic in her colonies. The Treaty of Paris in 1814, set in the suppression of the slave traffic. Loud voice was raised against the practice of slave trade in 1815, in the Vienna Congress. A number of treaties were brought in during 1815 and 1880. In the Berlin Conference an act was passed (1885) to forbid slave strade. An Anti Slavery Act was signed by 18 States in 1890. These are some of the international machineries that worked for the protection of human rights.

The League of Nations proclaimed in its Article 22, the principles for the well being and development of the peoples in the mandatory territories. The Convention of 1919, provided for the suppression of slavery and slave trade by land and sea. In 1926, the League of Nations created a special committee to study the problem of slavery. Since the inception of UN. It has taken up the work of the Leage of Nations by adopting the famous UDHR on 10 December 1948. This is the 'corner stone' of all human rights.

Humanitarian Law of Warfare

The International Law concerning the human rights focussed its attention on the humanitarian law of warfare. During war, any one may be taken as a prisoner of war. Up to middle ages, enslaving the prisoners of war was quite common. Law could not replace war. All efforts of men could not stop the horrors and terrors of war. In the 18th century the wounded and affected enemy soldiers were treated with humanity. The role of Florence Nightingale during the Crimean War (1854) is to be considered with worth. The Geneva Convention of 1864 paved the way for the treatment and care of the sick and wounded with humanism despite their nationality. The role of Red Cross is commendable in this regard.

After the World War I much improvement took place in implementing the humanitarian law of war force. The Hague rules of 1923 prohibited damaging private property and bombing neighbouring places of war. In 1938, a resolution was passed by the League of Nations stating that the international bombing of civilian population as illegal. So also, the use of bacterial weapons was stated as illegal.

The Red Cross is popularly known for its role as a care taker of prisoners of war. Red Cross also did the work of identifying the prisoners of war, informing their where about and their physical condition to their homeland. Providing medical care to the affected and visiting the camps of POWs are also undertaken by the Red Cross.

Protection of Minorities

The Treaty of Paris (1856) was the first to be mentioned in protection of minorities. The world countries by then, started to give much importance to the question of minorities. The Treaty of Berlin (1878) gave full religious freedom to the nationals of the signatories. By it is to be observed that the real spirit of action started to develop only with the inception of the League of Nations (1919). Countries like Poland, Greece etc. signed some special treaties which dealt with minorities. The principle of the protection of minorities was also recognised in Article 7 of the Treaty of Riga between Soviet Union and Poland. All sort of discriminations are to be weeded out to exercise the principle of the protection of minorities of life, liberty, religion etc. to all the nationals of the States.

Human rights development upto the establishment of the UNO is the next stage that throws light on the general condition of human rights and their early development. The American French and Russian revolutions awakened the masses to the rise of the occasion and imparted the human rights consciousness. The Virginian Declaration of Rights (1776) has helped for the recognition of fundamental rights of man and their protection. These rights are referred as the 'rights of mankind'. The international law guarantees these rights to each and every individual in the world. Even the individual members of armed forces who violate the laws of war are liable for punishment. The post war period of World Wars I and II realised the need for human rights and fundamental freedoms of mankind, which resulted in the outcome of the International Covenants *i.e.,* ICCPR and ICESCR.

Human Rights Development in India

There is an impression among the general public that the concept of human rights originated in the West. But the Indian civilisation and culture had the highest forms of human rights and values for thousands of years. Rights to happiness, equality, education, protection, practice of any religion, forming association, social security, human treatment in custody and in prison, impartial and speedy justice, fair and human treatment of employees, special rights of women and protection and promotion of human rights even during war time and after etc., are noted in various incidents in Indian History.

Hindu scriptures are authentic in the field of human rights. They are perennial sources of human rights and values. The Vedas and Upanishads were the primordial sources for all kinds of human rights and duties. References of civil rights and criminal liabilities are found in our Puranas. Dharma, stressed in Indian Hindu scriptures, makes code of rightous conduct. Indian Philosophy also speaks about Dharma and rights. Arthasthra enjoins the king to take an oath before assuming office, that the would rule strictly according to Dharma, safeguarding the happiness of all. During ancient period, efforts were taken to establish a duty based society guaranteeing human rights to all instead of making right as the foundation of social life. Right to equality is the most valuable right. *Bhagavad Gita* says, "your right is to perform your duty". Atharvaveda says "All should live together with harmony supporting one another like the spokes of a wheel". This correlates with the contents of the Article 14 of Indian Constitution. Vedas laid down the importance of education.

Education is the special manifestation of man. The right to education is provided in the Articles 29 and 30 (Part III) and Article 45-Part IV of the Indian Constitution. Article 26 (I) of the UDHR provides the right to education. The right to practice religion was provided in ancient

India. Special rights of women were protected by treating womanhood as motherhood and accorded highest consideration *i.e.*, the father protects the girl, the husband protects her after marriage and her son protects her in old age. In Manu Smiriti, there are references about the rules relating to treatment of conquered people and they constitute the watermark of the respect for the protection of human rights.

The Constitution makers while guaranteeing the fundamental rights, were also fully alive to the objective economic needs of the society and there was a general consensus over the obligation of the State to provide for welfare of the masses. This belief found expression in the form of Directive Principles of State Policy which lay down the social and economic rights of the people.

Human Rights in the Post Cold War Era

Everywhere on the Planet, human dignity is under assault. In most places human beings life is nasty, brutish and brief. To combat this an international human rights system is evolving. It continues to alleviate human sufferings. Some decades back, no importance was given towards this. A change came over in 1945, with the cooperation of UNO nations decided to promote human rights with the cooperation of UNO. Distinctive prescriptions and institutional arrangements were developed for the invocation and the application of human rights norms.

The basic purpose of the international law of human rights is that the government can no longer utilise any means against its own people even though it is acting against its own citizens and in its own territory. In January 1947, United Nations's Human Rights Commission held its session. It comprised of 18 nations. Its Chairman was Eleanor Roosevelt. The task of the Commission was to draft an international bill of human rights. That was the UDHR in 1948. It was presented to 55 member countries. It was a historic achievement and an improvement in the development of international human rights (For details refer UDHR).

Now, in the post Cold War era, our world community is facing some critical human rights challenges. "For each age is dream that is dying, or one that is coming to birth". We are on the verge of a new age. There are also new fault lines and conflicts among the nations. It is believed that such distinctions among nations will fade away and we may enter with an age of commonality. Anyhow it is difficult to ignore the conditions that characterise our international environment. The forces that challenge and test our human condition, the forces of technology, demography, political disintegration cultural animosities, ecological damage etc. are severe and in many respects increasing. These are the root of challenges that our human family now faces in efforts to uphold human dignity.

Our post-cold war order is characterised by disorder. Our planet is less characterised by interdependence than it is by interdetermination. The human rights abuses are conveyed about the planet. They are conveyed to the elites and to the masses.

The international system during this era is yielding new humanitarian crises, pattern of human rights violation on a massive scale, the denial of self determination, environmental destruction and compassion fatigue. It is observed that "Anyone who is not confused, does not understand the situation."

17

Role of Voluntary Organisations

1. Amnesty International

Amnesty International is a world wide voluntary organisation. It was established in 1961. The London based Amnesty International with a membership of over 10 lakh, monitors human rights in more than 192 countries.

The man aim of this organisation is to find out solutions for the human rights problems all over the world. Thousands of schools, universities, professionals and others from various countries have got registered in the Amnesty International. It is an out and out impartial body.

There is an International Secretariat of this organisation which carries on research into human rights violations. Individual victims are also helped by this Amnesty International. It works continuously to prevent the gravest violations of human rights. Its service to free the prisoners from inhuman treatment, torture, ill-treatment, execution etc. is praiseworthy. In short it works to promote the human rights that are enshrined in the UDHR and other International instruments. It is an independent body. But it has its formal relations with ECOSOC, UNESCO, OAS, OAU and the Inter-Parliamentary Union.

It is financed by the subscriptions and donations made by its members. No financial help is accepted from any of the governments.

Functions

It is focusing its attention exclusively on the rights of prisoners. It seeks the release of prisoners of conscience or the people who have been detained in violation of human rights. It also presses for the early trial of political prisoners. Amnesty International presents evidences in its reports then and there, that prisoners had been tortured or cruelly treated in 1/3 of the countries of the world. It has found out that the prisoners are being tortured in more than hundred countries. Turkey, Libya, Iran Pakistan and Chile are noted for their worst treatment. The atrocities committed to the Indian Prisoners also are brought into light by the Amnesty International. It also condemns the atrocities caused by the army against the minorities.

Eight years after the Chinese army crushed pro-democracy demonstrators in Tiananmen square, the Government of China still refuses to acknowledge the deaths of hundreds of workers, students and even children. In June 1997, the Amnesty International said, Beijing was continuing to harass relatives who had wanted to honour their dead on the emotive anniversary. The Amnesty International also called on the Chinese leadership to reassess its harsh verdict against the 1989 democracy movement in the wake of the death of paramount leader Deng Xiaopeng.

In November 1997, Amnesty International has accused Japan of human rights violation by its police and prison guards who subject foreign inmates to torture and forced confession. In its latest report on human rights violation in Japan, the Amnesty revealed how inmates are physically abused and urged the government to change the system without any delay.

Amnesty International condemned without hesitation, the Afghan rebels who executed the Afghan Leader Najibulla and his brother in September 1996. Since 1992 crores of unarmed and innocent Afghan Civilians were killed. Such tragics have become common in Afghanistan. The challenges posed by massive human rights abuses and the disintegration of State authority in many areas have led human rights campaingers to develop new strategies.

Amnesty International has always worked to persuade governments to safeguard human rights. It also works to help governments improve their system of accountability and training for military and law enforcement personnel.

Modern conflicts are accompanied almost by human rights abuses and international humanitarian law.

The Turkish military and police authorities attempted to stem international criticism of their human rights record by announcing new guidelines and human rights training measures for their personnel in 1995.

So also in Australia, this organisation campaigned against the transfer of assault rifles to the Indonesia armed forces.

In 1995, the Amnesty International took action to sustain a 1994 cessation of US military aid to the Cambodian army. It questioned the governments of China, France and US about the provision of military and police training and equipment also to the army, the Republican Guard and the gendarmerie in Chad.

The International community was warned of the dangers in Central Africa before the mass killings commenced in April 1994.

It also questioned about the armed embargo to Nigeria and a number of human rights violations occurred there in 1995.

Chain gang, a merciless action is reintroduced in USA. Prisoners are compelled to hard labour. As per the rule 33 of the (UN) Standard Minimum Rules for the Treatment of Prisoners, adopted by the International Community in 1955, the use of chains or irons is prohibited. Despite, in certain parts of US (Florida and Alabama) chain gang system is introduced. Amnesty International took action against it in 1995.

Prisoners in Greek police stations suffered severe ill-treatment, such as using electric shock devices. Amnesty International severely warned and opposed such ill-treatment. Possession of such electric shock weapons is also strictly prohibited.

Amnesty International has opposed the use of any form of tear-gas in confined spaces since 1988. When the Bahrain Security Police fired tear gas (September 1995) into homes, mosques and other places which caused deaths, was strongly protested by Amnesty International.

Amnesty International warns governments by asking a series of searching and thought provoking questions to stop human rights abuses. Besides it is doing its level best to secure the agreement of all governments to introduce proper monitoring and control over all sorts of military, security and police assistance. Eren Keskin, a human rights activist and Turkish lawyer was imprisoned in 1994 for she was found guilty of spreading separatist propaganda. 'She was one of the women featured in Amnesty International's campaign on women and human rights. Due to the efforts taken by Amnesty International, she was released in November 1995.

Amnesty International worked in close co-operation with women's organisations at all levels. The world conference on women, held in Beijing in 1995, provided opportunities for the Amnesty International to strengthen its measures for the protection of women's rights.

The Nigerian Section of Amnesty International launched the Campaign against human rights abuses in January 1995.

Aung San Suu Kyi, the Nobel Peace Price Laureate and opposition party leader of Myanmar was released from her house arrest only due to the efforts taken by Amnesty International.

Amnesty International has issued a broad condemnation of the US border patrol, saying detenus, sometimes including US citizens, are beaten, raped and maltreated; as per the investigation conducted in September 1997.

It visits almost all the countries wherever the violation of human rights occur.

Its services are welcome by human rights activists and others who work to defend human rights and realised the value of this organisation as priceless.

India

In India, there was no need for the interference of Amnesty International at the early days of Independence. But in due course human rights were violated in various parts of India. This made the Amnesty International to start its work in India too. In states like Jammu and Kashmir, Assam, Punjab etc. incidents of violation of human rights occurred in large numbers. The role of Amnesty International on such occasions is laudable. Some such incidents are : Sheik Abdullah spent his major part of his life time as a human rights activist and questioned the authorities about the violation of human rights in Kashmir. The government with its mighty hand put him in prison and ill-treated him. Amnesty International interfered in this and Sheik was set free. In West Bengal thousands of Naxalites were imprisoned and put into torture. Prisoners were ill-treated in the name of inquiry. Amnesty International directed the then Indian Premier Mrs. Indira Gandhi and Mr. S.S. Ray, the Chief Minister of West Bengal to submit a detailed report of the prisoners and their treatment on 14 June 1974. When emergency was proclaimed in India. (1975) the opposition party leaders were imprisoned under the MISA and treated cruelly.

Amnesty International never hesitated to check the violations of human rights in India. When Mrs. Indira Gandhi raised her accusations against this organisation, it explained that it is doing its duty impartially, as a non-governmental organisation. It also made it clear that its sole aim was to help the prisoners and safeguard them from torture and other inhuman treatment. It also made it clear that the organisation never bothers about the protests of the concerned governments. It further explained that the Indian government had violated the rights provided in the Constitution and directed the Government of India to submit its report giving the details of the number of prisoners released, date of release, their names etc. As such the Government of India came forward to release the political prisoners in 1977.

In 1978, The Amnesty International visited Tihar Jail (New Delhi) Presidency Jail (Calcutta) and Central Jail (Hyderabad), made enquiries and submitted a memorandum to the Government of India. It is, it recommended the Standard Minimum Rules for the treatment of prisoners. It also recommended for the establishment of an Independent Visitors Board to visit prisoners at any time and abolition of the use of iron fetters on political prisoners.

Amnesty International also wrote in 1980 to the Chief Ministers of the States of West Bengal, Uttar Pradesh, Madhya Pradesh and Karnataka where custodial deaths occurred due to the brutality of police. In 1981, the Amnesty international wrote to the Chief Minister of Tamil Nadu, in which it urged him for the judicial enquiries to investigate the reports where 13 alleged Naxalites had died in encounters in the State in 1980. When a communal violence broke out in Assam in 1983, thousands of immigrants were killed by Assameese. Amnesty International made the State government aware of the fact that no official reports about the killings were received by it. It also showed its concern for the killing of 2987 Sikhs as a result of the riots after the assassination of Mrs. Indira Gandhi on 31, October 1984. It has also shown its concern about the human rights violations in various parts of India. It attacked and raised objections about the National Security Act which allows detention without trial and the TADA Act of 1985.

Every year thousands of prisoners were and are being detained by the police without any charge or trial. Torture has become common routine throughout the country. Many people die during police custody. Some die due to torture. Many were extrajudicially executed. During the year 1995, three were judicially executed. In 1996 also, 2 others were executed, though execution is considered as an inhuman activity. Arbitrary killings also occur then and there in India.

Indian government face violent opposition from armed political groups in states like Jammu and Kashmir, Assam, Punjab and even in North Eastern States. Beant Singh, the Chief Minister of Punjab was assassinated in a bomb explosion. Every year, many undergo detention without trial; under the National Security Act, Public Safety Act and Terrorist and Disruptive Activities (Prevention) Act (TADA). The NHRC is at its swing to create public awareness of human rights and also has held some state governments accountable for human rights violations. As per the report submitted by the Government of India to the NHRC, 3007 people were under detention in Jammu and Kashmir alone. But the non-governmental organisations have estimated the figure at 20,000 in almost all the states in India, detainless are tortured by police in the name of inquiry. Most of the victims were only suspected criminals. They mostly belong to Scheduled Castes and Scheduled Tribes and other down-trodden groups. One Uzzal Dass was severely lathi charged which resulted in fracture of his legs. But no action was taken against the officers who were responsible for it.

Women prisoners and the women in North Eastern States are often raped by the security forces and armed forces. Such crimes occur mostly in Assam and Nagaland. Even pregnant women are not spared from this cruelty. If any one happens to complain about the human rights abuses he/she would be attacked by the security forces. In 1995, Parver Imroz, secretary to the Srinagar Branch of Peoples Union for Civil Liberties (PUCL) was shot by an unidentified gun man. As per the Annual Report (1995) of Amnesty International 23 people were killed in police custody in West Bengal alone. The period from 1986 to 1991, witnessed atleast 10 custodial deaths in Bihar. The Border Security Force personnel often violate human rights and they escape trial or punishment. When a custodial death was reported in 1981 in Madhya Pradesh, the Supreme Court of India sentenced 4 police officers to life imprisonment.

So also in Karnataka, eight police officers were sentenced to life imprisonment for the murder of two men. All these are brought into the notice of the public by Amnesty International's vigilant work in the field of human rights.

In Tamil Nadu, the police personnels involved in rape cases at Vachathi village were sentenced to imprisonment after a long period of trial. Thanks to the services of the NHRC and Amnesty International.

Scores of custodial disappearances are also reported in India. For example in 1995, J.S. Khalra, General Secretary of the Human Rights wing of the Akali Dal Party disappeared after being arrested by police. Deliberate and arbitrary killings are also questioned by Amnesty International. The fate of the five foreign nationals seized by Al-Faran group in Kashmir is due to arbitrary killing.

Prompt and fair trial is needed in dealing with the problems of prisoners in India. Amnesty International called on the Indian Government to ensure and implement safeguards against torture and to stop death sentences and abolish death penalty. It is also appealed by Amnesty International to stop human rights abuses. It has also urged the government to release the hostages held in Jammu and Kashmir. Undoubtedly, Amnesty International is an organisation that is committed to the protection and safeguard of human rights; a challenger to the human rights abuses and a path setter for all the countries to strive for the implementation of human rights instruments with safety measures so as to help the humans to enjoy their rights without any threat and discrimination.

All the countries should bear in mind, and Amnesty Internationals observations, and each and every country has an international responsibility to honour human rights standards and accept accountability in case of human rights violations.

Asia Watch

The role of NGOs in protecting human rights is noteworthy. At the International level, the Amnesty International, International Court Justice, Asia Watch, America Watch, Africa Watch etc. strive hard to promote human rights and stop violation of human rights, by taking, special efforts. All these organisations advice the countries where normally human rights abuses occur and suggest ways for protection of human rights. Once India never allowed any international organisation to visit India in order to conduct research on human rights. But, Asia Watch is allowed to come to India, whenever it wishes and conduct research on the existing human rights are function. India had also made arrangements for the Asia Watch to visit India on Tourist Visa. Its activities in India increased considerably since 1993. It arranged for a meeting comprising of human rights activists at Delhi in 1993. Since then, the Asia Watch along with the Joint Committee on Human Rights keenly observes the functioning of human rights in India, finds out human rights violations and abuses and based on its findings it submits its report to the concerned country. Thus, it makes the countries in the continent to be vigilant enough in implementing human rights.

In its 1993 report, it pointed out about the Kashmir people's sufferings on account of violation of human rights, the number of human rights abuses that had occurred in Kashmir, torture and harassment faced by the innocent people in various villages and the role of judiciary, police and medical department in dealing with human rights problems. Most of the observation reports of Asia Watch are about India *i.e.,* no incident of human rights violation in Kashmir could escape from the notice of Asia Watch.

Assam State also attracted the attention of Asia Watch on account of the atrocities against human rights. 'Operation Rhino' was started in September 1991 and Assam was virtually brought under military rule. The Army was operating under the provisions of the Acts (1) The Assam Disturbed Areas Act (1955) and (2) the Armed Forces Special Powers Act (1958). The army took the power in its hand and conducted mass raids and arrested innocent civilians. For days together mass atrocities were coming common. The army even raided the house of a Judicial Magistrate without proper warrants. It also indulged in torture. Suspicion and non-co-operation between civilian and armed forces as the reality of 'Operation Rhino'. People were humiliated and punished in various ways. Everyone was suspected that he is an ULFA. Deaths occurred commonly. Women and girls were raped by Army Jawans. All these details were brought out by the vigilant watch of 'Asia Watch'. The Assam government came forward to conduct enquiries about the atrocities only when the Students' Federation and the opposite political parties undertook fast unto death. In 1993, Asia Watch reported all these details in its annual report.

A human rights activist by name Dr. Farooq Abudllah of Kashmir was shot dead and no proper enquiry was conducted by the government. Asia Watch referred that Abdulla was killed because he questioned about the human rights violations in the state. The Asia Watch revealed the fact that one Jaspal Singh of Punjab was detained by the Punjab Police and was tortured inhumanly on 16 August 1993. He was released on 16 September 1993 that too on the advice of Human Rights Commission.

America Watch

It was established in 1981. It focusses its attention on the human rights abuses in South America, Central America and Caribbeans. It came into existence as a result of US Declaration. It differentiates human rights abuses of friendly authoritarian regimes and unfriendly totalitarian countries. The Lawyers Committee for International Human Rights (New York) is concerned with the human rights abuses in countries where the US is involved. It also assists asykum applicants in the US. Just like Asia Watch, the America Watch is to function for the American Continent.

Hot-Line

Hot line is nothing but a direct 'Secure' telephone link officially commissioned between nations. It helps tremendously in the field of human rights too. The incidents concerning human rights abuses and violations are made available immediately after the occurrence of incidents and even during such occurrences and proper measures are taken to protect human rights. Already ordinary hotline facilities are in existence between nations. In India it was commenced during the period of Mr. Morarji Desai. For the first time, it was used between Russia's Kremlin Palace and America's White House, to find out the dangers of war and prevent them. It is quite helpful for the NGOs which strive hard for the protection of human rights. China has entered into the big league of super powers when a direct secure telephone line was officially commissioned between the Chinese President Mr. Jiang Zemin and his Russian Counterpart, Mr. Boris Yelstin. The Beijing-Moscow link is the first of its kind between the Chinese President and any leader of a foreign country. Beijing and Washington had signed an agreement on 29 April 1998 to establish a similar hotline between Mr. Jiang Zemin and the US. President Mr. Bill Clinton, during the visit of the U.S. Secretary of State, Ms. Madeline Albright and it is expected that it will commission soon. No doubt it is a boon to human rights activists.

People's Union for Civil Liberties (PUCL)

People's Union for Civil Liberties is a voluntary organisation involved in fact finding. The members of the organisation visit the places where the violation of human rights takes place, conduct inquiries with the victims, police officers, public and others before it draws up a conclusion with regard to the violations of human rights. All its reports are based on the facts and no wonder it has been referred as a 'fact finding organisation'. It's reports help the people to acquire the knowledge about the value and importance of human rights and further help the people to get a first hand knowledge about the violations of the rights of Indians.

In its report entitled "PUCL" Investigates Police Atrocities in "Uttar Pradesh" the PUCL has brought out a number of incidents of police repression in Agra. It says that poor people's lands were grabbed by influential individuals which led to a clash, in which ordinary womenfolk also were injured. The report also highlights the attitude of police personnels that affected the human rights. In 1982, the PUCL also highlighted the incidents in Assam where the civil liberties of the people were denied in large scale. It sent an investigation team to the affected places to investigate the details. The team spent six days in Assam, and found out the facts as a fact finding organisation. It also spoke about the 'Black Laws' in India (NSA, The Armed Forces Act, TADA, Disturbed Areas Act etc.) that were in force, in its report entitled "The Black Laws 1984-85". There laws helped the police to violate the democratic rights of the people because several provisions of the said Acts seemed to be incompatible with the provisions of the Optional Protocol to the Covenant on Civil and Political Rights.

The PUCL along with Peoples 'Union for Democratic Rights presented a joint report under the title "Who are the guilty?". It stated the attacks on Sikhs in Delhi, following the assassination of Mrs. Indira Gandhi marked the acts of both ommissions and commissions by the top level Congress (I) authorities and alleged that certain politicians were responsible for instigating 'violence against the innocent people. The Ajmir unit of PUCL, has recently probed into the police firing and harassment of Muslims during the curfew in February 1998 following some incidents near the Dargah of Khwaja Moinuddin Chishti which were deliberately given a communal colour. The teams of NHRC and the Minorities Commission, which later visited ajmir to inquire into the violence, had largely relied upon the PUCL's report.

Atrocities against Dalits and women, custodial deaths and victimisation of the minority communities will get the highest priority in the agenda of the PUCL. It feels that it is unable to reach the scene of occurrences as the atrocities against common people are on the increase. It has decided in its annual meeting held in 1997, to strengthen its cadre by inviting the like-minded people working in different fields to join it. All the state wings are advised to take efforts and build up concrete steps unaniously to mobilise its activities. To make PUCL, more effective, its activists should pledge to devote more time and energy to the cause of social justice.

People's Union for Democratic Rights (PUDR)

It is also a fact finding voluntary organisation, it focuses its special attention in highlighting the violations of human rights in various parts of India. Its base is Delhi. PUDR assessed the role of non-congress governments in India for the protection of democratic rights. As such it assessed the Government of Andhra Pradesh during the Chief Ministership of Mr. N.T. Rama Rao. He was the first non-Congress Chief Minister of Andhra. As a leader of the regional party *i.e.,* Telugu Desam, he promised in his election manifesto that his government would give priority to protect the interests of the weaker sections and also promised to provide protection to women from the various atrocities caused to them. It was noted by PUDR that during the period of Mr. N.T. Rama Rao's Chief Ministership, police atrocities upon the weaker sections in the society increased day by the day and continued to affect the status of women, girl children, etc. Both PUCL and PUDR highlighted all these details in the report known as "NTR's one year in Andhra Pradesh".

Among the various States in India, Bihar is often noted for its local disturbances due to caste contradictions, due to difference of opinions between the workers and industrialists, tug with the tribals and forest officials etc. Thus, Bihar became a tension bound area. The PUDR by its enquiry found out that the main reason for the existing tension in Bihar State is the illegal attitudes and the atrocities of the wealthy and powerful landlords over the landless poor. This matter was taken to the court and the landless poor won the case. Even after the Court's verdict, the landlords in Bihar continue their hold, though illegal, over the lands of the poor people. It also made it clear that the police authorities exterminated the poor peasants in some of the villages. Sometimes the opposing peasants were killed by the landlords. In 1983, some individuals associated with Majdoor Kisam Sangharshi Samiti were also killed by the landlords in Saya District. The mere survival of the low caste peasants itself has become doubtful under these circumstances. In 1984, PUDR investigated the impact of various laws inforce which affected the people's normal course of life and led to communal terrorism. It also brought into light that these laws are 'Black laws' and 'anti-democratic' in nature (For details refer Black Laws).

Citizens for Democracy (CFD)

Another notable voluntary organisation in India that works for the protection of human rights is CFD. It started its role in 1977. Ordinary people in Andhra Pradesh underwent repression continuously by the police and other administrative authorities. During Emergency it reached its highest mark. Many a number were arrested and imprisoned without trial. Many were also killed. Mr. Jayapraksh Narayan, the President of Citizens for Democracy, set up a committee in April 1977 under the leadership of V.M. Tarkunde (The Tarkunde Commission) to investigate the reasons for the deaths. The CFD conducted extensive investigations and reported in 1977. The CFD found out that these deaths were either due to encounters, or murders in cold-blood and the to burtal torture. It reveals that the police indulged in cold blood liquidations. The reports of the CFD also include "Oppression in Punjab", operation Blue Star-the Untold Story" and "The Black Laws-Charter of Slavery". All these reports exhibit the atrocities committed against the innocent people in the name of law and order, violations of democratic rights and detention under the anti-terrorist law. No one knows what had actually happened inside the Golden Temple from 1-7th June 1984 *i.e.*, during the Blue Star Operation. It is accused by the CFD that the government has completely hidden the truth in its White Paper Statement. The fact is hundreds of pilgrims, staying in the Golden Temple were killed by the army's brutal action. This is nothing but an inhuman barbarity and ruthless killing.

The Turkish Human rights Foundation (1990), Peace Movement Focolare in Itlay (1981) and the Civil Rights Group CAJ in Northern Ireland (1981) are working towards protecting Human Rights in their respective countries.

If we analyse the various reports in favour of human rights protection released by different international organisations and other NGOs we can very well arrive at a decision that how in almost all parts of the world and in India too, violation of human rights are quite common. The atrocities faced by the innocent people, police's brutal behaviour towards the prisoners under trial custodial deaths, attacks and counter attacks, human rights abuses caused to women and children and other such activities pose a challenge to the human rights. It is also clear that even judiciary is not co-operating with the people, instead it is quite helpless. It is the duty of the concerned countries to provide social justice to the people. The role of governmental and non-governmental agencies are equally important in this regard. The non-governmental organisations have been rendering yeomen service at the world level by highlighting the need for proper enforcement of human rights.

Press and Human Rights

The UDHR ensures in its Article 19, stating "Everyone has the right to freedom of opinion and expression, this right includes freedom to hold opinions without interference and to seek, receive and impart information and ideas through any media and regardless of frontiers".

Article 19 of Indian Constitution lays down that all citizens shall have the right to freedom of speech and expression. The freedom of speech and expression means the right to express one's convictions and opinions freely by word or mouth, writing, printing pictures or any other mode. It also includes the freedom to propagate not only one's own views but also those of others. The fundamental right of the 'freedom of the press' is implicit in the right of freedom of speech and expression. The Supreme

Court has held that the liberty of press is included in the freedom of speech and expression.

The Press Council of India, a body constituted under the press Council Act (1978) was responsible for preserving the freedom of the press. UN Human Rights Commission has established three subcommissions; one deals with freedom of information and of the press — The Sub-Commission on freedom of Information and of the press was set up at the first session of the Commission on Human Rights in 1946. It is to examine what rights, obligations and practices should be included in the concept of freedom of information and to report to the commission on Human Rights. The most important work of the Sub-Commission consisted in its participation in the UN conference on freedom of Information, held at Geneva in 1948. According to the Conventions drafted at the Conference, the freedom of press is put into force.

The print media consists a number of dailies, weeklies, monthlies, bi-monthlies etc. They help the public to understand the day to day activities that occur at regional, national and international level. They bring a complete picture of human rights and their functions, violations of human rights and the problems that arise out of them. The Journal 'Women's Rights' Today published from Columbia University, speaks about the women's rights and their practice at the international level. *The American Journal of International Law, New York Times* (USA), *The Sunday Times* (UK), *Washington Post* (USA), *Red Flag* (China), *International Herald Tribune* (USA), *Toronto Star* (Canada), *Morning News*; *Ceylon Daily News* (Sri Lanka), *Berliner Zeibeg* (Germany), *Le Monde* (France) etc., are some of the international journals that help to know about the human rights and other incidents at the international level.

The print media in India circulate *Times of India* (English), *Malayala Manorama* (Malayalam), *Gujarat Samachar* (Gujarati), *Eenadu* (Telugu), *Indian Express* (English), *The Hindu* (English), *Dainik Jagaran* (Hindi), *Ananda Bazaar Patrika* (Bengali), *Aaj* (Hindi), *The Hindustan Times* (English), *Dhina Thanthi* (Tamil), *Dhina Malar* (Tamil) and *Dina Mani* (Tamil). These are the largest circulated dailies in India. There are some notable weeklies and monthly magazines which help to have a thorough knowledge about the functioning of human rights in India. Sunday, Front Line, India Today, The Lawyer, Junior Vikatan, Nakiran, Tharasu, Kalki etc., play a tremendous role in bringing into light about the human rights violations, the atrocities committed by the police and the ruling elite to the public, and the hardships faced by them.

India has four news agencies. They are (1) Press Trust of India (PTI), (2) United News of India (UNI), (3) Samachar Bharath and (4) Hindustan Samachar. The first two supply news is English. Others through Hindi and other Indian Languages.

Death in police custody has become the order of the day. It is due to the growing brutishness and unchecked power of the police. Torture is used to extort information from the persons under detention. *Indian Express Magazine*, 19-2-1989 has revealed the fact "The state has armed police aggression further through there cent laws such as the National Security Act (NSA) and the TADA, which have virtually formalised this licence to kill. Police encounter death are rampant and no longer investigated, particularly in Andhra Pradesh and Punjab........ the right to life".

"The Majority of the undertrials are those charged with petty offences like theft of a cycle, watch or ticketless travel. In most of such cases the accused admits the crime both in the police station and the court" (Plight of undertrials — Indian Express dated 1-5-1989).

"Women prisoners of a jail in Rajasthan just eat and sleep — The women have neither information about nor access to a Legal Aid Scheme" (*Indian Express,* dated 6-5-1989).

"How the Supreme Court uphold human rights. Through its judgements, the Supreme Court has been reiterating its stand on human rights *vis-a-vis* police behaviour" *(The Hindu* — open page dated 17-3-1998).

"Children freed to weave their own future".

Poverty drove the parents to send their children to work and the money supplemented the family earnings. The weavers engaged child labour because it came cheap. Many had pledged their children to the master weavers for several thousands of rupees *(The Hindu*, dated 6-4-1998).

The Print media play an important role in democratic nation to help the success of democracy. There is no substitute for press in helping the public to acquire a thorough of human rights and their functioning. Besides, the press also contribute much towards the understanding of political administrative and judicial activities in a democracy. Without media it is humanly impossible to survey the day today incidents that speak about human rights, their protection and promotion as well. The print media's role in the field of human rights is laudable. It even questions the judiciary and its responsibility in safeguarding human rights. At the world level there are provisions for interference of the press wherever the human rights are at stake.

Films and Human Rights

The role of films in modern society is no doubt a greater one. All world countries show much interest in film industry in recent days. As such, USA is a leading nation in producing larger number of films. Next to America, India stands second in the world in film production. Through audio and video aids the films penetrate into the minds of even the illiterates. In fact it is the most successful media.

Social dramas, historical dramas and artistic dramas also reach the stage of realism. The decade during which the Second World War was fought and Indian Independence won was a momentous period for cinematography all over the world. The Cinemas contribute on large scale to society in the form of different messages for *e.g.*, the poor and the rich, the haves and have-nots, employer and employee, upper and lower castes, untouchability, exploitation, high-handedness of landlords, bonded labour, child labour, communal clashes, illtreatment of women. Widows, religious reformation, lockup atrocities, human rights violations, property rights, national integrity. Liberty and equality, role of legal system, murder, looting rape and the like.

Among Indian films, Malayalam films derived much of its strength from literature. The New Indian Cinema emerged as a reaction to the popular cinemas of the world. Sathyajit Ray, Mrinal Sen and Ritwik Ghatak were the founding fathers of the new cinema in India. Sathyajit Ray has made a number of feature films and documentaries, tackling a wide range of rural, urban and historical themes. These films are infused with an unusual humaneness. "Pather Panchali" "Apur Sansar", "Charulata", Jalsaghar, Goopy, Gyne Bagha Byne Seemabadha, Jana Aranya, Ashani Sanket and Agantuk are some of his outstanding films. He was fortunate enough to present his films in almost all the leading films festivals of the world. The national and international awards won by Ray are numerous. Ritwik Ghatak swooped the Indian scene with new dynamism. His films constitute a record of the traumas of change from the desperation of the rootless and deprived refuges from East Bengal.

Over the years more than 15000 feature films have been produced in India. Most of the films speak about human rights. Dada Saheb Phalke, the 'Father of Indian Cinema' was noted for his outstanding contribution to Indian Cinema. There came a series of socially conspicuous films like Nirmalyam, Kaadu, Ghatasratha; K. Balachander's Arangetram, Avargal and Apoorva Ragangal; Adoors' Kodyettam etc. K. Balachander's 'Thanneer Thanneer' is also a social film that speaks about the hardships of the people in getting water. The film 'Tale of Two Cities' reveals the course and effects of French Revolution. Director Bharathi Raja's "Alaigal Oyvathillai", "Vetham Pudhitu", and Director Mani Rathnam's "Bombay" are some of the films that speak about the need for the abolition of caste system. The film "Evargal Indiyargal" portrays the suffering of a freedom fighter in enjoying his rights. Dowry system was condemned in the films "Thangaikor Geetham" and "Nengil oor Ragham". "The film "Karuthamma" is against female infanticide. The film 'Thozhilai' no doubt sentimentally touches the problems between the employer and employee. The exploitation of fishermen by the bureaucrats is portrayed the film "Meenava Nanbhan".

Further there are films which spread the news against some of the social evils like smuggling, black marketing, terrorism, using narcotics and the like. There are some other films which describe civil, political, economic, social and cultural rights and the need for safeguarding such rights. The film 'Porkalam' explains that there is no meaning in giving room for physical deficiencies like handicapped. Some films also portray the misdeeds of the police force and after effects, human rights violation and the need for the protection and promotion of human rights. The above mentioned facts reiterates the role of films in the field of human rights.

Mass Media today enjoys a distinctive status in Indian society. The nature of cultural experience is greatly affected by the development of media. Rural broadcasting was given emphasis in post independence India. Television arrived with the propose of the experimentation in social education. It was launched in rural areas selectively and cautious enough. In the beginning education was central to introduce T.V. Then, it was extended in various spheres. No doubt Media is a vehicle of collective expression for the citizens.

Further T.V. and radio also contribute much towards propagating human rights among the masses. Even the illiterates are able to understand this media easily and interestingly. This media is successful doing its job of helping the layman too, to realise the need for human rights and their role in their life. When compared with press media this is more attractive in a way as it provides both audio and video tracks.

18

Violation of Human Rights

Almost all the countries in the world have incorporated Human Rights in their Constitutions. The UN is a trend setter in this respect.

Human rights, undoubtedly are the inherent rights of a persons. In India, the rights of the people are incorporated under the chapter 'Fundamental Rights (Part III) and the Directive Principles of State Policy (Part IV) of the Indian Constitution. The rights guaranteed under Part III of the Constitution are enforceable in a Court of Law. Whereas the Directive Principles' contents are mere wishes—which cannot be enforced in a Court of Law. It mainly concerns with the poor, unemployed and destitute people. It is the duty of the State to apply the principles contained in Part IV to make laws. Part IV provides that the State Policy should aim at securing the rights of the citizens. It also provides for health and strength of workers, to safeguard men, women and children from abuses, protect children from exploitation and the like. All these come under 'human rights'. The Government of India and the State governments have enacted a number of legislations to provide the people with essential 'human rights'. In practice it is understood that they are inadequate and ineffective in fulfilling the aims.

Violation of Human Rights

Almost in all the countries of the world, violation of human rights has become a normal commitment. Even the organised governments could not prevent the violation of human rights. Police and custodians of Law cause atrocities against women, children, prisoners, poor and destitutes and the human rights are testified on various occasions. Police are expected to police. Instead, the police torture innocent young boys, girls, women and even youth. They employ barbaric techniques to torture the people. Some sorts of brutal means are used by the police to get forced confessions from the arrested ones. Beating, making the victims to sit on the top of a sharp bamboo, blinding, handing upside down from tree, pouring water constantly on the mouth of a person, staking, giving electric shock, kneeling down for hours together, burning with lighted cigars, burying in ground up to neck, hitting on genitalia and tests are some of the methods used by the police in the name of interrogation. Sometimes the innocent people die due to such inhuman activities of the police. Deaths in police custody has become a very common incident. Such deaths occur only on account of the torture of the police. No government has the right to kill its own citizens through its agencies. The police is expected to keep the alleged in safe custody. Enquiries show that only downtrodden people in the society become the victims of death penalty. Institutionalised torture also has become common in India. It has been established that torture has been institutionalised in Punjab and Haryana in the form of Criminal Interrogation Agencies. On 8, March 1980, a fifty year old Rattan Singh of Haryana was arrested by the police and thrashed the old man till he collapsed.

Encounter deaths also occur due to violation of human rights. It is just taking persons as prisoners into custody, torture them and subsequently get them murdered. In 1970s, it became familiar in States like Tamil Nadu, Andhra Pradesh and Uttar Pradesh. Such deaths were reported as having occurred in an encounter. Upto 1980, there was no officially recorded encounter in Tamil Nadu, But after that, Tamil Nadu has become an encounter area, especially the Naxalites. Police torture has been found throughout India. The police torture political prisoners, especially the Nexalites. Mrs. Indira Gandhi has condemned police brutality on various occasions. Torture includes deliberate blinding also. Many suspected criminals of Bihar (Bhagalpur jail) were blinded by the police in 1980. The only punishment given to the guilty officials was were 'suspension' from duty or just a transfer. Surprisingly after a lapse of period those officials were reinstated in the service. While some police officers are undoubtedly secular, others are highly or subtly communal and their bias reflects in their functioning. The may 1987 Meerut riots were the fiercest communal conflagration in Independent India. The city was not only tense but also trembling with fear till the first week of June 1987. The provincial armed constables turn into killers. Till today no action has been taken against the culprits and the poor affected people are waiting for justice. Our philosophy of maintaining law and order is far from democratic and the police have inherited colonical methods and there has been no improvement in the last fifty years. The police believe in strong-arm methods. The whole philosophy of policing has to be changed. Besides, many political bosses are quite communal and use police officials for their political agenda. This should immediately be changed through proper legislations.

Another incident that took place in Tamil Nadu (Virudunagar) also speaks about the police harassment in riot hit areas on 22, July 1997. It is learnt that there were instances in which the police themselves damaged the property of the Devendra Kula Vellalars. The Police also entered the homes, looted the belongings and took away the womenfolk and children to the police station. There is yet another incident, in Tamil Nadu, there was a general feeling among the police personnel that the enforcement of law might be affected by the insistence of human rights.

Police and Violation of Human Rights

Police repression is quite common in almost all states in India. The repressive action of police led to the violations of human rights and the ordinary people become the sufferers. During the past two decades, police atrocities became the order of the day in certain states like Madhya Pradesh, Karnataka, Haryana, Tamil Nadu, Andhra Pradesh, West Bengal Rajasthan, Delhi and Bihar, atrocities committed on 'Naxalites' are quite unbearable, violent and even alarming. Illegal confinement was common. Physical torture became all the more cruel. Beating with lathis, beating with rifle butt, stamping with heeled boots, slapping, burning with lighted sigars and a host of others are some of the brutal forms of torture. Sometimes, prisoners will be made to starve without food and water. Thus, there are no bounds for the lawlessness and unruly activities of police. The custodians of law converted themselves into law breakers. Police also torture young boys into impotence. To get forced confession, police never hesitate in using brutal methods of torture. There are incidents in Bihar, that the undertrials were blinded by police. As per the reports it is understood that about 27 suspects were blinded by police over a period of 10-11 months. Hundreds of suspects are dumb, caught in the Web of law, unable to understand what the charge against them is or, why they have been sent to jail. It establishes that the fundamental rights of the people are violated by the custodians of law. If the government becomes a law breaker it breeds contempt for the law, it invites everyman to become a law into himself. Torture also takes place in the forms of Criminal Interrogation Agencies. It is not prohibited by the Constitution of India.

But the Government claims that India laws contain needed provisions for safeguarding human rights and also needed safeguards against police brutality and torture exist. But a number of people become victims of police torture throughout India. Police also never hesitate to use methods of torture at the time of interrogation.

The Indian press also has condemned police brutality on several occasions. The Supreme Court of India itself has taken an active part in seeking protection to detainees and prisoners from torture. Because the police think that inaction was better than action wherever they feared that their action might attract the allegation of violation of human rights. Mrs. Archana Ramasundaram, DIG of police, vellore range requested the Commission to arrange for a healthy interaction between the police and the public on all aspects of the Human Rights.

The Court issued guidelines to be followed in all cases of arrest or detention till legal provision are made in that behalf as preventive measures.

The Guidelines are :

(1) The police, personnel carrying out the arrest and handling the interrogation of the arrestee should bear accurate, visible and clear identification and name tags with their designations. The particulars of all such police personnel who handle interrogation of the arrestee must be recorded in a register.

(2) The police officer executing the arrest shall prepare a memo at the time of arrest and shall be attested by atleast one witness. This may be either a member of the family of the arrested or a respectable person of the locality from where the arrest is made. It shall be countersigned by the arrestee and shall contain the time and date of arrest.

(3) A person who has been arrested or detained and is being held in custody in a police station or interrogation centre or other lockup, shall be entitled to have one friend or relative or other person known to him or having interest in his welfare being informed as soon as practicable that he has been arrested and is being detained in a particular place, unless the attesting witness of the memo of arrest is himself such a friend or a relative of the arreste.

(4) The time, place of arrest and venue of custody of an arrestee must be notified by the police where the next friend or relative of the

arrestee lives outside the district or town through the Legal Aid Organisation in the district and the police station of the area concerned telegraphically within 8-12 hours of the arreste.

(5) The person arrested must be made aware of his right to have some one informed of his arrest or detention as soon as he is put under arrest or is detained.

(6) An entry must be made in the diary at the place of detention regarding the arrest of the person which shall also disclose the name of the next friend of the person who has been informed of the arrest and the names and particulars of the police officials in whose custody the arrestee is.

(7) The arrestee should, where he so requests, be also examined at the time of his arrest the major and minor injuries if any present on his body must be recorded at that time. The 'Inspection of memo' must be signed by both the arrestee and the police officer effecting the arrest and a copy provided to the arrestee.

(8) The arrestee should be subjected to medical examination every 48 hours during his detention in custody by a doctor on the panel of approved doctors appointed by the Director, Health Services of the State concerned or Union Territory. He should prepare such a panel for all tehsils and districts as well.

(9) Copies of all the documents including the memo of arrest referred to above, should be sent to the Magistrate for his record.

(10) The arrestee may be permitted to meet his lawyer during interrogation though the latter may not be present throughout interrogation.

(11) A police control room should be provided at all District and State Headquarters where information regarding the arrest and the place of custody of the arrestee shall be communicated by the Officer carrying the arrest within 12 hours of effecting the arrest and at the police control room it should be displayed on a conspicuous notice board.

The requirements flow from the Articles 21 and 22(1) of the Indian Constitution and are to be strictly followed. These would apply with equal force to the other government agencies including the Directorate of Revenue Intelligence, Directorate of Enforcement, Coast Guard, Central Reserve Police Force (CRPF), Border Security Force (BSF) the Central Industrial Security Force (CISF), the State Armed Police, Intelligence

Agencies, such as the Intelligence Bureau, RAW, Central Bureau of Investigation (CBI), CID, Traffic Police, Mounted police and ITBP.

These guidelines are a few out of a large number of judgement of the Apex Court in which the Court upheld the human rights of the oppressed individuals of India. Police officers must learn lessons from these directions. If they commit mistakes they should be strictly punished and no sympathy should be shown on them.

Regarding Hand — cuffing also there are certain guidelines to be followed as directed by the Court.

They are :

(1) We declare, direct, and down as a rule that handcuffs or other fetters shall not be forced on a prisoner convicted or under trial while lodged in a jail anywhere in the country or while transporting or in transit from one jail to another or from jail to court and back. The police and jail authorities, on their own shall have no authority to direct the hand cuffing of any inmate of a jail in country or during transport from one jail in to another or from jail to court and back.

(2) Where police or jail authorities have well-grounded basis for drawing a strong influence that a particular prisoner is likely to jump jail or break out the custody then the said prisoner be produced before the Magistrate concerned and a prayer for permission to hand-cuff the prisoner be made before the Magistrate. Some in rare cases of concrete proof regarding proneness of the prisoner to violence, his tendency to escape, he being so dangerous, desperate and finding no other practical way of forbidding escape is available, the Magistrate may grant permission to hand-cuff the prisoner.

(3) In all the cases where a person arrested by the police is produced before the Magistrate and remand judicial or non-judicial is given, the person concerned shall not be hand-cuffed unless special orders in the respect are obtained from the Magistrate.

(4) When the police arrests a person in execution of a warrant of arrest obtained from a Magistrate, the person so arrested shall not be hand cuffed unless the police has also obtained orders from the Magistrate for the hand-cuffing of the person to be so arrested.

(5) When a person is arrested by the police without warrant, the police Officer concerned may if he is satisfied on the basis of

> the guidelines given by in the para above that it is necessary to hand-cuff such a person he may do so till the time he is taken to the police station and thereafter in production before the Magistrate. Further, use of fetters thereafter can only be under the orders of the Magistrate as already indicated.

Hand-cuffs are not summary punishments. In every special situation, the application of hand-cuffs is not ruled out. Even in extreme cases where hand-cuffs have to be put on the prisoner, the escorting authority must record contemporaneously the reason for doing so.

Custodial Deaths

Custodial deaths have always caused a furore. Of the heinous crimes reported in recent years, two cases are important. One was the case of rape of Padmini at Annamalainagar in 1997 and the other of a 10 year old boy at Dharmapuri in 1993. Both the cases would not have come to light and the culprits punished if for not a sustained public out-cry. A common feature noticed by inquiry commissions on custodial deaths was that in majority of the cases, the victims were either suspects handled up to the police stations at odd hours or those involved in petty thefts. The Khalid Commission appointed in 1991 to inquire into the series of charges of illegal custody against police, recommended that police should see that no women is taken into custody, arrested or brought to a police station except in the company of a women constable.

The police force in India must be reformed. Kins of lock up death victims should be provided with solatium so as to help them to build up their future. One Srinivasalu of Cuddapah (Andhra Pradesh) died under suspicious circumstances in police custody on 22, October 1997. Mystery deaths also occur in certain prisons. The two prisoners of the District, Jail, Nellore died mysteriously on 9, November 1997.

In Several cases in Bihar, people belonging to Scheduled Castes and Scheduled Tribes or backward classes have died in police custody apparently as a result of torture. Deliberate and unlawful police killing of unarmed individuals are also reported. In some areas our police are in the pockets of landlords. When atrocities are committed against untouchables, they do not take action against those who did it.

Indian Parliament enacted the Human Rights Act in 1993 and it provided for the constitution of Human Rights Commission at the National and State level and also human rights courts. The Commission has directed that all autopsy conducted in cases of custodial deaths should be video-filmed. As such, the Tamil Nadu government constituted SHRC in 1997 and the Commission has passed a resolution that it would take *Suo moto* cognisance of any human rights courts that were set up by the Tamil Nadu Government in March 1996. A political activist moved the Human Rights Court at Erode against the alleged killings and sexual abuse of the tribals by the police of the STF set up to apprehend Veerappan, the sandalwood smuggler. But the court returned the complaint, as the scope of its jurisdiction was not clear. The Madras High Court delivered a judgement on 23, August, 1997 to make Human Rights Courts workable. A special Bench observed that special Public prosecutors should be appointed for the prosecution of Human Rights offenders. It is necessary to set up an independent agency, directly responsible to the government to investigate custodial violence. Otherwise human rights offenders will continue to go scot-free. All these, warrants to humanise the police. There is a big challenge in front of us *i.e.,* to what extent have we been able to protect the 'Right to Life' of our people?

The NHRC has passed severe strictures against the Uttar Pradesh police for the custodial death of a Benaras Hindu University student happened in December 1997 and ordered the State Government to pay the highest ever compensation of Rs. 5 lakhs. Atal Bihari Mishra, a student of BHU was killed in custody after he was dragged to the police station on fictitious and frivolous charges because of the political differences between his father and a ruling party politician. This kind of torture meeted out to the youth was unparalleled. The police had registered a false case against the youth's family and there was delay in handing over the body of the boy. The police had also harassed the family by arresting all the members of the family after the death of the youth. The NHRC ruled that unless appropriate punishment was meted out to the officers responsible for this distantly crime it would be difficult to contain and control custodial deaths.

The police cannot take law into their own hands and systematically violate the basic rights of an individual or group of people leading their own lives. Use of excessive force and alleged punitive steps which result in the death of innocent people are all violative of human rights. Death in police custody has become today of the growing unchecked powers of the police. Custody deaths are not limited to any State or city. The ruthlessness of the police seems to be uniform in both rural and urban India. The human rights status of the humble people is sunken since the state has lost its sensitivity.

Violation of Human Rights in North Eastern States

Mass raids on villages of the North Eastern States have become common. It is held only on the basis of suspicion. In more than thousand villages such raids were undertaken by the army. In the name of interrogation innocent villagers were tortured by the army and the villagers were subjected to brutal beating with lathis, whips etc. Interestingly, the army failed to find out even a single hard-core insurgent. Electric shocks also were applied to the body of the suspected victims and even the private parts were not spared from torture. Indiscriminate arrests were also made by the army. The jawans in mufty, lifted the young ones from shops, homes, schools, colleges, playgrounds, roads etc. The innocent ones undergo torture for no reason. All interrogations conducted in the army camps are useless because of the language problem. The Jawans also misbehaved with the womenfolk. Attempted mollestation occur almost every day. Raping is quite common in these regions. Some girls were gangraped to death. Most of the rape cases were not brought into light. Young boys were also used for perverted sexual assaults. Torture leads to death also. During army raids in Assam, Manipur etc., a few people lost their lives too. This is due to excessive violence, beating point blank shooting of detained, gang rapes, mental shock etc. One Raj Kamal Choudhry (Assam) was lifted from his house by the army personnels and tortured continuously for two days then handed over his dead body on 1, October 1991. There were burn marks all over the body and marks of severe beating. Above all his bones and ribs were broken and the joints of hands were smashed. Such incidents are common in the army camps of North Eastern States.

All these prove that India is undeniably giving much room for the 'Violation of Human Rights'. But India is labelled as Champion of Human Rights in Africa and elsewhere. Violation of human rights in any part of the world is a threat to the human race as a whole. Thus, every one is concerned with the protection and promotion of human rights. In India a number of facts reveal that there occurs suppression of the basic rights of the people in one form or the other. The Naga people's Movement for Human Rights was formed on 9 September 1978 to protect and promote their human rights. The NPMHR moved a Habeas Corpus petition on behalf of two Women, whose husbands had been taken away by the army and who did not return at all. The Supreme Court of India directed the army to give one lakh rupees to each of the widows and also directed the DSP to initiate prosecuting the guilty army personnel. In order to save the innocent people from the torture of dehumanised forces, the NPMHR has urged the government to revoke the Black laws that are in force *e.g.*,

(1) Nagaland Security Regulation, 1962,
(2) Assam Maintenance of Public Order, 1953 and
(3) Armed Forces (Special Powers) Act 1958 *i.e.*, the North-East Armed Forces (Special Powers) Act, 1972.

Besides, a number of human rights abuses also have been reported in Manipur since 1950. On 9, September 1979, Manipur valley was declared as a disturbed area and army was deployed there. The armed forces were given the power to undertake searches and destroy the elements of insurgency. This paved the way to suppress the democratic rights of the people of Manipur in the name of maintaining law and order. Number of human rights violations took place in Manipur from March 1974 to March 1992. Among the violations, incidents of rape by the army, opening fire on innocent people, illegal detention, army atrocities and disappearance in army custody, are to be given importance. Among the combing Operations that took place in Manipur, the Oinam (a small village) operation is one of the highest degree on the scale of human rights violations. Amnesty International has made it clear that the security forces have exercised absolute powers in certain areas in the name of maintaining law and order. The Civil Liberties and Human Rights Organisation (CLAHRO) in Manipur is working for the restoration of Democracy and Rule of Law in the State.

Human Rights and Emergency

Articles 352, 353, 354, 355, 356, 357, 358, 359 and 360 of Indian Constitution deal with emergency provisions. In India Emergency was declared on 26 October 1962, during Chinese aggression. It was withdrawn in 1968. During emergency the President of India is empowered to suspend the Fundamental Rights except the rights provided in the Articles 20 and 21. During Indo-Pakistan War (1971) the president of India proclaimed another emergency in December 1971. It was withdrawn only in 1977. Even while the emergency was in force, a fresh emergency was proclaimed on 25, June 1975. The basic rights of the people were suppressed during this emergency. The right of people were put under threat. Compulsory sterilisation programme was insisted and implemented without caring the wishes of the people. This hurried programme led to number of deaths Kerala's concentration camps were noted for their notorious behaviour during emergency, which resulted in death of two suspects. "The roller treatment" in Kerala killed one engineering student P. Rajan on 23 May 1977. During emergency prisoners were hung upside down and beaten. It was also reported that even rats were tied inside the trousers of prisoners. When 'Emergency' itself is against one's right to life, the various excesses committed by police and others were a challenge to democracy. Besides, preventive detention laws were misused during emergency. The fundamental rights guaranteed by the Constitution were suspended during emergency. Above all the MISA and Defence of Indian Rules were extensively used during emergency to detain the opponents of the Government. It is believed that about 35,000 people were detained under MISA. When Janata Party came to power, it replaced the MISA in 1977.

Human Rights Violations — World Scenario

Democracy is essential to the strengthening of human rights. The Vienna Conference on human rights (1993) made it clear that human rights are not only universal, but also a legitimate subject for international organisations and institutions. The UN human rights Commission scrutinized the violation of human rights in 1995 and considered to build new institutions to improve human rights at the world level. Human rights are not just rhetoric nor they are universally held values. As such human rights system has to be implemented as a part of reconciliation process and peace. The human rights institutions will also emphasise justice. The only way to end human rights violations is to bring justice by tackling the problems of human rights. Mostly war crimes lead to the violation of human rights in a great ideal. In 1995 and 1966 in the Bosnian-Serb areas a number of human rights violations took place and a sort of terror created in the minds of people besides genocidal killings. This also lead to the people fleeing from their native land to find refuge, thus warranting the problem of refugees. A lot is to be done in connection with Haiti, as it is the poorest nation and its democratic institutions are fragile. To introduce reforms and ensure hope in the minds of the people, a better understanding between the government and the people and also among the people of Haiti themselves is to be fully established. The people of Haiti know it is their bounden duty to safeguard their freedom. The people of Haiti know it is their bounden duty to safeguard their freedom. Haiti has a national commission for Truth and Justice which aims at investigating human rights abuses. Even the developed countries in the world are continuously struggling to perfect their own democracy and no wonder the people of Haiti struggle hard to build their own.

Basic human liberties have been established around the world through legal measures. Justice is to be a reasoned one to protect basic human rights. The UN Security Council established the International Tribunal for prosecution of persons responsible for serious violations of International Humananitarian Law committed in the Territory of the former Yogoslavia since 1991 in order to restore and maintain peace. This tribunal incorporates positive developments, with respect to the rights of criminal defendants under international law.

In 1994, within a few weeks, horrific genocidal massacres took place at Rwanda and hundreds of Jutsis and Hutus were brutally slaughtered simply by violating human rights. In 1996, 70,000 Rwandans were detained in prisons. The prisoners were pur under torture and illtreatment. Criminal trials are the most obvious way of reckoning with genocide and other atrocities. Depending on the particular conditions in the country, justice for these crimes may entail a variety of alternative or supplemental approaches. In Greece, hundreds of soldiers and officers were prosecuted for torture of former prisoners. In South Africa, amnesty will be granted on a case-by-case basis to those committed abuses, but only after the individual offenders apply for the amnesty and provide detailed confessions of their crimes. In countries like Chile and El Salvador 'Truth Commissions' have produced a national historical accounting as a form of justice. In the Czesh Republic Lithuania and post-communist Germany, administrative purges have temporarily removed those affiliated with past abuses involve official recognition and rehabilitation of victims. But it is quite surprising that the Khmer Rouge leadership has never been persecuted, or punished for the atrocities they committed in Cambodia in the 1970s. The challenge is to achieve justice in a manner that facilitates a durable peace.

In 1975, the Khmer Rouge, a Marxist Guerrilla group took over Cambodia and ruled up to 1979. The new leaders exterminated large number of Cambodian civilians. People and other ethnic groups were tortured and killed. Nearly 15 million people had been tortured murdered or starved to death during the Pol Pot regime.

The Human Rights Group 'Africa Watch' says as many as 80,000 South Africans mainly blacks were detained and tortured during 1960-1993. It is learnt from the Washington Post that the former White apartheid regime of South Africa operated under a 'Skewed Moral Code' which could never acknowledge the secret hit squads, the torture and the fomenting of black-on-black-violence. It further stated that if the Truth Commission can document the crimes and force the perpetuators to acknowledge them, it will perform a great service for South Africa and its future. According to Prof. D.E. Orentlicher 'Deterrence is an important part of the process if dealing with human rights violations. She further said that the establishment if mechanisms that deal with massive injustices of the past, draw a line between the past and the future which is critical to a successful political transmission process'. It is understood that it is extremely difficult to carry around a template for universal justice, but there is certainly an international consensus now that a regime or government that practiced genocide or the wholesale violation of human rights of a particular group should face an authoritative judicial process.

It is also believed that Truth Commissions and such other bodies may serve as an exercise in purging the national consciousness concerning a country's previous record of human rights abuses. The human rights situation in Argentina has improved because the people have a civilian elected government, a free press and the political culture of the country has changed significantly since Falkands War (1982). With regard to the state of Human Rights in Argentina, it was found that about 2000 Agentines were killed between 1973 and 1976 but the Amnesty International fixed the number between 15,000 and 20,000. The UN received reports about 15,000 cases of human rights violations from 1980-91.

Human Rights groups and activists have been sharply critical of Mr. Chretien's visit to Cuba in April 1998 and have been insisting that the Prime Minister personally take up the case of high profile dissidents who have been detained as a part of the political round up. Officially Ottawa has been taking the stance that the Prime Minister will address this issue, but thus far Mr. Chretien has been very silent or has said very little directly to the issue of human rights and democracy.

Rural Injustice

Agriculture is the backbone of our country. More than 75 per cent are small and marginal farmers. Their problems are vast. They have to face a member of injustices *i.e.*, forced labour, low wages, bonded labour, child labour, exploitation, sexual harassment and suppression, atrocities is the name of caste, debt and fear and police atrocities in rural areas.

Poverty : Poverty is common among rural people. Poverty persists is almost all countries in the world. It is due to low income, decreased economic development low wages, disparity in wages, unemployment, only a few being rich, urban development, social stratification, illiteracy, exploitation and the like. Various steps have been taken to eradicate poverty.

Realities of Life : The UDHR and the provisions created a new era is the life and man. Well planned economy is a must for the progress and prosperity of man and the society.

Realities of various groups should be studied for their development.

Analysis of Family Problems : Family is a part of society. It is one among the social institutions. Family is either a joint family or a unclear family. In every family there are problems of various dimensions. Economic problems, unemployment and other problems, housing, education, property addiction to vices, water problems, health and hygiene, environment etc. Each and every adult in a family is expected to choose a job and earn to live. At present, unemployment is quite common. Even if one is fully qualified for a particular job, it is not easy to secure it. So, the family members depend on one man's earning *i.e.,* the income of father, to fulfil their needs. Under such circumstances, there arises a number of problems. The primary one is economic problem. Based on economy, people are divided into poor, middle class, rich etc. For rich people there is no chance for economic problem. India is one among the poor nations in the world. No wonder, most of the people are also poor and live below poverty line. Daily wage earner's family is the most affected one.

Man cannot live by bread alone. Every man need food, dress and shelter. But most of the people are homeless. A good lot suffer from starvation and die. Starvation deaths in all the developing countries have become quite common. The rising number of starvation deaths has drawn the attention of the NHRC (India) and it has recommended a number of preventing measures, including emergency feeding programmes, old age and disability pensions and other social security and employment generation programmes to be taken by the Central and State governments. In States like Orissa, Andhra Pradesh etc. a number of people died of starvation due to drought and other reasons. State governments should initiate measures to prevent such incidents. The Commission has also sought interim measure to prevent deaths by starvation that have reportedly occurred in various States. Programmes relating to rural drinking water supply, social security, soil conservation, irrigation, afforestation, primary health care etc. could lead a big way in curbing the starvation deaths. Emergency feeding programme should be made available to the people for each and every day and the nutritional quality of the food both in terms of types of items offered and their caloric value should be improved.

All the aged and disabled should be included in the feeding programme Government has come forward to solve these problems by providing facilities for the poor and downtrodden. At the same time, people are driven to unbearable hardships due to the various plans and policies of Government. Though free and compulsory educational system is in force, some parents never prefer to send their children to school. They consider their children is an economic asset and put them in work either in agriculture field or in other petti works.

Many parents suffer a lot in fulfilling the needs of their children. Some find it difficult to provide proper education to them. Some others find it hard to conduct the marriage of their female children. Dowry and other problems, pose a serious threat to them. As such they are driven to plunge into debts. There are others who become frustrated due to the family problems mar themselves and their families by becoming drug addicts. They stirk their responsibilities and such neglected families are put below poverty line, and suffer a lot. To pull on the life, women come forward to take up the responsibility and they are forced to go for work. There again, womenfolk face problems in their working places, some housewives are ill-treated by their husbands and in-laws and thereby life becomes a challenge to them. Of course life itself is a challenge. But challenges should not haunt one's life.

Now a days, joint families are quite rare. Rather it seems they are completely erased from society. In a nuclear family, that too when both husband and wife are employed, their problems are multifarious. They face problems not only at home but in working place too. Their children are left aloof. No proper care is taken by the parents. They think their rights to be cared for and love have been denied to them. Such children's future is spoiled in one way or other. All these could be overcome if one realise his place in society and utilizes his rights in a proper way. Some men waste a good part of their wages by drinking or gambling and care very little for the family. Their wives and children suffer from want of food and clothing. When a man marries, it is his responsibility to feed and cloth his family and educate children. His wife and children have the right to share his income.

Right follow duties. An individual who knows his rights and respects the rights of others will definitely be a responsible citizen. Responsible children grow up to be responsible parents. It is the responsibility of parents to look after the children, it is also the responsibility of the children to help the parents. Rights and responsibilities go side by side. If everybody respects the rights of everybody else, the world would be a wonderful place to live in.

PATHOLOGY AND PREVENTIVE MEDICINE FOR THE VIOLATION OF HUMAN RIGHTS

Pathology

Many pathogens cause various bodily diseases and such diseases need proper analysis, special care and application of powerful medicines to prevent them. So also in the field of human rights, the disease of violation of human rights has become common in almost all States in the world. India is no exception from this disease. As far as India is concerned, the number of violations of human rights is on its increase and many innocent people suffer from this acute disease. The need of the hour is to find out causes for this disease, at first. They are namely :

(l) Casteism and sectarianism are deeply rooted in our society and they have changed four society into a sick one and we are forced to live in that sick society. This stands as a main cause for the disease of violation of human rights in various parts of our society.

The communal clashes and atrocities in the name of castes are the best examples of this disease.

Further, discrimination in the name of caste, colour, creed, race, religion, sex, place of birth and the like is dominating in our society.

Even after 50 years of Indian independence, we still hear about the existence of untouchability, though it is banned by the government through proper legislations.

(2) Poverty and its sharp teeth bite the innocent lot and they are forced to undergo ill-treatment in the hands of haves. The social strata of haves and havenots, powerful and powerless, capitalists and labourers etc. create grounds for the violation of human rights. As most of the people live below the poverty line, they easily become the preys of the mighty hands.

(3) The high-handedness of the landlords also pose a threat to the peasants and agricultural coolies and they suffer a lot due to exploitation, bond etc. *i.e.*, violation of human rights.

(4) The police, who are the custodians of law, indulge in a number of atrocities and that lead to violation of human rights. Here, the police conduct themselves as law breakers. In the name of inquiry and interrogation number of violations occur for e.g. beating, torture, inhuman treatment, raping, custodial death, disappearance during custody, causing impotence; breaking legs and knuckle and the like. As such the police contribute much to the chronic disease of the violation of human rights.

(5) Misuse of administrative machinery also causes the disease of violation of human rights. The executive should not give room for unnecessary interference of the wealthy ones or bureaucrats for their benefit and lean towards them.

(6) Gender degradation is a massive slaughter of the rights of womanhood. Trafficking is a daily reality. Women being the weaker section of society, they are easily cheated, humiliated, harassed, exploited and even put under exposure. Even young girl children become the victims of such violations.

(7) The concept of equality is still not palatable to the common people. The equality that is expected by the common people in their day to day life differs from that under law and it is completely absent in society. This lands them mostly in confusion. In the Indian context, it is still more challenging in view of the institutionalised social hierarchy based on caste differences an entuated by class distinctions and varied economic levels of living. Achieving social and economic equality among all is a must to escape from the dangerous disease of violation of human rights.

(8) Illiteracy is also one among the causes for the violation of human rights. Illiteracy leads to ignorance. Most of the people affected by the violation of human rights are either poor or uneducated or down trodden, or Dalits or the penniless ones.

(9) Problems pertaining to environment, ecology etc. also create rooms for the violation of human rights (e.g., Narmada Bachao Andolen). Indian Constitution reflects the human rights approach to environment protection through various constitutional mandates (Articles 14, 21, 48 and 51). As such it is the basic human right of every individual to live in pollution free environment with human dignity. The problem of environmental pollution has posed a serious threat to the very existence of humans. But to our surprise, everywhere there is pollution *i.e.*, air, water, soil and environmental pollution as a whole. Modern tanneries, textile industries, sago industries and other chemical industries cause lot of pollution and contribute to the disease of violations of human rights.

(10) Children, the future builders of nation are most defenceless in society. The tender age of the children is abused and they are forced to indulge in child labour, that too in hazardous condition and they are exploited to the maximum. The very right to live is denied to such children and there occurs the violation of human rights.

(11) The greatest black mark on our civilization is the continued world wide violation of human rights and freedoms. A more dismal

picture is on, in the third world countries. A very small group of rich nations dominate over other world countries in possessing the world resources. It is nothing but a naked exploitation; which leads to hunger, sickness, illiteracy, poverty, unemployment or under employment etc.

(12) The ruling elites, in the name of development processes increase the burden of the people in various dimensions. Rather, the ruling minorities become richer and richer. The common people and driven to the verge of poverty and they are forced to indulge in communal violence, all sorts of agitations, riots etc.

(13) Absence of economic well being and social justice have been causing ever so many problems that affect the human rights and freedoms.

(14) The most heartening refugee problem is only due to the violation of human rights at various parts of the world. Here, the very right to live is testified. The affected persons become homeless and Stateless by losing their kith, kin, dwellings, positions, possessions and helps too.

(15) Some draconian laws passed by the Government of India and other state Governments made serious inroads on the rights of people and led to the violation of human rights.

Preventive Medicine

Thus, the list become a lengthy one when we analyse the pathology of the violation of human rights. Because, human rights are now a days recognised only theoretically and as such they are being violated to a greater extent. It is not sufficient to name to the causes for the disease; rather it becomes a must to provide suitable antidotes for preventing the violations of human rights. For that some suggestive medicine/measures are given below :

(1) Giving freedom to others is the real freedom. It goes without saying that one must respect the rights of others. When one human treats the other human with human dignity, there is no room for the violation of human rights. It should be practised in its real spirit.

(2) The human rights are the inherent right of man. No one should interfere in the rights of others. Tresspassers should be strictly prosecuted.

(3) There are ever so many constitutional provisions and guarantee in each and every nation State to safeguard human rights and freedoms, but they are decorated only in words. They must be put into practice in reality.

(4) "All are equal in front of law" — Quite an encouraging notion and appeals to the human mind. But unequal treatment of equals either by granting of favours or imposing of burdens creates social discrimination. It is quite unfair and discrimination should be uprooted at all levels. In a democracy all should have equal rights.

(5) The rights reflected in Indian Constitution are quite encouraging but still many of the violations of human rights remain unrepaired and unremedied. Proper steps should be taken with zeal to eradicate such violations. Responsibility rests with judiciary.

(6) Police atrocities and abuses are very frequent and they are left unnoticed. Whoever may be the violator of the rights. He/she must be punished without any deviation. The unruly police should be policed.

(7) Prison conditions are quite unsatisfied and unspeakable too. Prisoners too have their own rights as humans. They should not be neglected. Atleast minimum human treatment should be extended to the persons behind the bars. Exploitation of juvenile prisoners should be put an end with strict measures. Police is using brutal methods to get forced confessions from innocent people and destroy the life of many. It should be checked properly. The role of law should be prompt.

(8) Preventive Detensions laws should not be misused.

(9) Atrocities against women by the landlords, bosses in working centres, and by police are quite unbearable. Biting laws should be enacted and put into force to control such atrocities.

(10) Economic imbalances, social injustice, treat to external and internal security etc. are to be removed so as to make human rights available to every individual.

(11) Inculcating public awareness is the most needed measure to implement the human rights programme. Mass media should be utilised to the maximum in this regard.

(12) All adverse effects of Science and Technology that affect human rights and their promotion should he eliminated.

(13) Effective measures to check the violation of human rights should be adopted both at the international and national level without any further delay.

(14) Wherever the violations of human rights occur, proper inspections must be made by the authorities and other interested groups to investigate the exact affair.

(15) Concerned government alone can not play its role full well in arresting the violations of human rights; for that full support from the public; the youth, the human rights activists, political parties, pressure groups and legal system is a must.

(16) The PIL system introduced by the SC should be made available in the Constitution itself so as to enforce it with authority.

(17) More Powers should be accorded to the National Human Rights Commission and State Human Rights Commission so as to make them to function more effectively.

(18) As we live in a changing, moving, and developing society needed Constitutional amendments should be included where ever necessary to safeguard, and promote human rights.

(19) Above all, human rights education should be imparted from the school level itself. After laying foundation at the school level it should be made compulsory at the higher education level so as to create an awareness among youth to realise their rights, to protect and promote them at all possible ways.

(20) Human rights have to be defended everyday. For Freedoms and Rights battle once begun, must be fought with vigour. It will never be lost.

Black Laws in India and Violation of Human Rights

Some of the Acts passed by the Government of India and State governments made unwanted inroads on the very right to life of Indians. As the people underwent a number of hardships by these acts they are referred as 'Black Laws'. Some such Acts are :

1. The Armed Forces Act, 1958.
2. The Armed Forces Special Powers (Punjab and Chandigarh) Act 1983.
3. Chandigarh Disturbed Areas Act 1983.
4. National Security Act (Amendment Ordinance No. 5 and 6) 5 April 1984; 21 June 1984.
5. The Terrorists Affected Areas (Special Courts) Act, 1984.
6. The Terrorist and Disruptive Activities (Prevention) Act 1985.

7. The Uttar Pradesh Gangsters and Anti-Social Activities (Prevention) Act, 1986.
8. The Act of 1999 in Assam.

All the above said Acts in one way or other affected the normal course of human rights.

It is better and fitter to check the violations of human rights for the progress and prosperity of human beings.

19

Judiciary and Human Rights

Today human rights have become one of the central challenges of civilisations. No doubt Human Rights cover a vast territory.

These rights cannot be taken away by any person or authority arbitrarily. In the rapidly growing society the world recognizes these rights by incorporating them in the Constitution as Fundamental Rights. In some countries they are referred as Bill of Rights. These rights are considered as the basic rights for the people/citizens to live in this world. If these rights face any challenge the Supreme Court afford to play an active role. Human rights inherently belong to a person and affirm his human dignity. Right to personal liberty is embodied in Article 21 of the Indian Constitution. Though civil rights may not always be legal and justifiable and are protected by the Indian Constitution, the Supreme Court has been called upon to consider the nature and scope of civil rights. Civil liberty is essential for the preservation of various aspects of freedom. Therefore protection of rights has assumed paramount importance in view of the increasing threat to the rights and liberties of the people.

Right to life is the most important Human Rights. It is the base from which all other rights flow. So the violation of human rights affects the society at large. It creates social and political unrest which in turn leads to violence, chaos, conflict, and confusion. One who violates human rights is expected to undergo trial, that is the trial by judiciary. In each and every State, judiciary no doubt is the defender to human rights. Articles 32 and 226 allow the filing of writ applications in the Supreme Court and the High Courts for the protection of rights. The existing economic inequalities constitute a great impertinent to the realisation of rights and liberties of the people. Public interest litigation in the Indian Supreme Court aims at strengthening the moral authority. A right exists when there is a positive law on the subject and a liberty, where there is no law against it. Rights and duties are correlated with each other.

Law is a means to an end. To achieve this end law should function in a fulfledged way. Law must change with the changing needs of the society. In India, the task of interpreting the Constitution is entrusted with the judiciary. The Supreme Court of India for the first time in Menaka Gandhi *vs.* Union of India, made the procedure established by law in Article 21 of the Constitution as "just fair and reasonable". In India judiciary has played an important role in developing the concept of legal aid and experimenting its scope so as to enable the people to have access to courts in case of any violation of the human rights.

In M.H. Hoskot *vs.* State of Maharashtra, the Supreme Court held that the right to legal aid is one of the ingredients of fair procedure.

With regard to the rights to life, as guaranteed under Article 21 of the Indian Constitution, it is the most fundamental of all the rights. Without this right, other rights will not have any value. Articles 21 says "No person shall be deprived of his life or personal liberty except according to procedure established by law."

Article 39A emphasis that free legal service is an unalienable element of "reasonable fair and just" procedure — for, without it a person suffering from economic or other disabilities would be deprived of an opportunity for securing justice. The court emphasises that the state was bound to provide free legal services to an indigent accused person and could not plead financial and administrative inability.

In R.M. Wasawa *vs.* State of Gujarat, the Supreme court observed "Indigence should never be a ground for denying fair trial or equal justice.

The Supreme Court has also emphasised the role of people, voluntary organisations and social action groups in making legal aid meaningful, effective and purpose oriented.

There are two different opinions with regard to capital punishment. Through out the world two extreme approaches have been advocated. One is to retain the death sentence and the other is for abolition of death sentence. In India, the IPC provides for death penalty for seven types of offences. They are :

(1) For the offence of waging war against the government of India (Section 121).

(2) For abetment of mutiny by a member of the armed forces (Section 132).

(3) For giving false evidence leading to conviction of an innocent person and his execution (Section 194).

(4) For murder punishable with death (Section 302).

(5) For abetment of suicide of a person under 18 years of age or of an insane or delirious or idiot or intoxicated person (Section 306).

(6) For an attempt to murder by a life convict (Section 307, para 2).

(7) For dacoity accompanied by murder (Section 396).

There are certain safeguards against the death penalty too. Article 72 of the Constitution has empowered the President of India to grant pardons, commute, suspend or remit death penalty, in appropriate cases. If a sessions court passed a death sentence the proceedings shall be submitted to the High Court for confirmation without which the sentence cannot be executed. The CPC, 1973 provides that the execution of death sentence is to be postponed in case an appeal is pending before the Supreme Court. It also requires the High Court to postpone the execution of death sentence on pregnant women and may commute the sentence of imprisonment. The IPC contains special provisions to govern the situations of mass killing and murders. As such India has retained the death sentence in certain cases and at the same time it is evident that the basic human 'right to life' is well protected in India.

In Jagmohan Singh *vs.* State of U.P. the Supreme Court held that death sentence is constitutionally permissible and not violative of Article 14, 19 and 21 of the Constitution.

Indian Judiciary plays a vital role in safeguarding human rights whenever they are abused. Often the people face a number of cruel, degrading and inhuman ill-treatment. The Supreme Court has held in Mullin's case that any form of torture or degrading treatment would be offensive to human dignity and would, therefore, violate Article 21. In a earlier case, Justice Krishna Iyer observed that courts should come to the rescue of detenues who are tortured in prisons.

Custodial violence is yet another instance of inhuman, cruel and degrading treatment. Indian police personnel often break the laws in this regard. There are some policemen who are dedicated to the service and honest too. Judicial activism has not only protected the human rights of people, but it also led to the granting of exemplary compensation to the victims of police atrocities, which resulted in human rights violation.

Khatri *vs.* State of Bihar, also known as Bhagalpur Blinding case, was the first case of this type where the question of granting monetary compensation was considered by the Supreme Court. In this case, it was alleged that police had blinded certain prisoners and the State was liable to pay monetary compensation to them.

The Supreme Court brought about revolutionary break through in the "Human Rights Jurisprudence" in Rudul Sah *vs.* State of Bihar when it granted Monetary Compensation of Rupees 35,000 to the petitioner against the lawless acts of the Bihar Government which kept him in illegal detention for over 14 years after acquittal. Thus, the Supreme Court has openly declared that compensation ought to be paid for the violation of basic human right *i.e.,* right to life and liberty under Article 21 of the Constitution. Human right are being violated not only by the action or reaction of the state machinery but also by the other groups in society. Bhopal gas leakage case and the Delhi oleum gas leak case selected the ground for PIL. Here it is clear that even the private companies are brought with in the domain of human rights as per the Article 21 of the Indian Constitution.

Both in America and India, Supreme Courts exercise wide powers of review of legislation, especially in the field of human rights. The British Judiciary enjoys less powers in this regard than that of Indian and American Judiciaries. The Constitutions of developing countries also largely exclude the contents of Articles 8 to 10 and 14 of the ICCPR which prescribe standards concerning freedom from servitude, right to liberty and security of person freedom from arbitrary arrest and detention, right to trial within a reasonable time and pre-trial release, freedom from discrimination in the Administration of Criminal Justice, and right to a fair and public hearing by a competent, independent and impartial tribunal established by law.

In India the condition of prisons, prolonged detention and treatment of under trial prisoners are under fierce controversy. The Amnesty International in its report in 1973 observed that the Naxalites are ill-treated in prisons. Slow Judicial process causes over crowding in jails. Further the under trials are lodged with hardened criminals and this leads to unwanted tensions in jails and internal clashes among the prisoners. Till now the Judiciary didn't intervene to put and end to the callous administration of Indian prisons. Of late, the Supreme Court has realised its duties of reforming prisons.

Judiciary is no doubt the custodian of the Constitution. The judiciary has been performing positive function in securing and promoting human rights of the people. The judiciary in India is promising innovative remedial measures for vindication of the governmental commitment to the welfare and relief of the oppressed and in protecting and promoting human rights of the people.

Public Interest Litigation (PIL)

The concept and procedure of public interest litigation in India is fashioned by the Supreme Court of India. Indian Constitution is enshrined with civil, political, economic, social and cultural rights (Fundamental Rights) but they are yet to be implemented fully. However, the Supreme Court of India, by introducing PIL, has made possible to protect the human rights. The PIL helps to work in favour of the weaker sections of the people of India. In Fertilizer Corporation Kamgar Union, Sindri *vs.* Union of India case, Justice. Krishna Iyer emphasised the importance of PIL :

Law...........is a social auditor and this audit function can be put into action only when some one with real public interest ignites the jurisdiction...........In a society where freedoms suffer from atrophy and activism is essential for participative public justice. Some risks have to be taken and more opportunities opened for the public minded citizen to rely on the legal process and not be repelled, from it by narrow pendency now surrounding *locus standi.*

In S.P. Gupta *vs.* Union of India case, otherwise called as judges case, Justice Bhagwati observed : where a legal wrong or a legal injury is caused to a person or to a determinate class of person by reason of violation of any constitutional or legal right or any burden is imposed in contravention of any constitutional or legal provision or without authority or law or any such legal injury or illegal burden is threatened and such person or determinate class of persons is by reason of poverty, helplessness or disability or socially or economically is advantaged position, unable to approach the court for relief, any member of the public can maintain an application for an appropriate direction, order or writ in the High Court under Article 226 and case of breach of any fundamental right of such persons, in the court under Article 32 seeking judicial redress for the legal wrong or injury caused to such person or determinate class of persons. Thus the PIL came before the court and new jurisdiction was evolved by the Supreme Court. He further observed it must not be forgotten that "procedure is but a handmaid of justice and the cause of justice can never be thwarted by any procedural technicalities.

In PUDR *vs.* Union of India case, Justice Bhagwati elaborated the principle of PIL and explained the scope and importance of PIL in the legal aid movement, which is a part of "fair, just and reasonable" procedure under Article 21. He said that PIL which is a strategic arm of the legal aid movement and which is intended to bring justice within the reach of the poor masses, who constitute the low visibility within humanity, is a totally different kind of litigation from the ordinary traditional litigational which is essentially of an adversary character .... but it is intended to promote and vindicate public interest which demands that violations of constitutional or legal rights of a large number of people who are poor, ignorant or in a socially or economically disadvantaged position should not go unnoticed and unredressed. That would be destructive of the rule of law which forms one of the essential elements of public interest in any democratic form of Government.

Further, Justice Bhagwati elaborated the importance of PIL in Bandhua Mukti Morcha *vs.* Union of India Case :

PIL is not in the nature of adversary litigations but it is a challenge and an opportunity to the government and its officers to make basic human rights meaningful to the deprived and vulnerable sections of the community.

So also in the PIL case of Chaitanya Kumar *vs.* State of Karnataka, the Supreme Court observed "This court cannot close its eyes and persuade itself to uphold public by mischievous actions which have been so exposed. When arbitrariness and perversion are writ large and brought out clearly, the court can not shirk its duty and refuse its writs".

The judiciary has been cautions in entertaining the PILs. In each and every case it has evolved various principles. PIL espousing cause of an individual permissible if it falls within the purview of policy decision of general application. It can not be used to remove distress of nay particular individual or satisfy that individual's whims, however pious that may be. With regard to the en-mass arrests of hundreds of Tibetan refugees, Justice P.B. Sawant said that the "Tibetans may not be our citizens but they have legal rights."

All these prove that PIL for upholding the human rights is being nurtured by the court. The Supreme Court is doing its best to bring law into the service of the poor under the banner of PIL. Problems involving human rights like prisoners, ill-treatment of children in jail, sexual harassment, pollution, untouchables, bounded labours, starvation deaths, victimisation etc. are some that were covered by the Supreme Court in recent years.

Justice P.N. Bhagwati was the Chief Architect of PIL movement and was the votary of the protection of human rights of the poor. Most of the human rights have been evolved by the judiciary under the PIL. Thus the concept of PIL is being fostered by judicial activism in the field of human right and legal treatment for the poor, illiterate and downtrodden ones.

In India, the Supreme Court has been quite active in defence of human rights and has intervened to resist the repression of the poor and weaker sections of society. For a long time, the Supreme Court has been struggling to innovate a new jurisprudence to ensure justice to the weak and poor. It has used an effective strategy called the public interest or social litigation to make the legal system responsive to the needs of the weak. Public Interest Litigations has acquired a good deal of importance in Indian courts. The term PIL, originated in U.S. in 1960s and spread to other countries. In India it has great relevance as most of the people are poor and downtrodden. Creative activism of the court is at the very root of PIL. This reflects the potentiality of the legal system to give justice to the poor, oppressed, ignorant and illiterates.

The court has made it possible for the public to participate in judicial review of administrative action only through PIL. PIL has made the position of the judiciary paradoxical.

The progress of nation, its unity and integrity, rule of law and social equality depend on the judiciary to a great extent in India.

It is undeniable that the Supreme Court has done its job judiciously not withstanding the prejudices and predilections of individual judges. The existence of Supreme Court gives the people in general and the opposition groups in particular an easy feeling that there is an independent authority to check the arbitrary and extreme actions of the party in power and to uphold the Constitution. The Indian Supreme Court is exceptionally strong and its judges have played central role in sustaining Constitutional government in India. The Supreme Court has by and large acted as a watchdog of the Constitution and fundamental rights and as a defender of democracy. Judicial activism has widened the concept of civil liberties which are no longer confined to the fundamental rights but also include those civil liberties which have been created by the law and statues operating in the State. Today, civil liberty not only means freedom of speech or expression, right to life and personal liberty, but also right to the basic needs for civilized existence without which all other rights become meaningless.

Law cannot remain static : it is an effective weapon of social change and social welfare. It is for the Supreme Court to see that law responds to social change; otherwise the judicial process would become putrefied. No doubt, judiciary can play a complementary or a contradictory role in the sphere of civil liberties and social justice to safeguard human rights of the people. At the same time, it is to be remembered that the Supreme Court alone can not ensure the preservation of rights. The need of the hour is that the people should arise from their slumber and unite together in participatory organisations to demand their rights. Because, a majority of the people in India are ignorant of their fundamental rights.

The social action groups should come forward to galvanise the people into action to defend their basic rights and liberties and at the same time, it is to be borne in mind that judicial, legislative and executive operations are the means to achieve the ends that are intended in the field of human rights.

20

Human Rights Commission

The National Human Rights Commission (NHRC) was established as per its protection of Human Rights Act passed by the Government of India in 1993. It (NHRC) came into force on 12th October 1993.

This Commission shall consists of a Chairperson, who has been a Chief Justice of the Supreme Court; one member who is or who has been a Judge of the Supreme Court; one member who is or who has been the Chief Justice of a High Court and two other members to be appointed from amongst the persons having knowledge of or practical experience in matters relating to human rights. There shall be a Secretary General who shall be the Chief Executive Officer of the Commission. This is now held by R.V. Pillai. The Commissions headquarters is at Delhi and the Commission may with the previous approval of the Central Government, shift it to other places in India. Justice Venkata Chellaiya, the retired Chief Justice of the Supreme Court is its present Chairperson. The Chairperson and other members of the Commission are appointed by the President under the recommendations of a Committee consists of the Prime Minister, Speaker of the House of the People, Minister for Home Affairs, Leader of the Opposition in the House of the People, Leader of the Opposition in the Council of States and the Deputy Chairman of the Council of States. Any member of the Commission shall be removed from his office only by order of the President, on the grounds of proved misbehaviour or incapacity. The Chairperson shall hold office for a term of 5 years from the date of entering his office or until his age of 70 years whichever is earlier. The other members' terms of office is also for 5 years and are eligible for reappointment for another term of 5 years. When a Chairperson is not in a position to discharge his functions due to one reason or the other, one of the members of the Commission may be authorised by the President to discharge the functions of the Chairperson until the date on which the Chairperson resumes his duties.

The Commission shall meet at the time and place as proposed by the Chairperson. The Commission shall regulate its own procedures. All orders and decisions of the Commission shall be authorised by the Secretary General of the Commission. The salaries and other allowances payable to the members shall be as prescribed by it.

Functions

The Commission shall perform the following functions :

They are to inquire *suo moto* or no a petition presented to it by a victim or any person on his behalf, into complaint of violations, of human rights, negligence in the prevention of such violations, intervene in any proceedings involving any allegations of violation of human rights, visit prisons or other institutions under the control of state government where persons are lodged or detained, or to study the living conditions of the inmates and make recommendations and reports there on.

It also reviews the factors and acts of terrorism that obstruct human rights and recommend remedial measures.

It also reviews the safeguards provided in by the Constitution and other laws for the protection of human rights and makes suggestions for their effective implementation.

It undertakes research in the field of human rights. It also scrutinises the international instruments on human rights and recommends for their implementation.

It strives to create awareness among the people in society by spreading human rights literacy in the form of seminars, publications, media etc.

Proper encouragement is given to the NGOs and other institutions that are interested in the field of human rights.

Powers

The Commission enjoys all the powers of a Civil Court under the Code of Civil procedure. It sends summons to the concerned, enforces the attendance of witnesses and examines them on oath. It has the power of receiving evidence on affidavits. It can ask for any public record or copy thereof from any office or court to carry on its enquiry. The Commission shall have the power to require any person subject to any privilege which may be claimed by that person under any law for the time being in force, to furnish information on such points or matters as in the opinion of the Commission, may be useful, to or relevant to, the subject matter of inquiring any persons so required shall be deemed to be legally bound to furnish such information within the purview of Sections 176 and 177 of the IPC. Every preceding of the Commission shall be deemed to be judicial proceeding. The Commission may enter any place of office where the Commission has the reason to believe that any document relating to the subject matter of inquiry may be found. It may utilise the services of any officer, or agency if with Central and State governments with the concurrence of the Central and State governments as the case may be. After inquiry, the Commission shall send a copy of its inquiry report to the concerned government or authority within a period of one month. It shall also publish its inquiry reports with its recommendations to the concerned government or authority. The Commission shall also submit an annual report to the concerned government and the government in turn shall lay before each House of Parliament along with a memorandum of action taken or proposed to be taken on the recommendations of the Commission and the reasons for non-acceptance of the recommendation if any.

The regulations that govern the NHRC are referred as the NHRC Regulations. These regulations came into force on 1, March 1994. They include periodic meetings and venue of the meetings. Agenda, procedure for dealing with complaints, report of action taken, transaction of business, reports on complaints and inquiries, special reports, annual reports, printing of the reports and annual reports and an investigation team. The NHRC has the rights to add, delete and amend these regulations. The role of NHRC is made alive with these regulations.

State Human Rights Commission

Each state in India may constitute a body to be called as "State Human Rights Commission" to exercise its powers on human rights. The SHRC consists of a Chairperson, who has been a Chief Justice of a High Court, one member who is has been a Judge of a High Court, another member who is/has been a district judge in that State and two other members to be appointed from persons having knowledge of human rights.

Besides the above members, there shall be a Secretary, who is also the Chief Executive Officer of the State Commission. The headquarters of the SHRC shall be a such place as the State Government may specify. This commission may inquire into the matters concerned with List II and

III of the Seventh Schedule to the Indian Constitution. The Chairperson and other members of SHRC are appointed by the governor of the concerned State. Every appointment of the State Commission is made on the recommendations of a committee consisting of the Chief Minister of the State, the Speaker of the Legislative Assembly, Minister in charge of the Department of Home in that State and the Leader of the Opposition in the Legislative Assembly, the Chairman of Legislative Council and the Leader of the Opposition in that Council.

Any member if the SHRC shall be removed from his office only by order of the Governor on the ground of proved misbehaviour or incapacity. The term of office of each member is of five years from the date on which he enters upon his office. No member shall hold office after he has attained the age of 70 years. In the event of inactivity of the Chairperson, due to one reason or the other, the Governor may authorise by notification any one of the members of SHRC as the Chairperson until the appointment of a new Chairperson. The salaries and allowances of members shall be as prescribed by the State Government. The Commission shall be assisted by a Secretary, investigative Officer (Inspector General of Police) and other technical and scientific staff appointed by the Commission.

The SHRC shall submit an annual report to the State Government consisting of its work as well as recommendations on human rights. The functions and powers of the Commission are like that of the functions and powers of the NHRC but at the state level. The Commission shall also carry on the directions put forth by the NHRC.

Human Rights Courts

As the violation of human rights has become quite common, and the increasing number of cases and speedy trial of such offences have warranted for the establishment of Human Rights Courts at the District level. The State government by notification specify for each district a court; known as Human Rights Court to try the offences against human rights. A public prosecutor or an Advocate having atleast seven years experience also is appointed to these courts. He is in-charge of conducting cases in these courts and it may help for speedy trial of offences arising out of violation of human rights.

21

Services Rendered by Leaders for Women's Rights and their Upliftment

The position of women community has been a fluctuating subject since the early ages. With the ups and downs in the Hindu Society, the status of women has been affected.

During the Vedic period, the women enjoyed equal status with men. They were respected and honoured. Historical research and literary writing of the ancient period establish this fact. The education of women was looked upon so important. According to Atharva Veda, "the success of women is her married life depended upon her proper training during the Brahmacharya", Many Vedic women composed hymns, some of the revered Vedic women are Lopamudra, Viswavara, Sikata, Nivavari, Gosha and Aswalayana.

During the Upanishadic period there were great Brahmavadinis who were enriched with deep knowledge of philosophy. Gargi and Maitraye asked difficult questions in a challenge with their husband Yajnavolkya, the great thinker.

During the Buddhist period, great women lived who were in no way inferior to men. The status of women was highly appreciable during the time of Jainism.

In ancient India marriage for male and female was considered necessary from religious as well as social view point. It was also contended that an unmarried person cannot take part in Vedic rites. They had a choice in selecting their husbands. Widows were allowed to remarry. The early Dharmasastras allowed divorce, Kautilya dealt with the problem of divorce in detail. Ancient Hindu scripture does not mention the prevalence of sati system. According to Vedic hymns, wife and husband had joint ownership rights of the property.

The women were degraded to a very lower status after 300 B.C. During this period women's rights were strictly subjected to restrictions. Many young women renounced their homes and joined Buddhistic and the Jain monasteries. It led to drastic social changes.

Then came the impact of political intrusion by the Greeks and the Scythians. New developments affected the life of widow. The widow was confined to lead an ascetic life at home. During the 8th century purdah system became more and more accepted as a part of custom, specially among the middle class. Neera Desai comments. "Ideologically women were considered a completely inferior species, inferior to the male, having no significance, no personality socially she was kept in a state of utter subjection, denied by polygamy, the purdah, the property structure, early marriage, self-immolation of widows (Sati) or a state of permanent widowhood, all these contributed to the smoothening of the free development of women".

In the 19th century many thinkers in India rose against the evil practices and so called customs framed with the intention of exploiting women. B. Kuppuswamy has beautifully described the wave of reformist thought in the 19th century from Ram Mohan Rai to Gandhiji. Thereby the fight against women subjucation in India started in 19th century. Due to the efforts of Ram Mohan Rai, Lord William Bentinck, the Governor General of India, in 1829 abolished 'Sati' and declared that practice was a crime. The Brahmo Samajists, demanded widow remarriage as well as the freedom of equality of sexes. Iswarchandra Vidhyasagar campaigned tirelessly and it led to creation of Widow Remarriage Act, 1856. Keshab Chandra Sen was successful in getting passed the Civil Marriage Act, 1872. The striking feature of the Act was the enforcement of monogamy.

The restoration of property rights was given to the womenfolk by the Married Womens Property Right Act of 1874. Restriction on child marriages was brought by the efforts of Bekranji Malabari which led to the enactment of the Age of Consent Act of 1881.

Education is a catalystic agent for social change. Changes in life and position of women have been greatly accelerated by the spread of education. As a result women's organisations and a strong women's movement took place. Many greatest women emerged in the scene. Among them Rani Laxmi Bai of Jhansi, Pandita Rama Bai, Rama Bai Ranade, Madam Cama and Toru Dutt were prominent.

Jhansi Rani

Probably, Rani Laxmi Bai of Jhansi (1835-1858) inspired women as well as men of India regarding the potentialities of women by way in which she participated in the 1857 war of Indian Independence and died fighting valiantly on the battlefield. She has become a legendary figure since then.

There were also several Indian leaders who worked for the emancipation of women in the nineteenth century. Among them the work of some may be briefly recounted here.

Pandita Rama Bai

The foremost among them was Pandita Rama Bai (1858-1922). She came from a learned Brahmin family in Karnataka. She was a great scholar of Sanskrit and addressed many learned groups in different parts of the country and was given the title of "Pandita" and "Saraswat", for her deep knowledge of Sanskrit. After the death of her parents she and her brother travelled different parts of the country. She spoke about social injustice done to women in the society. They went to Calcutta in 1878. Two years later her brother also died. A little later in 1880 she married a Bengali pleader of a lower caste. Thus, even at that time she was bold enough to marry a man of a different caste and different language. After the death of her husband two years later she returned to Pune and started the Arya Mahila Samaj with the help of leaders like Ranade and Bhandarkar.

In 1882, She gave evidence before the Hunter Commission who were very happy to see 300 women being educated in the Samaj. She pleaded for facilities for women to qualify themselves in medicine. In 1883, she went to England and was baptized as a Christian. She went to America in 1886. On her return to Bombay in 1889, she started the Sharada Sadan to provide home for the destitute high caste widows again with the help of Ranade, Bhandarkar and others. In the institute many Hindus were converted to Christianity. So, a strong protest came from Tilak and others.

As a result of this even, liberal leaders like Ranade and Bhandarkar had to give up their connection with the Sadan. After this, she shifted to Khedgoan near Poona and established a Mukti Sadan. Soon there were 2000 children and women. Training was given from kindergarten to the teacher and the industrial section. In spite of the criticism against her, she was able to give general education and vocational training to several thousand women, who were able to become self-independent.

Rama Bai Ranade

Another outstanding women who contributed to the emancipation of women in the nineteenth century was Rama Bai Ranade (1862-1922).

She married the great economist and social reformer, Justice Mahadev Govind Ranade when she was just eleven. Ranade educated her and helped her in her various activities. She started the Hindu Ladies Club in her house in 1884 and later opened classes for illiterate women and widows. She also started the Poona Seva Sadan with branches in different parts of Maharashtra. Finally, she started a Nursing Medical Association and trained nurses.

Madam Cama

Another woman of outstanding merit was the great revolutionary Madam Cama (1861-1936). She was a pioneer in the struggle for freedom. She left India in 1902 and settled down in England and joined the Indian Revolutionary movement there.

Toru Dutt

Toru dutt (1855-1877) of Bengal was a great literary celebrity of the nineteenth century.

Swarnakumari

Another great writer was Swarnakumari Devi (1855-1932) of the famous Tagore family. She wrote historical and social novels in Bengali.

Para

Another outstanding woman was Para, a talented painter. She belonged to the Kangro school of Rajput Painting. She was a woman artist of great repute.

Karve

In the last decade of the century the great Indian figure Karve started the Hingne Women's Education Institution in Poona in 1896. There she imparted training not only in academic subjects but also in domestic economy, to unmarried, married, widowed and deserted women with branches in other parts of Maharashtra. Ultimately, she was responsible for starting the S.N.D.T. Women University in 1915, adopting the mother-tongue as the medium of instruction. It was recognised as a university in 1938. It has a number of high schools and colleges affiliated to it. Thus, it was a great step in the advance of women's education, particularly in Maharashtra.

Swami Vivekananda

Swami Vivekananda (1863-1902) gave a tremendous impetus to the emancipation of women from seclusion and bondage. He said, "That country and that nation which did not respect women have never become great nor will ever in the future".

Swami Vivekananda took a stand for the liberation of women and equality of treatment on the basis of the Vedantic ideals that "one and the same self is present in all beings". He attributed the helplessness and dependence of woman on man in the training given to her and asserted "However, when she is no longer oppressed she will become a lion". He emphasised the ideal that through education, women should be enabled to solve their own problems by thinking independently.

Mrs. Annie Besant

Annie Besant started Home Rule Movement not only for the emancipation of India, but also for the emancipation of women. When she was interned by the British, the Indian women led processions to temples to offer their prayers for her release. Then in the same year she was elected as the President of the Calcutta session of the Indian National Congress. In it she emphasised right to franchise and eligibility to all elective bodies concerned with the Local Government and Education for women.

After the Jallianwalabagh massacre in 1919, when hundreds of men, women and children were killed, a large contingent of women delegates, nearly 200, attended the Congress session at Nagpur. This was a striking evidence of the political awakening of the Indian women.

Gandhiji

Mahatma Gandhi rendered signal-service to the advancement of the women's movement by making thousands of them of all classes, to come out of their homes and participate in the political movement.

Amrit Kaur wrote that "Gandhiji's fundamental faith in the equality of women was based on the doctrine of non-violence."

From the very beginning Gandhiji preached against wrongs done to women in the name of Dharma Sastras, Law and tradition.

He was always a fighter for the equality of human beings and freedom for individuals. He also stood for the emancipation of women and untouchables. He wrote, "I passionately desire utmost freedom of our women." He asserted continuously that woman has the same right of freedom and liberty as man.

Though he himself was a victim of child marriage, he condemned child marriage in unequivocal terms. He had described in detail in his autobiography the sufferings he and his wife had to undergo because they were married as children.

With equal vehemence he condemned widowhood of children and strongly recommended widow remarriage. He wrote, ".....forced widowhood upon little girls is a brutal crime for which we Hindus are daily paying dearly....widowhood imposed by religion or custom is an unbearable yoke". Thus, he wanted to carry on two campaigns at the same time; he wanted to see that little girls are not married, and he also wanted to see that young men marry the girl widows so that such a widowhood is wiped out. So after freedom there was drastic change in the legal status of the women.

The most important thing he did, right from the years in South Africa, how to make women participate in social movements and public work. As a great campaigner and leader of social and political movements he could see and realise the importance of the participation of the women who constitute 50 per cent of the population. It is obvious that no movement could be popular, no movement could be mass movement, unless women participated in it. In the first non-co-operation movement and other movements a large number of women throughout the country participated enthusiastically. He wanted the women to participate in what he regarded as the vital tasks of constructive work, namely, picketing liquor shops and the shops which sold foreign cloth.

Even as early as 1921, he advocated the enfranchisement of women. Thus, the work of nineteenth century leaders and Gandhiji led to the emancipation of women.

Western Women

In the twentieth century new ideas swept across the country and a strong women's movement took shape. In this work three Western women played an important part. They are Margaret Nobel (1867-1911), later known as Sister Nivedita, Annie Besant (1847-1933) and Margaret Cousins (1878-1954). These three women were, as Homne Sen wrote, "Irish in origin, suffragette in sympathy and former participants in the Irish Home Rule agitation."

In 1917, some Indian ladies of the south established the Indian Women's Association in Madras and organised its branches in different parts of the country. Margaret Cousins started *Stree dharma* in order to mould public opinion in favour of women and to educate the women about their rights. In December, 1917 a deputation of women under the leadership of Sarojini Naidu (1879-1949) presented a memorandum to Montague, the British Secretary of State for India, demanding votes for women and also for increased educational and health facilities. No doubt in marked a new awakening of Indian women in the country.

Franchise Agitation

Then the women of India met the South Borough Committee appointed by the British Parliament regarding their franchise. In 1918 also the Indian National Congress as well as the Muslim League endorsed the demand of women for enfranchisement. But the committee ignored the demand of women for enfranchisement in its report published in 1919. Several protest meetings were organised by them and sent resolutions to the British Parliament. It entrusted the question of franchise to the Joint Select Committee. After its consideration, it was given to the Legislative Councils of India in each province. So the women appealed to the councils for their franchise. In March 1921 Krishna Nair, a prominent member of the Madras Legislative Council, introduced a resolution that women should be enfranchised on the same basis as the men. The resolution was adopted in a large majority. It was followed by Bombay Legislative Council and the Bengal Council. Later the princely states of Cochin and Travancore of south enfranchised women.

In 1926 Kamala Devi Chattopadhyaya stood for elections to the Madras Legislature. The Government of Madras nominated Muthulakshmi Ammal. She was elected by the Legislature as Deputy President.

Thus, within a period of ten years from 1917 the women's agitation for franchise bore fruit.

All India Women's Conference

In 1926, under Margaret Cousins, the secretary of the Women's Indian Association, many conferences were organised by women leaders in 22 places. As a result of this, All-India Women's Conference was established and it held the first session in January 1927 in Poona with representatives from all over the country. Thus they established all India organisation to help them in their struggle for rights.

In 1932, it established a National Education Fund and it set up the Lady Irvin College at New Delhi to give advanced education in Home Science for women. In the field of social reforms it carried on a propaganda against early marriage, polygamy, excessive expenditure at the time of marriage etc. It fought for equality in matters of property. It also fought for reasonable wages and healthy working conditions. As early as 1932 it demanded universal adult franchise. Very early it conducted a campaign in the field of family planning to prevent over population.

The All India Women's Conference is today a huge organisation with nearly 500 sub-branches and a membership of 3.25 million.

It conducts magazines and issues news letters. It has been very active in the starting of hostels for working women in the urban areas.

The Conference has played a very important part in supporting social legislation in India. It gave full support to Haribilas Sarada and mobilised public opinion so that the Act of 1929 raising the age of girls to 14 passed. Because of it many laws were passed during the fifties.

Many laws have been passed by the Parliament fo uplift the status of women in India. Notable among these are the following :

(1) Hindu Married Women's Rights to Separate Residence and Maintenance Act, 1946.
(2) Hindu Marriage Act, 1955.
(3) Hindu Succession Act, 1956.
(4) Hindu Adoptions and Maintenance Act, 1956.
(5) Hindu Minority and Guardianship Act, 1956.

Present Status

More than a hundred years ago, women took to the teaching profession and today, women constitute nearly 35 per cent of teachers in the country. Educated women are no longer confined to jobs such as those of school teachers, nurses etc. They have invaded the precints of commercial establishments, airlines, banking, government offices and institutions of local self-governments.

During the post-Independence period, women have been elevated to the most coveted posts of district officers, governors, ambassadors judges and even police officers. For instance, Vijayalakshmi Pandit has acted as ambassador of India. She has worked as Governor and also as the President of the U.N. General Assembly. Mrs. Indira Gandhi has had the distinction of being the first woman Prime Minister of the largest democracy in the world. Now Ms. J. Jayalalitha has become the Chief Minister of Tamil Nadu. Indeed, modern women have gone far beyond the problem relating to their personal rights. Moreover, women have a long way to go in order to emulate men in all fields of human endeavour.

There is a conspicuous drift of educated women to westernisation. The modern women may look westernised in form but, in spirit, she is Indian. It is only when women act as chaste wives, good mothers, responsible public servants and enlightened citizens of free India that success will kiss their feet.

22

Rise of Dissents for the Welfare of the People

The Right to Dissent is the personal right of every individual. The civilised world has acknowledged the rights of individuals including the right to dissent. The world has witnessed a number of dissents, who rose to the occasion to fight for the well being of the people in a particular territory or nation by establishing their ideals. It is desirable to discuss about them in this chapter.

1. Nelson Mondela

Nelson was born in 1918. He was a lawyer and politician. He was the leader of the blacks in South Africa. It is the right to dissent that made him to fight against apartheism in South Africa. He fought against social discrimination. He was threatened with life by the then White Government and put him behind the bars. For 27 years (1964-1990) he was in the cell. The most important period of his life was spend by him in prison. A number of world countries and the UN interfered in the matter. Atlast the South African White regime came forward to free him. He followed the principle of non-violence to achieve his goals. He was awarded Nehru Peace Prize in 1979. He was freed from imprisonment on 10 February 1990. He was given arousing welcome with mammoth support and he constantly fought for the right of the blacks. He was awarded Bharat Ratna in 1990. In the general elections that held in 1994, he contested and was elected as President of South Africa, after first non-racial elections in April, 1994. His success was behind his principle of non-violence. He attached greatest importance to truth and non-violence and not through violence. This helped to rise to the highest pedestal of social, national and international life. Under his leadership the ANC South Africans to a non-racist democracy.

2. Aung San Suu Kyi

Man's life is short. Within a short span of life many establish indelible crusades with courage and strength that too in a non-violence manner. Credit goes to Aung San Suu Kyi, the 1991 Nobel Peace Prize laureate and the recipient of the 1990 Sakharov Peace Prize for Freedom, the Jawaharlal Nehru Award for International Understanding in 1993 for the silent penetration in world politics.

She was born in 1945 to General Aung San, one of Myanmar's greatest leaders. Suu Kyi had her school education in New Delhi where she developed an obsession for non-violence which was inspired by her leaning towards Mahatma Gandhi's ideals. Then she pursued her studies at Oxford, got married and settled down in Britain.

In 1980s, she started to study the contemporary history of Myanmar. In 1985, she returned to Myanmar to look after her ailing mother. There she entered into the national movement. She founded National League for democracy with a view to making Myanmar a democratic country. The League gathered momentum and became a mighty storm. The State Law and military Government of Myanmar did not want to give way to this new movement. It is not power that corrupts, but fear. In the violence many were killed. But Suu Kyi kept stressing the need to adhere to the principle of non-violence. The students' revolt was crushed and Suu Kyi was placed under house arrest in Yangon (Rangoon) for transgression of laws. She was under the vigilence of soldiers. The period of cruel imprisonment changed her status from that of a little known political prisoner to that of a symbol of universal courage. She continued to be a source of powerful inspiration to her people. She was world's most famous prisoner of conscience and champion of democracy.

In the General Election that held in 1990, she and her National League for Democracy made a clean sweep at the polls. Her party won 392 out of 485 seats. But the military junta brushed aside the verdict and she continued to be confined to her home. She refused to compromise with the harsh regime of Myanmar. She was offered release if she agreed to leave the country and promised never to return; but Suu Kyi did not give a thought to live in exile. Rather, she wanted to stay in her homeland and fight for the noble cause of freeing the country from its fetters. After six years of her detention and incarceration, she was set free unconditionally on 11 July 1995 by SLORC. (State Law and Order Restoration Council). But she wanted to achieve her goal. This is only a beginning. Her journey is long and the road is rough. Yet she believes that it might pave the way for democracy. Most of her supporters too believe the same. Suu Kyi is free; but peace is far.

3. Taslima Nasreen

She is 31 years old and a native of Bangladesh. She is famous writer. Her novel 'Lajja' focuses on a Hindu family that was attacked in Bangladesh by Muslims following the Ayodhya incident. It was her freedom of expression which made her to write the novel with such a theme. But her life was threatened by Muslim fundamentalists and they demanded death punishment for her. This made her to leave the country and took asylum in Sweden. She was awarded French Human Rights Prize.

4. Medha Patkar

She was born in 1956. She was a college professor. She did her Ph. D. on tribals and their life. She is an Indian social activist and an environmentalist. She is the fire brand leader of 'Save Narmada Movement' *i.e.,* 'Narmada Bachavo Andolen'. She was given Right Livelihood Award in 1991 often called the alternative Nobel Prize. The US government honoured her by giving 'Gold Man Environmental Prize' in 1992.

5. Ken Saro Wiwa

Saro Wiwa was born in 1954. He was a human rights activist and environmentalist. He fought relentlessly for the minority rights of the Ogoni community — the race of his birth in Nigeria. As a leader of the 'Movement for Salvation' of the Ogoni people, a half million strong minority living in Southern Nigeria, Saro Wiwa had been fighting for his peoples' self determination and protection of environment. The Anglo-Dutch Oil Company 'Shell' developed the oil field of Ogoniland in Niger delta four decades ago and the excessive drilling of oil wells affected the region and its surrounding. It also led to severe ecological imbalances in the region. The Ogonis have been exploited and many of them are today hiding in the forests and swamps of the region. The 'Shell' was driven out of the Ogoni region in 1993. Saro Wiwa won the alternative Nobel Prize in 1994 and it was awarded by a Swedish Foundation.

6. Leeh Walesa

He was born in 1943. He became an electrician at the Lenin Shipyard in Gdansk in 1970. After 10 years, he became the leader of the strikers in the same shipyard and became the recognised leader of 'Solidarity' *i.e.* Poland's Free Trade Union Movement, run by his followers. He fought for the rights of the workers in the shipyard. He was imprisoned by the Polish Military Government in 1981 and freed only in 1989. He was awarded the Nobel Peace Prize in 1983. Then he became the President of Poland in 1990.

Recently China has released two prominent dissidents from jail Wei Jingskeng and Wang Dan, sending them into US exile. While the release have been welcomed by the human right advocates, they have cautioned the United States not to become complacent and believe the problem of repression in China has been alleviated. Thus, he Chinese government's repression of dissent and religious freedom has not ceased.

Thus, there arose a number of dissents in different parts of the world to fight for the development, progress, peace, unity etc. of a group or sect or region or nation. Such personalities with their different ideals have contributed much to the protection and promotion of human rights and left an indelible mark in the history of human rights and set an example to be emulated.

23

UDHR-ICCPR and ICESCR-Text

UNIVERSAL DECLARATION OF HUMAN RIGHTS (UDHR)

Adopted and Proclaimed by General Assembly resolution 217 A (III) of 10 December 1948

PREAMBLE

Whereas recognition of the inherent dignity and of the equal and inalienable rights of all members of the human family is the foundation of freedom, justice and peace in the world.

Whereas disregard and contempt for human rights have resulted in barbarous acts which have outraged the conscience of mankind, and the advent of a world in which human beings shall enjoy freedom of speech and belief and freedom from fear and want has been proclaimed as the highest aspiration of the common people.

Whereas it is essential, if man is not to be compelled to have recourse, as a last resort, to rebellion against tyranny and oppression, that human rights should be protected by the rule of law.

Whereas it is essential to promote the development of friendly relations between nations.

Whereas the peoples of the United Nations have in the Charter reaffirmed their faith in fundamental human rights, in the dignity and worth of the human person and in the equal rights of men and women and have determined to promote social progress and better standards of life in larger freedom.

Whereas Member States have pledged themselves to achieve, in cooperation with the United Nations, the promotion of universal respect for and observance of human rights and fundamental freedoms.

Whereas a common understanding of these rights and freedoms is of the greatest importance for the full realization of this pledge.

Now, therefore

The General Assembly.

Proclaims the Universal Declaration of Human Rights as a common standard of achievement for all peoples and all nations, to the end that every individual and every organ of society, keeping this Declaration constantly in mind, shall strive by teaching and education to promote respect for these rights and freedoms and by progressive measures, national and international, to secure their universal and effective recognition and observance, both among the peoples of Member States themselves and among the people of territories under their jurisdiction.

ARTICLE 1

All human beings are born free and equal in dignity and right. They are endowed with reason and conscience and should act towards one another in a spirit of brotherhood.

ARTICLE 2

Everyone is entitled to all the rights and freedom set forth in this Declaration, without distinction of any kind, such as race, colour, sex, language, religion. Political or other opinion, national of social origin, property, birth or other status.

Furthermore, no distinction shall be made on the basis of the political jurisdictional or international status of the country or territory to which a person belongs, whether it be independent, trust, non-self-governing or under any other limitation of sovereignty.

ARTICLE 3

Everyone has the right to life, liberty and security of person.

ARTICLE 4

No one shall be held in slavery or servitude; slavery and the slave trade shall be prohibited in all their forms.

ARTICLE 5

No one shall he subjected to torture or to cruel, inhuman or degrading treatment or punishment.

ARTICLE 6

Everyone has the right to recognition everywhere as a person before the law.

ARTICLE 7

All are equal before the law and are entitled without any discrimination to equal protection of the law. All are entitled to equal protection against any discrimination in violation of this Declaration and against; any incitement to such discrimination.

ARTICLE 8

Everyone has the right to an effective remedy by the competent national tribunals for acts violating the fundamental rights granted him by the constitution or by law.

ARTICLE 9

No one shall be subjected to arbitrary arrest, detention or exile.

ARTICLE 10

Everyone is entitled in full equality to a fair and public hearing by an independent and impartial tribunal, in the determination of his rights and obligations and of any criminal charge against him.

ARTICLE 11

1. Everyone charged with a penal offence has the right to be presumed innocent until proved guilty according to law in a public trial at which he has had all the guarantees necessary for his defence.
2. No one shall be held guilty of any penal offence on account of any act or omission which did not constitute a penal offence, under national or international law, at the time when it was committed. Now shall a heavier penalty be imposed than the one that was applicable at the time the penal offence was committed.

ARTICLE 12

No one shall be subjected to arbitrary interference with his privacy, family, home or correspondence, nor to attacks upon his honour and reputation. Everyone has the right to the protection of the law against such interference or attacks.

ARTICLE 13

1. Everyone has the right to freedom of movement and residence within the border of each State.
2. Everyone has the right to leave any country, including his own, and to return to his country.

ARTICLE 14

1. Everyone has the right to seek and to enjoy in other countries asylum from persecution.
2. This right may not be invoked in the case of prosecutions genuinely arising from non-political crimes or from acts contrary to the purposes and principles of the United Nations.

ARTICLE 15

1. Everyone has the right to a nationality.
2. No one shall be arbitrarily deprived of his nationality nor denied the right to change his nationality.

ARTICLE 16

1. Men and women of full age, without any limitation due to race, nationality or religion, have the right to marry and to found a family. They are entitled to equal rights as to marriage, during marriage and at its dissolution.
2. Marriage shall be entered into only with the free and full consent of the intending spouses.
3. The family is the natural and fundamental group unit of society and is entitled to protection by society and the State.

ARTICLE 17

1. Everyone has the right to own property alone as well as in association with others.
2. No one shall be arbitrarily deprived of his property.

ARTICLE 18

Everyone has the right to freedom of thought, conscience and religion; this right includes freedom to change his religion or belief, and freedom, either alone or in community with others and in public or private, to manifest his religion or belief in teaching, practice, worship and observance.

ARTICLE 19

Everyone has the right to freedom of opinion and expression; this right includes freedom to hold opinions without interference and to seek, receive and impart information and ideas through any media and regardless of frontiers.

ARTICLE 20

1. Everyone has the right to freedom of peaceful assembly and association.
2. No one may be compelled to belong to an association.

ARTICLE 21

1. Everyone has the right to take part in the government of his country, directly or through freely chosen representatives.
2. Everyone has the right to equal access to public service in his country.
3. The will of the people shall be the basis of the authority of government; this will shall be expressed in periodic and genuine elections which shall be by universal and equal suffrage and shall be held by secret vote or by equivalent free voting procedures.

ARTICLE 22

Everyone, as a member of society, has the right to social security and is entitled to realization through national effort and international co-operation and in accordance with the organization and resources of each State, of the economic, social and cultural rights indispensable for his dignity and the free development of his personality.

ARTICLE 23

1. Everyone has the right to work, to free choice of employment, to just and favourable conditions of work and to protection against unemployment.
2. Everyone, without any discrimination, has the right to equal pay for equal work.
3. Everyone who works has the right to just and favourable remuneration ensuring for himself and his family an existence worthy of human dignity, and supplemented, if necessary, by other means of social protection.

4. Everyone has the right to form and to join trade unions for the protection of his interests.

ARTICLE 24

Everyone has the right to rest and leisure, including reasonable limitation of working hours and periodic holidays with pay.

ARTICLE 25

1. Everyone has the right to a standard of living adequate for the health and well-being of himself and of his family, including food, clothing, housing and medical care and necessary social services, and the right to security in the event of unemployment, sickness, disability, widowhood, old age or other lack of livelihood in circumstances beyond his control.
2. Motherhood and childhood are entitled to special care and assistance. All children, whether born in or out of wedlock, shall enjoy the same social protection.

ARTICLE 26

1. Everyone has the right to education. Education shall be free, at least in the elementary and fundamental stages. Elementary education shall be compulsory. Technical and professional education shall be made generally available and higher education shall be equally accessible to all on the basis of merit.
2. Education shall be directed to the full development of the human personality and to the strengthening of respect for human rights and fundamental freedoms. It shall promote understanding tolerance and friendship among all nations, racial or religious groups, and shall further the activities of the United Nations for the maintenance of peace.
3. Parents have a prior right to choose the kind of education that shall be given to their children.

ARTICLE 27

1. Everyone has the right freely to participate in the cultural life of the community, to enjoy the arts and to share in scientific advancement and its benefits.
2. Everyone has the right to the protection of the moral and material interests resulting from any scientific, literary of artistic production of which he is the author.

ARTICLE 28

Everyone is entitled to a social and international order in which the rights and freedoms set forth in this Declaration can be fully realized.

ARTICLE 29

1. Everyone has duties to the community in which alone the free and full development of his personality is possible.
2. In the exercise of his rights and freedoms, everyone shall be subject only to such limitations as are determined by law solely for the purpose of securing due recognition and respect for the rights and freedoms of others and of meeting the just requirements of morality, public order and the general welfare in a democratic society.
3. These rights and freedom may in no case be exercised contrary to the purposes and principles of the United Nations.

ARTICLE 30

Nothing in this Declaration may be interpreted as implying for any State, group or person any right to engage in any activity or to perform any act aimed at the destruction of any of the rights and freedoms set forth herein.

INTERNATIONAL COVENANT ON CIVIL AND POLITICAL RIGHTS (ICCPR)

Adopted and opened for signature, ratification and accession by General Assembly resolution 2200A (XXI) of 16 December 1966

ENTRY INTO FORCE : 23 MARCH 1976, IN ACCORDANCE WITH

ARTICLE 49

PREAMBLE

The State Parties to the Present Covenant,

Considering that, in accordance with the Principles proclaimed in the Charter of the United Nations, recognition of the inherent dignity and of the equal and inalienable right of all members of the human family is the foundation of freedom, justice and peace in the world.

Recognizing that these rights drive from the inherent dignity of the human person.

Recognizing that, in accordance with the Universal Declaration of Human Rights, the ideal of free human beings enjoying civil and political freedom and freedom from fear and want can only be achieved if conditions are created whereby everyone may enjoy his civil and political rights, as well as his economic, social and cultural rights.

Considering the obligation of States under the Charter of the United Nations to promote universal respect for, and observance of, human rights and freedoms.

Realizing that the individual, having duties to other individuals and to the community to which he belongs, is under a responsibility to strive for the promotion and observance of the rights recognized in the present Covenant.

Agree upon the following articles :

PART I

Article 1

1. All peoples, have the right of self-determination. By virtue of that right they freely determine their political status and freely pursue their economic, social and cultural development.
2. All peoples may, for their own ends, freely dispose of their natural wealth and resources without prejudice to any obligations arising out of international economic co-operation, based upon the principle of mutual benefit, and international law. In no case may a people be deprived of its own means of subsistence.
3. The States Parties to the present Covenant, including those having responsibility for the administration of Non-Self-Governing and Trust Territories, shall promote the realization of the right of self-determination, and shall respect that right, in conformity with the provisions of the Charter of the United Nations.

PART II

Article 2

1. Each State Party to the present Covenant undertakes to respect and to ensure to all individuals within its territory and subject to its jurisdiction the rights recognized in the present Covenant, without distinction of any kind, such as race, colour, sex, language,

religion, political or other opinion, national or social origin, property, birth or other status.

2. Where not already provided for by existing legislative or other measures, each State Party to the Present Covenant, undertakes to take necessary steps, in accordance with its constitutional processes and with the provisions of the present Covenant, to adopt such legislative or other measures as may be necessary to give effect to the rights recognized in the present Covenant.
3. Each State Party to the present Covenant undertakes;
   (a) To ensure that any person whose rights of freedoms as herein recognized are violated shall have an effective remedy, notwithstanding that the violation has been committed by person acting in an official capacity;
   (b) To ensure that nay person claiming such a remedy shall have his right thereto determined by competent judicial, administrative or legislative authorities, or by any other competent authority provided for by the legal system of the State, and to develop the possibilities of judicial remedy;
   (c) To ensure that the competent authorities shall enforce such remedies when granted.

Article 3

The State Parties to the present Covenant undertake to ensure the equal right of men and women to the enjoyment of all civil and political rights set forth in the present Covenant.

Article 4

1. In time of public emergency which threatens the life of the nation and the existence of which is officially proclaimed, the States Parties to the present Covenant may take measures derogating from their obligations under the present Covenant to the extent strictly required by the exigencies of the situation, provided that such measures are not inconsistent with their other obligations under international law and do not involve discrimination solely on the ground of race, colour, sex, language, religion or social origin.
2. No derogation from articles 6, 7, 8 (paragraphs 1 and 2), 11, 15, 16 and 18 may be made under this provision.

3. Any State Party to the present Covenant availing itself of the right of derogation shall immediately inform the other States Parties to the present Covenant, through the intermediary of the Secretary-General of the United Nations, of the provisions from which it has derogated and of the reasons by which it was actuated. A further communication shall be made, through the same intermediary, on the date on which it terminates such derogation.

Article 5

1. Nothing in the present Covenant may be interpreted as implying for any State, group or person any right to engage in any activity or perform any act aimed at the destruction of any of the rights and freedoms recognized herein or at their limitation to a greater extent than is provided for in the present Covenant.
2. There shall be no restriction upon derogation from any of the fundamental human rights recognized or existing in any State Party to the present Covenant pursuant to law, conventions, regulations or custom on the pretext that the present Covenant does not recognize such rights or that it recognizes them to a lesser extent.

PART III

Article 6

1. Every human beings has the inherent right to life. The right shall be protected by law. No one shall be arbitrarily deprived of his life.
2. In countries which have not abolished the death penalty, sentence of death may be imposed only for the most serious crimes in accordance with the law in force at the time of the commission of the crime and not contrary to the provisions of the present Covenant and to the Convention on the Prevention and Punishment of the Crime of Genocide. This penalty can only be carried out pursuant to a final judgement rendered by a competent court.
3. When deprivation of life constitutes the crime of genocide, it is understood that nothing in this article shall authorize any State Party to the present Covenant to derogate in any way from any

obligation assumed under the provisions of the Convention on the Prevention and Punishment of the Crime of Genocide.

4. Anyone sentenced to death shall have the right to seek pardon or commutation of the sentence. Amnesty, pardon or commutation of the sentence of death may be granted in all cases.
5. Sentence of death shall not be imposed for crimes committed by persons below eighteen years of age and shall not be carried out on pregnant women.
6. Nothing in this article shall be invoked to delay or to prevent the abolition of capital punishment by any State Party to the present Covenant.

Article 7

No one shall be subjected to torture or to cruel, inhuman or degrading treatment or punishment. In particular, no one shall be subject without his free consent to medical or scientific experimentation.

Article 8

1. No one shall be held in slavery; slavery and the slave-trade in all their forms shall be prohibited.
2. No one shall be held in servitude.
3. (a) No one shall be required to perform forced or compulsory labour,

   (b) Paragraph 3(a) shall not be held to preclude, in countries where imprisonment with hard labour may be imposed as a punishment for a crime, the performance of hard labour in pursuance of a sentence to such punishment by a competent court;

   (c) For the purpose of this paragraph the term "forced or compulsory labour" shall not include :

   (i) Any work or service, not referred to in sub-paragraph (b), normally required of a person who is under detention in consequence of a lawful order of a court, or of a person during conditional release from such detention;

   (ii) Any service of a military character and, in countries where conscientious objection is recognized, any national service required by law of conscientious objectors;

(iii) Any service exacted in cases of emergency or calamity threatening the life or well-being of the community;

(iv) Any work or service which forms part of normal civil obligations.

Article 9

1. Everyone has the right to liberty and security of person. No one shall be subjected to arbitrary arrest or detention. No one shall be deprived of his liberty except on such grounds and in accordance with such procedure as are established by law.
2. Anyone who is arrested shall be informed, at the time of arrest, of the reasons for his arrest and shall be promptly informed of any charges against him.
3. Anyone arrested or detained on a criminal charge shall be brought promptly before a judge or other officer authorized by law to exercise judicial power and shall be entitled to trial within a reasonable time or to release. It shall not be the general rule that persons awaiting trial shall be detained in custody, but release may be subject to guarantees to appear for trial, at any other stage of the judicial proceedings, and, should occasion arise, for execution of the judgement.
4. Anyone who is deprived of his liberty by arrest or detention shall be entitled to take proceedings before a court, in order that court may decide without delay on the lawfulness of his detention and order his release if the detention is not lawful.
5. Anyone who has been the victim of unlawful arrest or detention shall have no enforceable right to compensation.

Article 10

1. All persons deprived of their liberty shall be treated with humanity and with respect for the inherent dignity of the human person.
2. (a) Accused persons shall, save in exceptional circumstances, be segregated from convicted persons and shall be subject to separate treatment appropriate to their status as unconvicted persons;

   (b) Accused juvenile persons shall be separated from adults and brought as speedily as possible for adjudication.
3. The penitentiary system shall comprise treatment of prisoners the essential aim of which shall be their reformation and social

rehabilitation. Juvenile offenders shall be segregated from adults and be accorded treatment appropriate to their age and legal status.

Article 11

No one shall be imprisoned merely on the ground of inability to fulfil a contractual obligation.

Article 12

1. Everyone lawfully within the territory of a State shall, within that territory, have the right to liberty of movement and freedom to choose his residence.
2. Everyone shall be free to leave any country, including his own.
3. The above mentioned rights shall not be subject to any restrictions except those which are provided by law, are necessary to protect national security, public order (Order public), public health or morals or the rights and freedoms of others, and are consistent with the other rights recognized in the present Covenant.
4. No one shall be arbitrarily deprived of the right to enter his own country.

Article 13

An alien lawfully in the territory of a State Party to the present Covenant may be expelled therefrom only in pursuance of a decision reached in accordance with law and shall, except where compelling reasons of national security otherwise require, be allowed to submit the reasons against his expulsion and to have his case reviewed by, and be represented for the purpose before, the competent authority or a person or persons especially designated by the competent authority.

Article 14

1. All persons shall be equal before the courts and tribunals. In the determination of any criminal charge against him, or of his rights and obligations in a suit at law, everyone shall be entitled to a fair and public hearing by a competent, independent and impartial tribunal established by law. The press and the public may be excluded from all or part of a trial for reasons of morals, public order (order public) or national security in a democratic society, or when the interest of the private lives of the parties so requires, or to the extent strictly necessary in the opinion of the

court in special circumstances were publicity would prejudice the interests of justice; but any judgement rendered in a criminal case or in a suit at law shall be made public except where the interest of juvenile persons otherwise requires or the proceedings concern matrimonial disputes or the guardianship of children.

2. Everyone charged with a criminal offence shall have the right to be presumed innocent until proved guilty according to law.
3. In the determination of any criminal charge against him, everyone shall be entitled to the following minimum guarantees, in full equality :
   (a) To be informed promptly and in detail in a language which he understands of the nature and cause of the charge against him;
   (b) To have adequate time and facilities for the preparation of his defence and to communicate with counsel of his own choosing;
   (c) To be tried without undue delay;
   (d) To be tried in his presence, and to defend himself in person or through legal assistance of his own choosing; to be informed, if he does not have legal assistance, of this right; and to have legal assistance assigned to him, in any case where the interests to justice so require, and without payment by him in any such case if he does not have sufficient means to pay for it;
   (e) To examine, or have examined, the witnesses against him and to obtain the attendance and examination of witnesses on his behalf under the same conditions as witnesses against him;
   (f) To have the free assistance of an interpreter if he can not understand or speak the language used in court;
   (g) Not to be compelled to testify against himself or to confess guilt.
4. In the case of juvenile persons, the procedure shall be such as will take account of their age and the desirability of promoting their rehabilitation.
5. Everyone convicted of a crime shall have the right to his conviction and sentence being reviewed by a higher tribunal according to law.
6. When a person has by a final decision been convicted of a criminal offence and when subsequently his conviction has been

reversed or he has been pardoned on the ground that a new or newly discovered fact shows conclusively that there has been a miscarriage of justice, the person who has suffered punishment as a result of such conviction shall be compensated according to law, unless it is proved that the non-disclosure of the unknown fact in time is wholly or partly attributable to him.

7. No one shall be liable to be tried or punished again for an offence for which he has already been finally convicted or acquitted in accordance with the law and penal procedure of each country.

Article 15

1. No one shall be held guilty of any criminal offence on account of any act or omission which did not constitute a criminal offence, under national or international law, at the time when it was committed. Nor shall a heavier penalty be imposed than the one that was applicable at the time when the criminal offence was committed. If, subsequent to the commission of the offence, provision is made by law for the imposition of the lighter penalty, the offender shall benefit thereby.
2. Nothing in this article shall prejudice the trial and punishment of any person for any or omission which, at the time when it was committed, was criminal according to the general principles of law recognized by the community of nations.

Article 16

Everyone shall have the right to recognition everywhere as a person before the law.

Article 17

1. No one shall be subjected to arbitrary or unlawful interference with his privacy, family, home or correspondence, not to unlawful attacks on his honour and reputation.
2. Everyone has the right to the protection of the law against such interference or attacks.

Article 18

1. Everyone shall have the right to freedom of thought conscience and religion. The right shall include Freedom to have or to adopt a

religion or belief of his choice, and freedom, either individually or in community with others and in public or private, to manifest his religion or belief in worship, observance, practice and teaching.

2. No one shall be subject to coercion which would impair his freedom to have or to adopt a religion or belief of his choice.
3. Freedom to manifest one's religion or beliefs may be subject only to such limitations as are prescribed by law and are necessary to protect public safety, order, health, or morals or the fundamental rights and freedoms of others.
4. The States Parties to the present Covenant undertake to have respect for the liberty of parents and, when applicable, legal guardians to ensure the religious and moral education of their children in conformity with their own convictions.

Article 19

1. Everyone shall have the right to hold opinions without interference.
2. Everyone shall have the right to freedom of expression; this right shall include freedom to seek, receive and impart information and idea of all kinds, regardless of frontiers, either orally, in writing or in print, in the form of art, or through any other media of his choice.
3. The exercise of the rights provided for in paragraph 2 of this article carries with it special duties and responsibilities. It may therefore be subject to certain restrictions, but these shall only be such as are provided by law and are necessary :
   (a) For respect of the right of reputations of others;
   (b) For the protection of national security or of public order (order public), or of public health or morals.

Article 20

1. Any propaganda for war shall be prohibited by law.
2. Any advocacy of national, racial or religious hatred that constitutes incitement to discrimination, hostility or violence shall be prohibited by law.

Article 21

The right of peaceful assembly shall be recognized. No restrictions may be placed on the exercise of this right other than those imposed in conformity with the law and which are necessary in a democratic society in the interests of national security or public safety, public order (order public), the protection of public health or morals or the protection of the rights and freedoms of others.

Article 22

1. Everyone shall have the right to freedom of association with others, including the right to form and join trade unions for the protection of his interest.
2. No restrictions may be placed on the exercise of this right other than those which are prescribed by law and which are necessary in a democratic society in the interests of national security or public safety, public order (order public), the protection of public health or morals or the protection of the rights and freedoms of others. This article shall not prevent the imposition of lawful restrictions on members of the armed forces and of the police in their exercise of this right.
3. Nothing in this article shall authorize States Parties to the International Labour Organisation Convention of 1948 concerning Freedom of Association and Protection of the Right to Organize to take legislative measures which would prejudice, or to apply the law in such a manner as to prejudice, the guarantees provided for in that Convention.

Article 23

1. The family is the natural and fundamental group unit of society and is entitled to protection by society and the State.
2. The right of men and women of marriageable age to marry and to found a family shall be recognized.
3. No marriage shall be entered into without the free and full consent of the intending spouses.
4. State parties to the present Covenant shall take appropriate steps to ensure equality of rights and responsibilities of spouses as to marriage, during marriage and at its dissolution. In the case of dissolution, provision shall be made for the necessary protection of any children.

Article 24

1. Every child shall have, without any discrimination as to race, colour, sex, language, religion, national or social origin, property

or birth, the right to such measures of protection as are required by his status as a minor, on the part of his family, society and the State.

2. Every child shall be registered immediately after birth and shall have a name.
3. Every child has the right to acquire a nationality.

Article 25

Every citizen shall have the right and the opportunity, without any of the distinctions mentioned in article 2 and without unreasonable restrictions :

(a) To take part in the conduct of public affairs, directly or through freely chosen representatives;

(b) To vote and to be elected at genuine periodic elections which shall be by universal equal suffrage and shall be held by secret ballot, guaranteeing the free expression of the will of the electors;

(c) To have access, on general terms of equality, to public service in his country.

Article 26

All persons are equal before the law and are entitled without any discrimination to the equal protection of the law. In this respect, the law shall prohibit any discrimination and guarantee to all persons equal and effective protection against discrimination on any ground such as race, colour, sex, language, religion, political or other opinion, national or social origin, property, birth of other status.

Article 27

In those States in which ethnic, religious or linguistic minorities exist, persons belonging to such minorities shall not be denied the right, in community with the other members of their group, to enjoy their own culture, to profess and practise their own religion, or to use their own language.

PART IV

Article 28

1. There shall be established a Human Rights Committee (hereafter referred to in the present Covenant as the Committee). It shall consist of eighteen members and shall carry out the functions hereinafter provided.

2. The Committee shall be composed of nationals of the States Parties to the present Covenant who shall be persons of high moral character and recognized competence in the field of human rights, consideration being given to the usefulness of the participation of some persons having legal experience.
3. The members of the Committee shall be elected and shall serve in their personal capacity.

Article 29

1. The members of the Committee shall be elected by secret ballot from a list of persons possessing the qualifications prescribed in article 28 and nominated for the purpose by the State Parties to the present Covenant.
2. Each State Party to the Present Covenant may nominate not more than two persons. These persons shall be nationals of the nominating State.
3. A person shall be eligible for renomination.

Article 30

1. The initial election shall be held not later than six months after the date of the entry into force of the present Covenant.
2. At least four months before the date of each election to the Committee, often than an election to fill a vacancy declared in accordance with article 34, the Secretary-General of the United Nations shall address a written invitation to the States Parties to the present Covenant to submit their nominations for membership of the Committee within three months.
3. The Secretary-General of the United Nations shall prepare a list in alphabetical order of all the persons thus nominated, with an indication of the State Parties which have nominated them, and shall submit it to the States Parties to the present Covenant not later then one month before the date of each election.
4. Elections of the members of the Committee shall be held at meeting of the States Parties to the present Covenant convened by the Secretary-General of the United Nations at the Headquarters of the United Nations. At that meeting, for which two thirds of the States Parties to the present Covenant shall constitute a quorum, the persons elected to the Committee shall be those nominees who obtain the largest number of votes and an absolute majority

of the votes of the representatives of States Parties present and voting.

Article 31

1. The Committee may not include more than one national of the same State.
2. In the election of the Committee, consideration shall be given to equitable geographical distribution of membership and to the representation of the different forms of civilization and of the principal legal systems.

Article 32

1. The members of the Committee shall be elected for a term of four years. They shall be eligible for re-election if renominated. However, the terms of nine of the members elected at the first election shall expire at the end of two years; immediately after the first election, the names of these nine members shall be chosen by lot by the Chairman of the meeting referred to in article 30, paragraph 4.
2. Elections at the expiry of office shall be held in accordance with the preceding articles of this part of the present Covenant.

Article 33

1. If in the unanimous opinion of the other members, a member of the Committee has ceased to carry out his functions for any cause other than absence of a temporary character, the Chairman of the Committee shall notify the Secretary-General of the United Nations, who shall then declare the seat of that member to be vacant.
2. In the event of the death or the resignation of a member of the Committee, the Chairman shall immediately notify the Secretary-General of the United Nations, who shall declare the seat vacant from the date of death or the date on which the resignation takes effect.

Article 34

1. When a vacancy is declared in accordance with article 33 and if the term of office of the member to be replaced does not expire within six months of the declaration of the vacancy, the Secretary-

General of the United Nations shall notify each of the State Parties to the present Covenant, which may within two months submit nominations in accordance with article 29 for the purpose of filling the vacancy.

2. The Secretary-General of the United Nations shall prepare a list in alphabetical order of the persons thus nominated and shall submit it to the States Parties to the present Covenant. The election to fill the vacancy shall then take place in accordance with the relevant provisions of this part of the present Covenant.
3. A member of the Committee elected to fill a vacancy declared in accordance with article 33 shall hold office for the remainder of the term of the member who vacated the seat on the Committee under the provisions of that article.

Article 35

The members of the Committee shall, with the approval of the General Assembly of the United Nations, receive emoluments from United Nations resources on such terms and conditions as the General Assembly may decide having regard to the importance of the Committee's responsibilities.

Article 36

The Secretary-General of the United Nations shall provide the necessary staff and facilities for the effective performance of the functions of the Committee under the present Covenant.

Article 37

1. The Secretary-General of the United Nations shall convene the initial meeting of the Committee at the Headquarters of the United Nations.
2. After its initial meeting, the Committee shall meet at such times as shall be provided in its rules of procedure.
3. The Committee shall normally meet at the Headquarters of the United Nations or at the United Nations Office at Geneva.

Article 38

Every member of the Committee shall, before taking up his duties, make a solemn declaration in open committee that he will perform his functions impartially and conscientiously.

Article 39

1. The Committee shall elect its officers for a term of two years. They may be re-elected.
2. The Committee shall establish its own rules of procedure, but these rules shall provide, *inter alia,* that :
   (a) Twelve members shall constitute a quorum;
   (b) Decisions of the Committee shall be made by a majority vote of the members present.

Article 40

1. The State Parties to the present Covenant undertake to submit reports on the measures they have adopted which give effect to the rights recognized herein and on the progress made in the enjoyment of those rights.
   (a) Within one year of the entry into force of the present Covenant for the States Parties concerned :
   (b) Thereafter whenever the Committee so requests.
2. All reports shall be submitted to the Secretary-General of the United Nations, who shall transmit them to the Committee for consideration. Reports shall indicate the factors and difficulties, if any, affecting the implementation of the present Covenant.
3. The Secretary-General of the United Nations may, after consultation with the Committee, transmit to the specialized agencies concerned copies of such parts of the reports as may fall within their field of competence.
4. The Committee shall study the reports submitted by the States Parties to the present Covenant. It shall transmit its reports, and such general comments as it may consider appropriate, to the State Parties. The Committee may also transmit to the Economic and social Council these comments along with the copies of the reports it has received form States Parties to the present Covenant.
5. The States Parties to the present Covenant may submit to the Committee observations on any comments that may be made in accordance with paragraph 4 of this article.

Article 41

1. A state Party to the present Covenant may at any time declare under this article that it recognizes the competence of the

Committee to receive and consider communications to the effect that a State Party claims that another State Party is not fulfilling its obligations under the present Covenant. Communications under this article may be received and considered only if submitted by a State Party which has made a declaration recognizing in regard to itself the competence of the Committee. No communication shall be received by the Committee if it concerns a State Party which has not made such a declaration. Communications received under this article shall be dealt with in accordance with the following procedure.

(a) If a State Party to the present Covenant considers that another State Party is not giving effect to the provisions of the present Covenant, it may, by written communication, bring the matter to the attention of that State Party. Within three months after the receipt of the communication the receiving State shall afford the State which sent the communication an explanation, or any other statement in writing clarifying the matter which should include, to the extent possible and pertinent, reference to domestic procedures and remedies taken, pending, or available in the matter.

(b) If the matter is not adjusted to the satisfaction of both States Parties concerned within six months after the receipt by the receiving State of the initial communication, either State shall have the right to refer the matter to the Committee, by notice given to the Committee and to the other State.

(c) The Committee shall deal with a matter referred to it only after it has ascertained that all available domestic remedies have been invoked and exhausted in the matter, in conformity with the generally recognized principles of international law. This shall not be the role where the application of the remedies is unreasonably prolonged.

(d) The Committee shall hold closed meetings when examining communications under this article.

(e) Subject to the provisions of sub-paragraph (c), the Committee shall make available its good offices to the States Parties concerned with a view to a friendly solution of the matter on the basis of respect for human rights and fundamental freedoms as recognized in the present Covenant;

(f) In any matter referred to it, the Committee may call upon the State Parties concerned, referred to in sub-paragraph (b), to supply any relevant information.

(g) The States Parties concerned, referred to in subparagraph (b) shall have the right to be represented when the matter is being considered in the Committee and to make submission orally and/or in writing.

(h) The Committee shall, within twelve months, after the date of receipt of notice under sub-paragraph (b), submit a report.

(i) If a solution within the terms of sub-paragraph (c) is reached, the Committee shall confine its report to a brief statement of the facts and of the solution reached.

(ii) If a solution within the terms of sub-paragraph (e) is not reached, the Committee shall confine its report to a brief statement of the facts; the written submissions and record of the oral submissions made by the States Parties concerned shall be attached to the report.

In every matter, the report shall be communicated to the States Parties concerned.

2. The provisions of this articles shall come into force when ten States Parties to the present Covenant have made declarations under paragraph 1 of this article. Such declarations shall be deposited by the States Parties with the Secretary-General of the United Nations, who shall transmit copies thereof to the other States Parties. A declaration may be withdrawn at any time by notification to the Secretary-General. Such a withdrawal shall not prejudice the consideration of any matter which is the subject of a communication already transmitted under this article; no further communication by any State Party shall be received after the notification of withdrawal of the declaration has been received by the Secretary-General, unless the State Party concerned has made a new declaration.

Article 42

1. (a) If a matter referred to the Committee in accordance with article 41 is not resolved to the satisfaction of the States Parties concerned, the Committee may, with the prior consent of the States Parties concerned, appoint and *ad hoc* Conciliation Commission (hereinafter referred to as the

Commission). The good offices of the Commission shall be made available to the States Parties concerned with a view to an amicable solution of the matter on the basis of respect for the present Covenant;

(b) The Commission shall consist of five persons acceptable to the States Parties concerned. If the States Parties concerned fail to reach agreement within three months on all or part of the composition of the Commission, the members of the Commission concerning whom no agreement has been reached shall be elected by secret ballot by a two-third majority vote of the Committee from among its members.

2. The members of the commission shall serve in their personal capacity. They shall not be nationals of the States Parties concerned, or of a State not Party to the present Covenant, or of a State Party which has not made a declaration under article 41.
3. The Commission shall elect its own Chairman and adopt its own rules of procedure.
4. The meetings of the Commission shall normally be held at the Headquarters of the United Nations or at the United Nations Office at Geneva. However, they may be held at such other convenient places as the Commission may determine in consultation with the Secretary-General of the United Nations and the States Parties concerned.
5. The secretariat provided in accordance with article 36 shall also service the commission appointed under this article.
6. The information received and collated by the committee shall be made available to the Commission and the Commission may call upon the States Parties concerned to supply any other relevant information.
7. When the Commission has fully considered the matter, but in any event not later than twelve months after having been seized of the matter, it shall submit to the Chairman of the Committee a report for communication to the States Parties concerned.

   (a) If the Commission is unable to complete its consideration of the matter within twelve months, it shall confine its report to a brief statement of the status of its consideration of the matter;

   (b) If an amicable solution to the matter on the basis of respect for human rights as recognized in the present Covenant is reached, the Commission shall confine its report to a brief statement of the facts and of the solution reached;

(c) If a solution within the terms of sub-paragraph (b) is not reached, the Commission's report shall embody its findings on all questions of fact relevant to the issues between the States Parties concerned, and its views on the possibilities of an amicable solution of the matter. This report shall also contain the written submissions and a record of the oral submissions made by the States Parties concerned;

(d) If the Commission's report is submitted under sub-paragraph (c), the States Parties concerned shall, within three months of the receipt of the report, notify the Chairman of the Committee whether or not they accept the contents of the report of the Commission.

8. The provisions of this article are without prejudice to the responsibilities of the Committee under article 41.
9. The States Parties concerned shall share equal all the expenses of the members of the Commission in accordance with estimates to be provided by the Secretary-General of the United Nations.
10. The Secretary-General of the United Nations shall be empowered to pay the expenses of the members of the Commission, if necessary, before reimbursement by the States Parties concerned, in accordance with paragraph 9 of this article.

Article 43

This members of the Committee, and of the *ad hoc* conciliation commissions, which may be appointed under article 42, shall be entitled to the facilities, privileges, and immunities of experts of mission for the United Nations as laid down in the relevant sections of the Convention on the Privileges and Immunities of the United Nations.

Article 44

The provisions for the implementation of the present Covenant shall apply without prejudice to the procedures prescribed in the field of human rights by or under the constituent instruments and the conventions of the United Nations and of the specialized agencies and shall not prevent the States Parties to the present Covenant from having recourse to other procedures for settling a dispute in accordance with general or special international agreements in force between them.

Article 45

The Committee shall submit to the General Assembly of the United Nations, through the Economic and Social Council, an annual report on its activities.

PART V

Article 46

Nothing in the present Covenant shall be interpreted as impairing the provisions of the Charter of the United Nations and of the Constitutions of the specialized agencies which define the respective responsibilities of the various organs of the United Nations and of the specialized agencies in regard to the matters dealt with in the present Covenant.

Article 47

Nothing in the present Covenant shall he interpreted as impairing the inherent right of all peoples to enjoy and utilize fully and freely their natural wealth and resources.

PART VI

Article 48

1. The present Covenant is open for signature by any State Member of the United Nations or member of any of its specialized agencies, by any State Party to the Statute of the International Court of Justice, and by any other State which has been invited by the General Assembly of the United Nations to become a Party to the present Covenant.
2. The present Covenant is subject to ratification. Instruments of ratification shall be deposited with the Secretary-General of the United Nations.
3. The present Covenant shall be open to accession by any State referred to in paragraph 1 of this article.
4. Accession shall be effected by the deposit of an instrument of accession with the Secretary-General of the United Nations.
5. The Secretary-General of the United Nations shall inform all States which have signed this Covenant or acceded to it of the deposit of each instrument of ratification or accession.

Article 49

1. The present Covenant shall enter into force three months after the date of the deposit with the Secretary-General of the United Nations of the thirty-fifth instrument of ratification or instrument of accession.
2. For each State ratifying the present Covenant or acceding to it after the deposit of the thirty-fifth instrument of ratification or instrument of accession, the present Covenant shall enter into force three months after the date of the deposit of its own instrument of ratification or instrument of accession.

Article 50

The provisions of the present Covenant shall extend to all parts of federal States without any limitations or exceptions.

Article 51

1. Any State Party to the present Covenant may propose an amendment and file it with the Secretary-General of the United Nations. The Secretary-General of the United Nations shall thereupon communicate any proposed amendments to the States Parties to the present Covenant with a request that they notify him whether they favour a conference of State Parties for the purpose of considering and voting upon the proposals. In the event that at least one third of the States Parties favours such a conference, the Secretary-General shall convene the conference under the auspices of the United Nations. Any amendment adopted by a majority of the States Parties present and voting at the conference shall be submitted to the General Assembly of the United Nations for approval.
2. Amendments shall come into force when they have been approved by the General Assembly of the United Nations and accepted by a two-third majority of the States Parties to the present Covenant in accordance with their respective constitutional processes.
3. When amendments come into force, they shall be binding on those States Parties which have accepted them, other States Parties still being bound by the provisions of the present Covenant and any earlier amendment which they have accepted.

Article 52

Irrespective of the notifications made under article 48, paragraph 5, the Secretary-General of the United Nations shall inform all States referred to in paragraph 1 of the same article of the following particulars :

(a) Signatures, ratifications and accessions under article 48;

(b) The date of the entry into force of the present Covenant under article 49 and the date of the entry into force of any amendments under article 51.

Article 53

1. The present Covenant, of which the Chinese, English, French, Russian and Spanish texts are equally authentic, shall be deposited in the archives of the United Nations.
2. The Secretary-General of the United Nations shall transmit certified copies of the present Covenant to all States referred to in article 48.

OPTIONAL PROTOCOL TO THE INTERNATIONAL COVENANT ON CIVIL AND POLITICAL RIGHTS

Adopted and opened for signature, ratification and accession by General Assembly resolution 2200 A (XXI) of 16 December 1966

ENTRY INTO FORCE : 23 MARCH 1976, IN ACCORDANCE WITH ARTICLE 9

The State Parties to the present Protocol

Have agreed as follows :

Article 1

A State Party to the Covenant that becomes a Party to the present Protocol recognizes the competence of the Committee to receive and consider communications from individuals subjects to its jurisdiction who claim to be victims of a violation by that State Party of any of the rights set forth in the Covenant. No communication shall be received by the Committee if it concerns a State Party to the Covenant which is not a Party to the present Protocol.

Article 2

Subject to the provisions of article 1, individuals who claim that any of their rights enumerated in the Covenant have been violated and who have exhausted all available domestic remedies may submit a written communication to the Committee for consideration.

Article 3

The Committee shall consider inadmissible any communication under the present Protocol which is anonymous, or which it considers to be an abuse of the right of submission of such communications or to be incompatible with the provisions of the Covenant.

Article 4

1. Subject to the provisions of article 3, the Committee shall bring any communications submitted to it under the present Protocol to the attention of the State Party to the present Protocol alleged to be violating any provision of the Covenant.
2. Within six months, the receiving State shall submit to the Committee written explanations or statements clarifying the matter and the remedy, if any, that may have been taken by the State.

Article 5

1. The Committee shall consider communications received under the present Protocol in the light of all written information made available to it by the individual and by the State Party concerned.
2. The Committee shall not consider any communication from an individual unless it has ascertained that:
   (a) The same matter is not being examined under another procedure of international investigation or settlement;
   (b) The individual has exhausted all available domestic remedies. This shall not be the rule where the application of the remedies is unreasonably prolonged.
3. The Committee shall hold meetings when examining communications under the present Protocol.
4. The Committee shall forward its views to the State Party concerned and to the individual.

Article 6

The Committee shall include in its annual report under article 45 of the Covenant a summary of its activities under the present Protocol.

Article 7

Pending the achievement of the objectives of resolution 1514 (XV) adopted by the General Assembly of the United Nations on 14 December 1960 concerning the Declaration on the Granting of Independence to Colonial Countries and peoples, the provisions of the present Protocol shall in no way limit the right of petition granted to these peoples by the Charter of the United Nations and other international conventions and instruments under the United Nations and its specialized agencies.

Article 8

1. The present Protocol is open for signature by any State which has signed the Covenant.
2. The present Protocol is subject to ratification by any State which has ratified or acceded to the Covenant. Instruments of ratification shall be deposited with the Secretary-General of the United Nations.
3. The present Protocol shall be open to accession by any State which has ratified or acceded to the Covenant.
4. Accession shall be effected by the deposit of an instrument of accession with the Secretary-General of the United Nations.
5. The Secretary-General of the United Nations shall inform all states which have signed the present Protocol or acceded to it of the deposit of each instrument of ratification or accession.

Article 9

1. Subject to the entry into force of the Covenant, the present Protocol shall enter into force three months after the date of the deposit with the Secretary-General of the United Nations of the tenth instrument of ratification or instrument of accession.
2. For each State ratifying the present Protocol or acceding to it after the deposit of the tenth instrument of ratification or instrument of accession, the present Protocol shall enter into force three months after the date of the deposit of its own instrument of ratification or instrument of accession.

Article 10

The provisions of the present Protocol shall extend to all parts of federal States without any limitations or exceptions.

Article 11

1. Any State Party to the present Protocol may propose an amendment and file it with the Secretary-General of the United Nations. The Secretary-General shall there upon communicate any proposed amendments to the State Parties to the present Protocol with a request that they notify him whether they favour a conference of State Parties for the purpose of considering and voting upon the proposal. In the event that at least one third of the State Parties favours such a conference, the Secretary-General shall convene the conference under the auspices of the United Nations. Any amendment adopted by a majority of the State Parties present and voting at the conference shall be submitted to the General Assembly of the United Nations for approval.
2. Amendments shall come into force when they have been approved by the General Assembly of the United Nations and accepted by a two-third majority of the State Parties to the present Protocol in accordance with their respective constitutional processes.
3. When amendments come into force, they shall be binding on those States Parties which have accepted them, other State Parties still being bound by the provisions of the present Protocol and any earlier amendment which they have accepted.

Article 12

1. Any State party may denounce the present Protocol at any time by written notification addressed to the Secretary-General of the United Nations. Denunciation shall take effect three months after the date of receipt of the notification by the Secretary-General.
2. Denunciation shall be without prejudice to the continued application of the provision of the present Protocol to any communication submitted under article 2 before the effective date of denunciation.

Article 13

Irrespective of the notifications made under article 8, paragraph 5, of the present Protocol, the Secretary-General of the United Nations shall inform all States referred to in article 48, paragraph, 1, of the Covenant of the following particulars :

(a) Signatures, ratifications and accessions under article 8;

(b) The date of the entry into force of the present Protocol under article 9 and the date of the entry into force of any amendments under article 11;

(c) Denunciations under article 12.

Article 14

1. The Present Protocol, of which the Chinese, English, French, Russian and Spanish texts are equally authentic, shall be deposited in the archives of the United Nations.
2. The Secretary-General of the United Nations shall transmit certified copies of the present Protocol to all States referred to in article 48 of the Covenant.

SECOND OPTIONAL PROTOCOL TO THE INTERNATIONAL COVENANT ON CIVIL AND POLITICAL RIGHTS, AIMING AT THE ABOLITION OF THE DEATH PENALTY

Adopted and proclaimed by General Assembly resolution 44/128 of 15 December 1989.

The State Parties to the present Protocol,

Have agreed as follows :

Article 1

1. No one within the jurisdiction of a State Party to the present Protocol shall be executed.
2. Each State Party shall take all necessary measures to abolish the death penalty within its jurisdiction.

Article 2

1. No reservation is admissible to the present Protocol, except for a reservation made at the time of ratification or accession that provides for the application of the death penalty in time of war pursuant to a conviction for a most serious crime of a military nature committed during war time.

2. The State Party making such a reservation shall at the time of ratification or accession communicate to the Secretary-General of the United Nations the relevant provisions of its national legislation applicable during wartime.
3. The State Party having made such a reservation shall notify the Secretary-General of the United Nations of any beginning or ending of a state of war applicable to its territory.

Article 3

The State Parties to the present Protocol shall include in the reports they submit to the Human Rights Committee, in accordance with article 40 of the Covenant information on the measures that they have adopted to give effect to the present Protocol.

Article 4

With respect to the State Parties to the Covenant that have made a declaration under article 41, the competence of the Human Rights Committee to receive and consider communications when a State Party claims that another State Party is not fulfilling its obligations shall extend to the provisions of the present Protocol, unless the State Party concerned has made a statement to the contrary at the moment of ratification or accession.

Article 5

With respect to the State Parties to the first Optional Protocol International Covenant on Civil and Political Rights adopted on 16 December 1966, the competence of the Human Rights Committee to receive and consider communications for individuals subject to its jurisdiction shall extend to the provisions of the present Protocol, unless, the State Party concerned has made statement to the contrary at the moment of ratification or accession.

Article 6

1. The provisions of the present protocol shall apply as additional provisions to the Covenant.
2. Without prejudice to the possibility of a reservation under article 2 of the present Protocol, the right guaranteed in article 1, paragraph 1, of the present Protocol, shall not be subjected to any derogation under article 4 of the Covenant.

Article 7

1. The present Protocol is open for signature by any State that has signed the Covenant.
2. The present Protocol is subject to ratification by any State that has ratified the Covenant or acceded to it. Instruments of ratification shall be deposited with the Secretary-General of the United Nations.
3. The present Protocol shall be open to accession by any State that has ratified the Covenant or acceded to it.
4. Accession shall be effected by the deposit of an instrument of accession with the Secretary-General of the United Nations.
5. The Secretary-General of the United Nations shall inform all States that have signed the present Protocol or acceded to it of the deposit of each instrument or ratification or accession.

Article 8

1. The present Protocol shall enter into force three months after the date of the deposit with the Secretary-General of the United Nations of the tenth instrument of ratification or accession.
2. For each State ratifying the present Protocol or acceding to it after the deposit of the tenth instrument of ratification or accession, the present Protocol shall enter into force three months after the date of the deposit of its own instrument of ratification or accession.

Article 9

The provision of the present Protocol shall extend to all parts of federal States without any limitations or exceptions.

Article 10

The Secretary-General of the United Nations shall inform all States referred to in article 48, paragraph 1, of the Covenant of the following particulars :

(a) Reservations, communications and notifications under article 2 of the present Protocol;

(b) Statements made under articles 4 or 5 of the present Protocol;

(c) Signatures, ratifications and accessions under article 7 of the present Protocol;

(d) The date of the entry into force of the present Protocol under article 8 thereof.

Article 11

1. The present Protocol, of which the Arabic, Chinese, English, French, Russian and Spanish texts are equally authentic, shall be deposited in the archives of the United Nations.
2. The Secretary-General of the United Nations shall transmit certified copies of the present Protocol to all States referred to in article 48 of the Covenant.

INTERNATIONAL COVENANT ON ECONOMIC, SOCIAL AND CULTURAL RIGHTS (ICESCR)

Adopted and opened for signature, ratification and accession by General Assembly resolution 2200 A (XXI) of 16 December 1966

ENTRY INTO FORCE

3 JANUARY 1976, IN ACCORDANCE WITH ARTICLE 27

PREAMBLE

The State Parties to the Present Covenant,

Considering that, in accordance with the principles proclaimed in the Charter of the United Nations, recognition of the inherent dignity and of the equal and inalienable rights of all members of the human family is the foundation of freedom, justice and peace in the world,

Recognizing that these rights derive from the inherent dignity of the human person,

Recognizing that, in accordance with the Universal Declaration of Human Rights, the ideal of free human beings enjoying freedom from fear and want can only be achieved if conditions are created whereby every one may enjoy his economic, social and cultural rights, as well as his civil and political rights.

Considering the obligation of State under the Charter of the United Nations to promote universal respect for, and observance of, human rights and freedoms,

Realizing that the individual, having duties to other individuals and to the community to which he belongs is under a responsibility to strive for the promotion and observance of the rights recognized in the present Covenant,

Agree upon the following articles :

PART I

Article 1

1. All peoples have the right of self-determination. By virtue of that right they freely determine their political status and freely pursue their economic, social and cultural development.
2. All peoples may, for their own ends, freely dispose of their natural wealth and resources without prejudice to any obligations arising out of international economic co-operation, based upon the principle of mutual benefit, and international law. In no case may a people be deprived of its own means of subsistence.
3. The State Parties to the present Covenant, including those having responsibility for the administration of Non-Self-Governing and Trust Territories, shall promote the realization of the right of self-determination, and shall respect the right, in conformity with the provisions of the Charter of the United Nations.

PART II

Article 2

1. Each State Party to the present Covenant undertakes to take steps, individually and through international assistance and co-operation, especially economic and technical, to the maximum of its available resources, with a view to achieving progressively the full realization of the rights recognized in the present Covenant by all appropriate means, including particularly the adoption of legislative measures.
2. The State Parties to the present Covenant undertake to guarantee that the rights enunciated in the present Covenant will be exercised without discrimination of any kind as to race, colour, sex, language, religion, political or other opinion, national or social origin, property, birth or other status.
3. Developing countries, with due regard to human rights and their national economy, may determine to what extent they would guarantee the economic rights recognized in the present Covenant to non-nationals.

Article 3

The State Parties to the present Covenant undertake to ensure the equal right of men and women to the enjoyment of all economic, social and cultural rights set forth in the present Covenant.

Article 4

The States Parties to the present Covenant recognize that, in the enjoyment of those rights provided by the State in conformity with the present Covenant, the State may subject such rights only to such limitations as are determined by law only in so far as this may be compatible with the nature of these rights and solely for the purpose of promoting the general welfare in a democratic society.

Article 5

1. Nothing in the present Covenant may be interpreted as implying for any State, group or person any right to engage in any activity or to perform any act aimed at the destruction of any of the right or freedoms recognized herein, or at their limitation to a greater extent than is provided for in the present Covenant.
2. No restriction upon or derogation from any of the fundamental human rights recognized or existing in any country in virtue of law, conventions, regulations or custom shall be admitted on the pretext that the present Covenant does not recognize such right or that it recognizes them to, a lesser extent.

PART III

Article 6

1. The State Parties to the Present Covenant recognize the right to work, which includes the right of everyone to the opportunity to gain his living by work which he freely chooses or accepts, and will take appropriate steps to safeguard this right.
2. The steps to be taken by a State Party to the present Covenant to achieve the full realization of this right shall include technical and vocational guidance and training programmes, policies and techniques to achieve steady economic, social and cultural development and full and productive employment under conditions safeguarding fundamental political and economic freedoms to the individual.

Article 7

The State Parties to the present Covenant recognize the right of everyone to the enjoyment of just and favourable conditions of work which ensure, in particular.

(a) remuneration which provides all workers, as a minimum, with :

(i) Fair wages and equal remuneration for work of equal value without distinction of any kind, in particular women being guaranteed conditions of work not inferior to those enjoyed by men, with equal pay for equal work;

(ii) A decent living for themselves and their families in accordance with the provisions of the Covenant;

(b) Safe and healthy working conditions;

(c) Equal opportunity for everyone to be promoted in his employment to an appropriate higher level, subject to no considerations other than those of seniority and competence;

(d) Rest, leisure and reasonable limitation of working hours and periodic holidays with pay, as well as remuneration for public holidays.

Article 8

1. The State Parties to the present Covenant undertake to ensure :

(a) The right of everyone to form trade unions and join the trade union of his choice, subject only to the rules of the organization concerned, for the promotion and protection of his economic and social interest. No restrictions may be placed on the exercise of this right other than those prescribed by law and which are necessary in a democratic society in the interests of national security or public order of for the protection of the rights and freedoms of others;

(b) The right of trade unions to establish national federations or confederations and the right of the latter to form or join international trade-union organisations;

(c) The right to trade unions to function freely subject to no limitations other than those prescribed by law and which are necessary in a democratic society in the interests of national security or public order or for the protection of the rights and freedoms of others;

(d) The right to strike, provided that it is exercised in conformity with the laws of the particular country.

2. This article shall not prevent the imposition of lawful restrictions on the exercise of these rights by members of the armed forces or of the police or of the administration of the State.
3. Nothing in this article shall authorize State Parties to the International Labour Organisation Convention of 1948 concerning Freedom of Association and protection of the Right to Organize to take legislative measures which would prejudice, or apply the law in such a manner as would prejudice, the guarantees provided for in the Convention.

Article 9

The State Parties to the present Covenant recognize the right of everyone to social security, including social insurance.

Article 10

The State Parties to the Present Covenant recognize that :

1. That widest possible protection and assistance should be accorded to the family, which is the natural and fundamental group unit of society, particularly for its establishment and while it is responsible for the care and education of dependent children. Marriage must be entered into with the free consent of the intending spouses.
2. Special protection should be accorded to mothers during a reasonable period before and after child birth. During such period working mothers should be accorded paid leave or leave with adequate social security benefits.
3. Special measures of protection and assistance should be taken on behalf of all children and young persons without any discrimination for reasons or parentage or other conditions. Children and young persons should be protected from economic and social exploitation. Their employment in work harmful to their morals or health or dangerous to life or likely to hamper their normal development should be punishment by law. States should also set age limits below which the paid employment of child labour should be prohibited and punishable by law.

Article 11

1. The State Parties to the present Covenant recognize the right of everyone to an adequate standard of living for himself and his family, including adequate food, clothing and housing, and to the

continuous improvement of living conditions. The State Parties will take appropriate steps to ensure the realization of this right recognizing to this effect the essential importance of international co-operation based on free consent.

2. The State Parties to the present Covenant recognizing the fundamental right of everyone to be free from hunger, shall take, individually and through international co-operation the measures, including specific programmes, which are needed;
   (a) To improve methods of production, conservation and distribution of food by making full use of technical and scientific knowledge, by disseminating knowledge of the principles of nutrition and by developing or reforming agrarian systems in such a way as to achieve the most efficient development and utilization of natural resources;
   (b) Taking into account the problems of both food-importing and food-exporting countries, to ensure an equitable distribution of world food supplies in relation to need.

Article 12

1. The State Parties to the present Covenant recognize the right of everyone to the enjoyment of the highest attainable standard of physical and mental health.
2. The steps to be taken by the State Parties to the present Covenant to achieve the full realization of this right shall include those necessary for:
   (a) The provision for the reduction of the stillbirth-rate and of infant mortality and for the healthy development of the child;
   (b) The improvement of all aspects of environmental and industrial hygiene;
   (c) The prevention, treatment and control of epidemic, endemic, occupational and other diseases;
   (d) The creation of conditions which would assure to all medical service and medical attention in the event of sickness.

Article 13

1. The State Parties to the present Covenant recognize the right of everyone to education. They agree that education shall be directed to the full development of the human personality and the sense of its dignity, and shall strengthen the respect for human rights

and fundamental freedoms. They further agree that education shall enable all persons to participate effectively in a free society, promote, understanding, tolerance and friendship among all nations and all racial, ethnic or religious groups, and further the activities of the United Nations to the maintenance of peace.

2. The State Parties to the Present Covenant recognize that, with a view to achieving the full realization of this right:
   (a) Primary education shall be compulsory and available free to all;
   (b) Secondary education in its different forms, including technical and vocational secondary education, shall be made generally available and accessibly to all by every appropriate means, and in particular by the progressive introduction of free education;
   (c) Higher education shall be made equally accessible to all, on the basis of capacity, by every appropriate means, and in particular by the progressive introduction of free education;
   (d) Fundamental education shall be encouraged or intensified as far as possible for those persons who have not received or completed the whole period of their primary education;
   (e) The development of a system of schools at all levels shall be actively pursued, an adequate fellowship system shall be established, and the material conditions of teaching staff shall be continuously improved.
3. The State Parties to the present Covenant undertake to have respect for the liberty of parents and, when applicable, legal guardians to choose for their children schools, order than those established by the public authorities, which conform to such minimum educational standards as may be laid down or approved by the State and to ensure the religious and moral education of their children in conformity with their own convictions.
4. No part of this article shall be construed so as to interfere with the liberty of individual and bodies to establish and direct educational institutions, subject always to the observance of the principles set forth in paragraph 1 of this article and to the requirement that the education given in such institutions shall conform to such minimum standards as may be laid down by the State.

Article 14

Each State Party to the present Covenant which at the time of becoming a Party, has not been able to secure in its metropolitan territory or other territories under its jurisdiction compulsory primary education, free of charge, undertakes, within two years, to work out and adopt a detailed plan of action for the progressive implementation, within a reasonable number of years, to be fixed in the plan, of the principle of compulsory education free of charge for all.

Article 15

1. The State Parties to the present Covenant recognize the right of everyone :
   (a) To take part in cultural life;
   (b) To enjoy the benefits of scientific progress and its applications;
   (c) To benefit from the protection of the moral and material interests resulting from any scientific, literary or artistic production of which he is the author.
2. The steps to be taken by the State Parties to the present Covenant to achieve the full realization of this right shall include those necessary for the conservation, the development and the diffusion of science and culture.
3. The States Parties to the Present Covenant undertake to respect the freedom indispensable for scientific research and creative activity.
4. The States Parties of the present Covenant recognize the benefits to be derived from the encouragement and development of international contacts and co-operation in the scientific and cultural fields.

PART IV

Article 16

1. The States Parties to the present Covenant undertake to submit in conformity with this part of the Covenant reports on the measures which they have adopted and the progress made in achieving the observance of the rights recognized herein.
2. (a) All reports shall be submitted to the Secretary-General of the United Nations, who shall transmit copies to the Economic and Social Council for consideration in accordance with the provisions of the present Covenant;
   (b) The Secretary-General of the United Nations shall also transmit to the specialized agencies copies of the reports,

or any relevant parts therefrom, from State Parties to the present Covenant which are also members of these specialized agencies in so far as these reports, or parts therefrom, relate to any matters which fall within the responsibilities of the said agencies in accordance with their constitutional instruments.

Article 17

1. The State Parties to the present Covenant shall furnish their reports in stages, in accordance with a programme to be established by the Economic and Social Council within one year of the entry into force of the present Covenant after consultation with the State Parties and the specialized agencies concerned.
2. Reports may indicate factors and difficulties affecting the degree of fulfilment of obligations under the present Covenant.
3. Where relevant information has previously been furnished to the United Nations or to any specialized agency by any State Party to the present Covenant, it will not be necessary to reproduce that information, but a precise reference to the information so furnished will suffice.

Article 18

Pursuant to its responsibilities under the Charter of the United Nations in the field of human rights and fundamental freedoms, the Economic and Social Council may make arrangements with the specialized agencies in respect of their reporting to it on the progress made in achieving the observance of the provisions of the present Covenant falling within the scope of their activities. These reports may include particulars of decisions and recommendations on such implementation adopted by their competent organs.

Article 19

The Economic and Social Council may transmit to the Commission on Human rights for study and general recommendation or, as appropriate, for information the reports concerning human rights submitted by States in accordance with articles 16 and 17, and those concerning human rights submitted by the specialized agencies in accordance with article 18.

Article 20

The States Parties to the present Covenant and the specialized agencies concerned may submit comments to the Economic and Social Council on any general recommendation under article 19 or reference to such general recommendation in any report of the Commission on Human Rights or any documentation referred to therein.

Article 21

The Economic and Social Council may submit from time to time to the General Assembly reports with recommendations of a general nature and a summary of the information received from the States Parties to the present Covenant and the specialized agencies on the measures taken and the progress made in achieving general observance of the rights recognized in the present Covenant.

Article 22

The Economic and Social Council may bring to the attention of other organs of the United Nations, their subsidiary organs and specialized agencies concerned with furnishing technical assistance any matters arising out of the reports referred to in this part of the present Covenant which may assist such bodies in deciding, each with its field of competence, on the advisability of international measures likely to contribute to the effective and progressive implementation of the present Covenant.

Article 23

The States Parties to the present Covenant agree that international action for the achievement of the rights recognized in the present Covenant includes such methods as the conclusion of conventions, the adoption of recommendations, the furnishing of technical assistance and the holding of regional meetings and technical meetings for the purpose of consultation and study organized in conjunction with the Governments concerned.

Article 24

Nothing in the present Covenant shall be interpreted as impairing the provisions of the Charter of the United Nations and of the constitutions of the specialized agencies which define the respective responsibilities of the various organs of the United Nations and of the specialized agencies in regard to the matters dealt with in the present Covenant.

Article 25

Nothing in the present Covenant shall be interpreted as impairing the inherent right of all people to enjoy and utilize fully and freely their natural wealth and resources.

PART V

Article 26

1. The present Covenant is open for signature by any State Member of the United Nations or member of any of its specialized agencies, by any State Party to the Statute of the International Court of Justice, and by any other State which has been invited by the General Assembly of the United Nations to become a party to the present Covenant.
2. The present Covenant is subject to ratification. Instruments of ratification shall be deposited with the Secretary-General of the United Nations.
3. The present Covenant shall be open to accession by any state referred to in paragraph 1 of this article.
4. Accession shall be effected by the deposit of an instrument of accession with the Secretary-General of the United Nations.
5. The Secretary-General of the United Nations shall inform all States which have signed the present Covenant or acceded to it of the deposit of each instrument of ratification or accession.

Article 27

1. The present Covenant shall enter into force three months after the date of the deposit with the secretary-General of the United Nations of the thirty-fifth instrument of ratification or instrument of accession.
2. For each State ratifying the present Covenant or acceding to it after the deposit of the thirty-fifth instrument of ratification or instrument of accession, the present Covenant shall enter into force three months after the date of the deposit of its own instrument of ratification or instrument of accession.

Article 28

The provisions of the present Covenant shall extend to all parts of federal States without any limitations or exceptions.

Article 29

1. Any State Party to the present Covenant may propose an amendment and file it with the Secretary-General of the United Nations. The Secretary-General shall thereupon communicate

any proposed amendments to the State Parties to the present Covenant with a request that they notify him whether they favour a conference of State Parties for the purpose of considering and voting upon the proposals. In the event that at least one third of the state Parties favour such a conference, the Secretary-General shall convene the conference under the auspices of the United Nations. Any amendment adopted by a majority of the State Parties present and voting at the conference shall be submitted to the General Assembly of the United Nations for approval.

2. Amendments shall come into force when they have been approved by the General Assembly of the United Nations and accepted by two-thirds majority of the States Parties to the present Covenant in accordance with their respective constitutional processes.
3. When amendments come into force they shall be binding on those States Parties which have accepted them, other State Parties still being bound by the provisions of the present Covenant and any earlier amendment which they have accepted.

Article 30

Irrespective of the notifications made under article 26, paragraph 5, the Secretary-General of the United Nations shall inform all States referred to in paragraph 1 of the Same article of the following particulars;

(a) Signatures, ratifications and accessions under article 26;
(b) The date of the entry into force of the present Covenant under article 27 and the date of the entry into force of any amendments under article 29.

Article 31

1. The present Covenant, of which the Chinese, English, French, Russian and Spanish text are equally authentic, shall be deposited in the archives of the United Nations.
2. The Secretary-General of the United Nations shall transmit certified copies of the present Covenant to all States referred to in article 26.

Abbreviations

01.	ADRD	The American Declaration of the Rights and Duties of Man
02.	AIDWA	All India Democratic Women's Association
03.	AMR	The American Convention on Human Rights
04.	ANC	African National Congress
05.	CFD	Citizens For Democracy
06.	CHR	Commission on Human Rights
07.	CLA	Criminal Interrogation Agencies
08.	ECHR	European Convention on Human Rights
09.	ECOSOC	Economic and Social Council
10.	FIR	First Information Report
11.	HRC	Human Rights Committee
12.	ICCPR	International Covenant on Civil and Political Rights
13.	ICESCR	International Covenant on Economic, Social and Cultural Rights
14.	ICI	International Court of Justice
15.	IDC	Institute for Development and Communication
16.	ILO	International Labour Organisation
17.	IMR	Infant Mortality Rate
18.	IPC	Indian Penal Code
19.	MISA	Maintenance of Internal Security Act
20.	NABARD	National Bank for Agriculture and Rural Development
21.	NCW	National Commission for Women
22.	NCOS	Non-Governmental Organisations

23.	NHRC	National Human Rights Commission
24.	NIAS	National Institute of Advanced Studies
25.	NREP	National Rural Employment Programme
26.	NSA	National Security Act
27.	OAS	Organisation of American States
28.	OAU	Organisation of African Unity
29.	PIL	Public Interest Litigation
30.	PTI	Press Trust of India
31.	PUCL	People's Union for Civil Liberties
32.	PUDR	People's Union for Democratic Rights
33.	SAARC	South Asian Association for Regional Cooperation
34.	SCs	Scheduled Castes
35.	SHRC	State Human Rights Commission
36.	SLORC	State Law and Order Restoration Council
37.	STs	Scheduled Tribes
38.	TADA	Terrorist and Disruptive Activities (Prevention) Act
39.	UDHR	Universal Declaration of Human Rights
40.	UK	United Kingdom
41.	UN	United Nations
42.	UNDP	United Nations Development Programme
43.	UNESCO	United Nations Educational Scientific and Cultural Organisation
44.	UNHCR	United Nations High Commissioner for Refugees
45.	UNI	United News of India
46.	UNICEF	United Nations International Children's Emergency Fund
47.	USA	United States of America
48.	WHO	World Health Organisation
49.	WOPRA	Women's Policy Research and Advocacy

Bibliography

Agarwal H.O.	Implementation of Human Rights, Covenants with special reference to India, Kitab Mahal, Allahabad 1983.
Agarwal R.S.	Human Rights in the modern world, Chetana Publications-New Delhi 1979.
Amnesty International	1974, 75, 78, 79, 83, 94, 95 Reports.
Aparajit	Equality and Compensatory Discrimination, under the Indian Constitution Dattsons, Nagpur 1992, India.
Bajwa G.S.	Human Rights in India, Ammol Publications Pvt. Ltd. 1995, New Delhi - India.
Castleberg F.	National Law & Human Rights Inter Science Publishers, Newyork 1968.
Columbia University	Human Rights Today.
Desai A.R.	Violations of Democratic Rights in India, Popular Prakashna, Bombay 1986.
Dr. Aggarval R.N.	Constitutional History of India and National Movement, Metropolitan Book Company, Delhi 1984.
Dr. Subbaian. A.	Manitha Kudumbathin Maatramudiyatha, Urimaigal.
George H. Sabine	History of Political Theory, Oxford and JBH publishing Co. Delhi 1961.

Humphrey P.	The Universal Declaration of Human Rights — Its History, Impact and Judicial Character, Martinus Nijhoff, 1979.
Krishna Jyer V.R.	Human Rights and Law, Vedpal Law House, Indore, 1984.
International Bill on Human Rights	Amnesty International Publication 1988.
Josef L. Kunz	The Declaration of Human Rights 1949.
Justice Krishna Iyer V.R.	Dr. B.R. Ambedkar and the Dalit Future Publishing Co. 1990 Delhi-India.
Justice Krishna Iyer V.R.	Human Rights and Inhuman Wrongs B.R. Publishing Co. 1990 Delhi-India.
Justice Krishna Iyer VLR	Police Ethos and Human Rights Hindu, 27 June 1995.
Mahajan V.D.	Select Modern Governments, S. Chand & Co. Ltd., Ram Nagar, New Delhi 1988.
Pathak R.S.	Human Rights in the Changing World International Law Association, New Delhi 1988.
Pondey J.N.	Constitutional Law of India, Central Law Agencies, Allahabad 1992.
Singh D.K.	Emergency and Constitution of India.
Singh S.K.	Bonded Labour and the Law, Deep & Deep Publication, New Delhi, 1994.
Sir. Alladi Krishnaswami Iyer	Human Rights. The Indian year Book of International affairs Vol. 1, 1952.
Subramaniyan T.R.	Rights and Status of the Individual in International Law, Deep & Deep Publications, New Delhi, 1984.
NEWSPAPERS :	*The Hindu* *Indian Express* *Times of India* *Dina Mani* *Swadesamitran.*

Index

V

W

X

Y

Z